The FOURTH COMMANDMENT

Also by Francine Klagsbrun

WORDS OF WOMEN (editor)

THE FIRST MS. READER (editor)

FREE TO BE . . . YOU AND ME (editor)

TOO YOUNG TO DIE: *Youth and Suicide*

VOICES OF WISDOM:
Jewish Ideals and Ethics for Everyday Living

MARRIED PEOPLE:
Staying Together in the Age of Divorce

MIXED FEELINGS:
*Love, Hate, Rivalry and Reconciliation Among
Brothers and Sisters*

JEWISH DAYS:
A Book of Jewish Life and Culture Around the Year

Books for Young Readers

SIGMUND FREUD: *A Biography*

THE STORY OF MOSES

THE FIRST BOOK OF SPICES

PSYCHIATRY: *What It Is, What It Does*

FREEDOM NOW! *The Story of the Abolitionists*

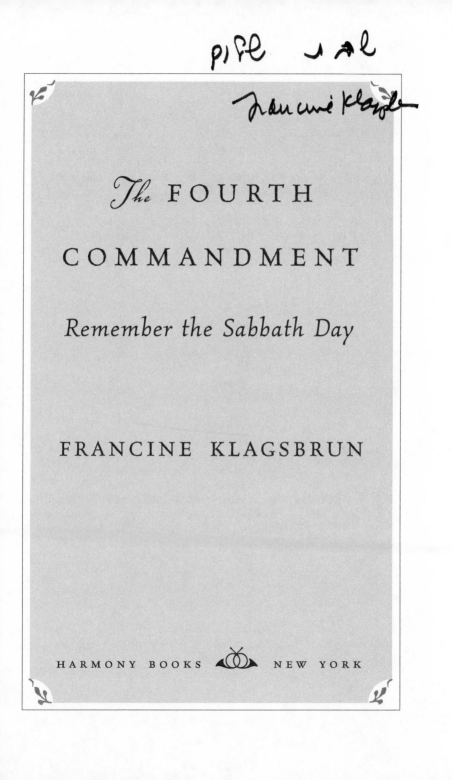

The FOURTH

COMMANDMENT

Remember the Sabbath Day

FRANCINE KLAGSBRUN

HARMONY BOOKS NEW YORK

Published by Harmony Books, New York, New York.
Member of the Crown Publishing Group,
a division of Random House, Inc.
www.randomhouse.com

HARMONY BOOKS
is a registered trademark
and the Harmony Books
colophon is a trademark
of Random House, Inc.

Printed in the
United States of America

DESIGN BY BARBARA STURMAN

Library of Congress
Cataloging-in-Publication Data
Klagsbrun, Francine.
The Fourth Commandment : remember the Sabbath day /
Francine Klagsbrun.—1st ed.
Includes bibliographical references.
1. Ten commandments—Sabbath.   2. Sabbath (Jewish law).   I. Title.
BV4670 .K53   2002
296.4'1—dc21   2002004692

ISBN 0-609-60745-6

10 9 8 7 6 5 4 3 2 1

First Edition

For Eliana Rose Hannah
Who brought Sabbath light into our lives
and
For Benjamin Salo
Who helps to sustain it, always

Contents

[vii]

INTRODUCTION

Uncle Zalman and the Sabbath Rest

In the small Russian village where my father's family had its roots, my great-uncle Zalman became known as a ne'er-do-well, a schlemiel. My father's uncle—his father's younger brother—Zalman could quote Jewish law and legend. He could recount the exploits of a biblical hero, explain a simple passage in the Talmud, and pray with more fervor than most. What he could not do was earn a living. Urged by his family to find an occupation after he married, he decided to use his dowry money of 300 rubles to become a fur merchant, traveling about local villages to buy and sell animal skins. The time to do this was in the winter, the height of the animal trapping season. But, here, as my father would tell it, is what happened.

On Sunday morning Zalman began planning his route for visiting the trappers. Because the Sabbath had so recently ended, however, he felt the spirit of the day still upon him. It would be best, he decided, to postpone his journey until the next day when he could get a fresh start for the week. On Monday morning he awoke early and went to prayer services before setting out. He happened to live near the local *heder,* the Jewish schoolhouse, so he stopped off to say good-bye to the teacher, his friend. The teacher had him wait until the lessons came to a close, and soon it was lunch time. After lunch, the two fell into animated conversation about the portion of the Torah read in shul on the previous Sabbath. By the time they finished their discussion, the short winter day had turned dark. It was too late, Zalman decided, to begin his journey. The same routine occurred the next day, except that this time the conversation revolved around the Torah portion to be read on the following Sabbath. By mid-week, Zalman was finally ready to take leave of the teacher, but now his mind turned to the approaching Sabbath. This was Wednesday. By Friday, the Sabbath eve, he would need to be home. What could he accomplish in two days? And wasn't he already enwrapped in Sabbath thoughts? Better to prepare himself for that holy day and get a fresh start for work after it ended.

So it went, week after week.

The story of Uncle Zalman and his Sabbath rest has become part of our family lore, always good for a laugh. Zalman well knew the Fourth Commandment that calls for a complete rest from all manner of work on the seventh day of the week. He simply managed to forget the first part of that commandment, which calls for working on the other six days.

Yet Zalman's misplaced Sabbath zeal points to something serious about the Sabbath's true position in Jewish tradition: It forms the center of Jewish life and thought. The Sabbath is not just part of the weekend; it is the essence of the week. In Hebrew it is the only day that has a name—Shabbat, or in its Yiddish version, *Shabbos*. The others are simply numbered by their proximity to it, "first day toward Shabbat," "second day," and so on. Early mystics portrayed the Sabbath as a time when the light of heaven bursts into the world on earth. As the day ends and the new week begins, that light grows dimmer and dimmer. It comes alive again in the middle of the week, and like an ember that glows with new life, it bathes the three days leading to Shabbat with a heavenly glow until it bursts out on Shabbat in full strength once more.

The Sabbath is the most mysterious and unique of all days. Mysterious, because as deeply as one probes its origins and impact, there is always more to uncover. According to tradition, the Sabbath came into being at the beginning of time, at the moment the cosmos was created, a divinely inspired institution. In the Bible, it exists from the earliest days of Israel's history. It shapes the life of the Israelites as they flee Egypt and wander in the desert, giving substance and rhythm to their days even before they receive the commandment at Mount Sinai to remember and observe it. For thousands of years, it has continued to shape the pattern of Jewish life in lands throughout the globe, wherever Jews have lived.

It is unique, because, until the Hebrew Bible, there had never been another day like it. All people developed feasts and festivals based on planting and harvest times. All people fixed their holidays according to the calendar, grounding them in the yearly rotation of the earth around the sun or the monthly cycles of the moon or a combination of both. But the Sabbath has no ties to solar rotations or lunar cycles. Set aside as a sacred day, it became the source for the seven-day week, a time period unrelated to planting or harvesting. With its emphasis on rest and sanctity for every person, the Sabbath transformed human dependence on nature into something moral and, in doing so, it transformed the world.

Ancient Roman writers mocked the Jews for their "laziness" in abstaining from work on the Sabbath. Still, the day appealed to many ancients, who incorporated it into their own lives. Eventually the Jewish Shabbat also became the basis for Christian and Muslim forms of Sabbath observance. For Jews, the Sabbath has been entwined in every aspect of existence—in family and community life, in law and ethics, in philosophy and theology, in literature and language. When the Bible describes the holiest day of the Jewish year, Yom Kippur, or the Day of Atonement, it does so in terms of the Sabbath. Yom Kippur is a *shabbat shabbaton,* it says, a Sabbath of complete rest, or more exactly, a Sabbath-like day. When, over the centuries, Jews wanted to indicate that someone adhered to Jewish law and practices, they spoke of that person as *shomer Shabbos,* a Sabbath observer. Nothing more was needed to vouch for the person's Jewish credentials and overall integrity.

We live in an age when such Sabbath observers comprise only a small minority of the Jewish community, yet knowledge of the Sabbath seems more urgent than at almost any time in the past. We live in an age when people have the capability for rest and recreation that previous generations could envision only in the fantasy realm of science fiction.

We have automated equipment to clean houses, wash clothes, organize documents, fly airplanes, run trains, answer telephones, regulate television sets, conduct commerce, and guide medical procedures. We have instant messages and global communication. We have every possible gadget to make life easier, but it seems to be getting harder all the time.

I can remember when social scientists worried about how people would spend the unprecedented amount of leisure time our rapidly growing technology was going to create. Now the term "leisure time" itself is becoming obsolete, like the leisure suits for men manufacturers optimistically made. Today, people are "wired" incessantly to their cell phones and beepers and reachable at any hour of the day or night by e-mail or fax. A sign I saw on a truck read, IS IT US, OR DIDN'T THEY SAY TECHNOLOGY WOULD MAKE THINGS BETTER? Yes, they did say that, but, instead, technology has made it possible to be in constant contact with the office even if you are vacationing on a remote island in the South Pacific. Technology has made it possible to talk on the phone while walking in the street, eating in a restaurant, flying on a plane, or pushing a child on a park swing. There's no place to hide anymore, and little time to focus on a single task, like playing with that child on the swing.

Work-related activities have become so pervasive that a man I met at a dinner party looked at me in astonishment when I told him I was writing a book about the Sabbath. "It must take enormous discipline to stop work on Friday evening and shut down for a full day," he said. "Most of us would give anything to add an hour, even a few minutes to the day." Earlier generations would give anything to gain an hour or even a few minutes of liberation from work, but our generation, supposedly more liberated than any before it, longs only for additional work time.

The Sabbath presents a different perspective, an alternative approach to all that. Contrary to Uncle Zalman's attitude, the Sabbath affirms the dignity of work. But it also asserts that people have the right to limit their work, for endless toil enslaves, draining the person of human dignity. The Sabbath offers a balance to the bonds of boundless labor, an opportunity one day a week to shut down the phones and faxes and reconnect instead with family and friends—and with oneself.

Paradoxically, or perhaps expectedly, in the midst of our work-intensive culture, people have longed for spiritual satisfactions beyond their material achievements. Some have taken up eastern religions. Some have reached for oneness with God through meditation or self-contemplation. Some have turned to esoteric teachings. In Jewish thought, the Sabbath provides the finest path to spiritual nourishment. Its rituals and customs, its combination of study and prayer, and its symbols of light and joy place the day outside our usual understanding of time and space. The most mysterious and unique of days, the Sabbath is also the most romantic. "If you want to know about true spirituality," a rabbi said to me, "you will find it in one word, Shabbat."

This book explores the spiritual dimensions of Shabbat. It examines the day from many angles to arrive at its deepest meanings and intentions. Neither a polemic nor a step-by-step manual on observing Shabbat, the book aims to show the complexities of this sacred day, the ethical values that define it, and the beauty—the breathtaking beauty—inherent in it. Above all, it aims to show how this ancient and hallowed tradition still has much to say to us today, and how it can enrich people's lives at whatever level they wish to approach it.

The exploration relies heavily on basic Jewish sources: the Bible and Talmud, classical commentators and modern ones, and the midrash—the legends, teachings, and interpretations of early times. It also includes many references to mystical sources. So many mysteries surround the Sabbath and so many mystical traditions cling to it that without those sources, much of the day's depth and texture would be lost. At the other end of the spectrum, this study takes into account the burgeoning body of biblical scholarship and criticism. And that requires a brief explanation.

Through archaeological investigations and other research, Bible critics have given us a world of insights into the lives and struggles of early people. Based on their findings, they've dated events in the Bible and presented theories on how and when various parts of the Scriptures were redacted. Most controversial, some have questioned the reality of biblical events that tradition has always accepted as factual, such as the exodus from Egypt or the great expanse of King Solomon's empire. I have not engaged in such controversies in this book. As I see it, whether an event took place exactly as the Bible records it is far less significant than the impact that event has had on Jewish life and history. However, I do refer to comparisons scholars make between biblical narratives and the stories and myths of other nations. Those comparisons help clarify biblical teachings and demonstrate the differences between Jewish ideals and those of other groups. Knowing someone else's culture aids in understanding one's own.

Finally, Jewish women have always embraced the Sabbath, with candle lighting and cooking, personal prayers and—for many contemporary women—increasing participation in leading synagogue services. Accordingly, wherever relevant, this book includes women's perspectives on Shabbat ceremonies, laws, and practices—and their concerns. It highlights the place Shabbat has held in women's lives and the place women have made and preserved for Shabbat in Jewish life.

When Uncle Zalman immigrated to America, my grandfather, who had arrived a few years earlier, went to fetch him at Ellis Island. My grandfather did not hug Zalman or shake his hand. He did not ask after the younger man's health. He did not even say hello. He said, "Zalman, what are you doing here?" My grandfather feared that Zalman's pattern of Sabbath rest would extend to the New World, and he was right. Zalman continued to make the Sabbath not only the heart of his week but a substitute for the week itself. It might be supposed that Zalman honored the Sabbath by devoting himself so fully to it. In fact, he misused the day. Shabbat stands apart from the remainder of the week. It is a different kind of day, a timeless day that contrasts with everything around it. It alone is a day of rest and holiness.

The FOURTH
COMMANDMENT

PROLOGUE

Sabbath Lights

The Sabbath day. From all sides light, in every corner a spark. The symbol of revelation.

FRANZ ROSENZWEIG

The last sentient act my mother performed on earth was to light the Sabbath candles. Ill with cancer, she had undergone a minor hospital procedure to ease some of her symptoms. It was Friday, the Sabbath eve, and she was eager to return home to light the candles that begin the Sabbath and to share the evening meal with my father. They were both deep into old age, she at ninety-four, he just turned one hundred. Their bodies were giving out, but their minds had remained intact and alert. In their seventy-two years of marriage, she had never been late in kindling the Sabbath lights, but this was January, the days were short, and she worried that she might not reach home before sundown. So she anxiously

[1]

hurried her discharge along and blew me a quick kiss good-bye as an aide wheeled her into the ambulette that would carry her home. She made it on time. She lit three household candles in the set of brass candlesticks that had belonged to her mother, and said the blessing as she had so many times before. Shortly afterward she suffered such severe pain that she had to be given a massive dose of drugs. She died two days later, never fully emerging from her drugged state.

When I think of my mother's death, I like to believe that she may have been comforted a bit in her illness by that last ritual act. Although Jewishly observant, my mother rarely discussed her religious feelings, and was not much given to sentiment. Yet she loved candlelighting, and could not imagine a Friday evening without it. In this she was not alone. Shabbat lights, more than any other symbol, have represented to Jews in all times and places the seventh day of the week, the Sabbath of complete rest. Many who observe little else about the day kindle lights to mark its beginning, and on occasion non-Jews have also taken up the practice. The first-century Jewish historian Josephus relates that across the Roman Empire—in every city of the "Grecians," the "barbarians," and "any nation whatsoever"—people lit oil lamps at the start of the Sabbath in imitation of the Jewish custom.

For Jews, light surrounds the Sabbath like parentheses, enclosing this time and setting it apart from the rest of the week. Simple white candles usher in the day and a colorful twisted candle escorts it out, the one announcing the stoppage of all creative activity, the other its beginning again. Before we can speak about rites or rules, prayers or practices, we need to speak about the light that sheds its glow over the Sabbath day, illuminating its essence.

Traditionally, the woman of the house lights the candles that open Shabbat, circling her hands over the flames as if to draw their luster toward her before she covers her eyes and recites the blessing. Through the ages, poets and artists have tried to capture the emotional impact of that moment of lighting and blessing. To thirteen-year-old Ozzie, the protagonist in Philip Roth's story "The Conversion of the Jews," at that instant "there should be no noise; even breathing, if you could manage it, should be softened." At that instant, his mother, ordinarily tired and bent, looks "like a woman who knew momentarily that God could do anything." The Israeli poet Zelda saw in the candles "the mystery of the fire of sunset."

According to early mystics, the lighted candles represent the masculine and feminine aspects of God, which, joined together, create *shalom bayit*, peace and harmony in the home. Therefore they called the candles themselves *shalom bayit*. Others hold that the Shekhinah, the feminine aspect of God, disperses the candlelight as she spreads her wings over the world, sheltering it in divine peace. Indeed, people often speak of an almost palpable sense of peace that lighting the Sabbath candles brings, what the liturgy calls poetically "a canopy of peace" that envelops the home.

The early rabbis supposed that the matriarch Sarah was the first person to light a lamp in honor of the Sabbath. "As long as Sarah was alive," the medieval commentator Rashi (Rabbi Solomon ben Isaac) explained, "there was a lamp lit from Sabbath eve to Sabbath eve." When she died, those lights ceased, until her son Isaac married Rebecca, who kindled the lights again. Actually, the Hebrew Bible does not mention Sabbath lights and no biblical law dictates their kindling. But the Bible does include a command, its only one, about the need to kindle lights for sacred purposes. The command addresses Aaron, the brother of Moses, directing him to light the menorah, the seven-branched golden candelabrum, that stood in the wilderness sanctuary, and in later years would stand in the Temple in Jerusalem. The thirteenth-century Spanish commentator Nahmanides (Rabbi Moses ben Nahman) saw in that command to Aaron a promise for the future. Even when the Temple no longer existed, the promise held, lights would be kindled in its memory.

Nahmanides was referring mostly to the Hanukkah lights that celebrate the rededication of the Temple after the Maccabees, Aaron's descendants, reclaimed it from the Syrians, who had desecrated it. But the Sabbath flames also memorialize the ancient Temple and its candelabrum. With the Temple gone, the talmudic sages said, the home would become a center of holiness. The Sabbath lights, which cast an aura of sacredness in the home, bear out the promise of remembrance inherent in Aaron's obligation to kindle the menorah.

The Shabbat flames form a counterpoint to a different biblical ruling, this one forbidding the kindling of fire on the Sabbath. And herein lies some history. During Second Temple times, some two thousand years ago, the aristocratic and priestly Sadducees took that rule literally to mean that no lights at all were permitted from the beginning of the Sabbath through its conclusion. They and the Karaites, who followed their thinking about eight hundred years later, observed the evening and day in cold darkness. Scholars have found fragments of Karaite betrothal contracts stipulating that a woman may not kindle Sabbath lights, even if her husband is not a Karaite. The Pharisees, forerunners of the talmudic masters, interpreted the rule differently. They permitted the making of a fire just before the Sabbath (but not on it) and allowing the fire to burn so that people could enjoy the day in light and warmth. That permission meant also that women could light oil lamps before sundown to enhance the festive Sabbath evening meal. Later sages thumbed their noses even further at the literalists by turning the practicality of a Sabbath eve lamp into law and mandating that a blessing be said over the lights. By the twelfth century, the great scholar Maimonides (Rabbi Moses ben Maimon) could write, "Lighting the Sabbath lights is not optional . . . but compulsory. . . . Even if you have nothing to eat, beg or borrow to find oil and light the lamp, for light is the essence of Sabbath joy." The Sabbath lights had come to define the day. In time, the light of oil lamps gave way to the candles that most people now use.

What is it about the Sabbath flames that gives them an air of transcendence, drawing us toward them long after we have ceased needing them for practical purposes? Partly, I suppose, it's the enchantment of light itself. Light makes it possible for the eye to see, and, say scientists, our brains receive more information through our eyes than through any other sense organ. The light that enters the retina affects our body temperature and influences our moods. So much so that some people experience deep depressions in wintertime, when daylight is scarce, and special lamps and light boxes are needed to fool the body into thinking it's springtime in December.

Light has always held special fascination for artists. Renaissance painters crowned their saints with halos of light and poked holes in the background of their canvases to let in the light of summer days. The French Impressionists often painted the same objects again and again at different hours of the day to capture the effects of the changing light. In nineteenth-century America, a group of landscape painters calling themselves Luminists focused their attention on the way light colored the sky and water and shaped the land's hills and crevices. Light had a spiritual presence for them, and they bathed their canvases in it.

Many early peoples also viewed light in spiritual terms. To them the changing light of each new season seemed magical and the power of light to make vegetation grow made it godlike. They prayed to the sun, the moon, and the stars, believing them to control the mysteries of the universe. To the sixteenth-century kabbalists light itself was one of the world's mysteries. The letters of the Hebrew word for light, *or,* they showed, have the same numeric value as the letters of the Hebrew word *raz,* meaning mystery.

The Sabbath candles embody the awe and mystery basic to all light. But they embody much more besides. In the interplay between their brightness and the shadows they cast, they seem a metaphor for themes of light and darkness that hover about the day. And in their golden luminosity they symbolize the light that in tradition infuses the Sabbath with warmth and sanctity and embraces all who enter it.

Shabbat begins in shadows. "The sun over the treetops is vanishing," wrote the twentieth-century Hebrew poet Hayim Nahman Bialik in a poem describing the onset of the Sabbath eve (a poem I sang in Hebrew as a schoolchild). Twilight has arrived, and as time wavers between day and night, the Sabbath lamps are kindled, pushing back the descending darkness.

"What is twilight," the sages asked. Rabbi Yose answered, "Twilight is like the twinkling of an eye, one (night) entering and the other (day) departing and it is impossible to determine it exactly." Intrigued by the twilight that brings on the Sabbath, the rabbis imagined all sorts of wondrous things that might have been fashioned in the chiaroscuro hours just before the first Sabbath of creation. Among them were the tablets upon which the Ten Commandments would be engraved. Among them also was the rainbow that would form an arc in the sky after Noah's flood, an emblem of God's pledge never again to destroy humanity with floodwaters. (The Sabbath lights have a connection to that rainbow. If you look at the yellow flame of a candle through a prism you will see a rainbow, a spectrum of colors that together create the appearance of a single light.)

On their most immediate level, however, the Sabbath lights connect us to all of creation and the light with which the world began. "Let there be light" is the first command given in the Bible, not to be heard by human ears but to establish a new cosmic order. Just as creation begins with light, so does the Sabbath, which celebrates the process of creation and its completion.

God's words bring the first light into being and that light illumined the universe from one end to the next, according to the midrash, the collection of talmudic legends and interpretations. It was a light, legend continues, that originated at the center of the earth, in the land of Israel. On that spot the

Temple would later be built, and from that primal beam the Temple menorah would glean its light. In the biblical account this supernal glow remained the only source of light in the world for three days, until God formed the heavenly bodies on the fourth day. (A scientific tease: Astronomers note a faint glow of radiation that fills the universe and whose origin remains unclear. Some believe it is the oldest light in the world, left over from the Big Bang explosion that brought the cosmos into being.)

The Bible's order in the creation of light makes a powerful statement about its theology and later Jewish belief. The first light on earth does not radiate from the sun or moon, those balls of fire and ice so many early peoples worshiped as gods. Nor do trees and plants sprout because of them—vegetation begins to grow on the third day, before the luminaries come into existence. The message the Torah wants to convey is that the lights in the sky are no more gods than are the plants and fruits on earth. All depend on the one God who created the world and the light within it.

God also separates time into day and night, light and darkness. Like the lights and shadows that play off each other when a candle is lit, light and darkness play off each other in the rhythmic repetition of days created. As each new day comes into being, the Bible proclaims, "And there was evening and there was morning. . . ." Those statements mean to inform us that the evening and the morning and the darkness and light that accompany them are part of a unified universe, under the domain of the same single God. This is an important teaching, for in other early religions, light and darkness often appear as separate gods, vying with each other for control of the universe. In Persian Zoroastrianism, for example, Ahura Mazda, the good spirit of light, struggles against Ahriman, the bad spirit of darkness, and as a result the original goodness and light of creation become mixed with evil and darkness.

No such dualism exists in the biblical description of the world's beginnings. The prophet Isaiah asserts in God's name, "I form light and create darkness, / I make peace and create woe." The prayer book echoes that thought in the Sabbath and daily evening service with the words "You create day and night, rolling light away from darkness and darkness away from light." Although light is often associated with righteousness and darkness with misfortune and evil, in Jewish thought God alone remains the source of all aspects of creation. In celebrating creation, the Sabbath attests to that oneness.

Yet Shabbat differs from the other days of creation. As the days progress in the Bible, evening and morning alternate with each other in a regular pattern. But with God's rest on the seventh day, the pattern disappears. Now we read nothing about evening arriving at day's end. Moreover, God blesses the Sabbath day and declares it sacred, the first time in the Torah that the word *kadosh,* or holy, is used. This blessing differs from the blessings animals and humans receive on previous days. This blessing is for the day itself.

Noting the omission of evening in the biblical description of the first Sabbath, the rabbis asked, "With what did God bless this day?" Some answered, "With light." When the sun set on the first Sabbath eve, they theorized, the primordial light—that light called into being on the first day of creation—continued to burn. Rabbi Levi said the light remained active for thirty-six hours, twelve hours on Friday, twelve during Friday night, and twelve on Saturday, the Sabbath day. Darkness would come again when the Sabbath ended, but the Sabbath eve and day were continuous light.

A midrash elaborates on that first light-filled Shabbat. Actually, those thirty-six hours of light, it says, was a time of grace for Adam and Eve. The first couple had been created on Friday, the sixth day, and on that very same day they committed their sin of eating from the forbidden tree of knowledge. On that day also they were expelled from Eden, toward evening as the Sabbath approached. By rights, the primeval light, which had allowed Adam unlimited vision of the universe, should have vanished after the expulsion. But in reverence for the Sabbath, God allowed the light to shine throughout the evening and day, a touch of paradise for the banished couple.

When Shabbat ended, the midrash continues, God hid the primordial light, foreseeing that corrupt generations would arise in the future and misuse it. Where did God hide that light? Some say in the Garden of Eden, stored there for the righteous of the world in a time to come. That is why the Psalmist sang "Light is sown for the righteous, and joy for the upright of heart." In kabbalistic thought that hidden light in Eden doesn't shine. It is a light of understanding and insight with which the righteous are blessed. Some say the primordial light is hidden within the Torah, which enlightens minds and hearts. And some say rays of that light remain embedded in the Sabbath, partially revealed in the lights that we kindle. Rabbi Liezer said, "I once lit a lamp for the beginning of the Sabbath night, and when the day had ended I found the lamp still burning and not at all dimmed." For Rabbi Liezer, that undimmed lamp hinted at the concealed celestial light that in legend shines through every Sabbath day.

It makes sense for the Shabbat candles to be associated with the creation of the world and its variegated lights, for Shabbat is like a new creation each week, a day different and apart from everything that comes before it. But while those candles tie us to creation, they also tie us to the Creator. We rest on Shabbat in commemoration of God's ceasing from creation, and we light the candles to sanctify the day, as God sanctified it. The lights help lift the day out of ordinary time, giving it an air of sublimity. In the words of the medieval Spanish poet Judah Halevi, "The lamp of my holy day is from the light of my Holy One."

God is often portrayed in language of light. The Psalmist described God as beginning the great work of creation "wrapped in a robe of light," creating new light from that light. Later mystics built on that image to picture the deity dressed in several garments of light on Shabbat, when the work was finished. Throughout the Bible, God's light leads the Jewish people. Moses encounters God through fire within a bush that burns but is not consumed. Atop Mount Sinai smoke and fire surround the drama of revelation, when the Israelites receive the Torah. Afterward, a pillar of cloud by day and a pillar of fire by night guide them on their journey through the wilderness.

The Talmud states that instead of drawing light in, the windows in Solomon's Temple were built in a way that cast the divine light of the building outward to enrich the world. God's splendor also blazed through the seven-branched menorah, a tree of life that was also a tree of light. The Shabbat candles recall those sacred branches of light.

By the blaze of the candles on Friday evening, parents bless their daughters and sons with the priestly blessing, asking, among other things, that the light of God's countenance shine upon the children and enhance their lives. In the Zohar, the major sourcebook of mystical thought, the candle flames represent the Shekhinah's rule on earth. The angels have authority in the world during the week, the mystics say, but on the Sabbath the Shekhinah enfolds them within her. Her light alone gleams through the fire, a token of God's presence in the home.

But if God is light, why try to add in any way to that light? That is a question the rabbis raised and answered in a variety of ways. Discussing the Temple menorah, they imagined asking God, "Ruler of the universe, You are the light of the world and brightness dwells within you. Yet you command us to light a lamp for You?" To which they fantasized God responding, "It is not that I need your service, but in order that you may give me light as I have given you light. To what purpose? That you may be raised up in the eyes of the nations of the world, who will say, 'See how Israel gives light to the One who gives light to the entire world!'"

The message here is that God has no need of the light from the Temple menorah, the Shabbat candles, or any other human source. But kindling those lights is a signal to people everywhere of Israel's attachment to God's teachings. That is what the prophets meant when they spoke of Israel as a "light unto the nations." Like the Sabbath candles that throw off light all around them, Jews can spread the light of the commandments to the world beyond them through their own behavior.

In another version of this conversation, God replies, "I told you to kindle lamps only in order to elevate you."

Ultimately, that response captures the significance of the Shabbat lights perhaps more than anything else does. Ultimately, in Jewish thought, the lights that we kindle on Friday evening stand for the totality of the day and the spiritual elevation of those who participate in it.

The book of Proverbs compares both the human soul and the Torah to a lamp. Of the soul it states, "The lifebreath of a person is the lamp of God." About the Torah, it says, "For the commandment is a lamp, the teaching is a light." What is the connection between the soul and the Torah? A midrash has God telling Israel, "If My light will be in your hand, your light will be in My hand." The implication is that if we keep the Torah alive, our souls will also remain alive. The two lamps come closest together on the Sabbath, when Jews read the Torah in the synagogue and study it during the day. On Shabbat, the lamp of the soul keeps the lamp of the Torah burning and the lamp of the Torah intensifies the lamp of the soul.

According to a familiar tradition, our souls are further uplifted on this day when we receive an extra soul that heightens our sense of well-being. The kabbalists, who spread that tradition, believed that at candlelighting on Shabbat eve an additional soul for each person descends from the cosmos to take its place alongside the regular soul. Some mystical writings portray these extra souls as "candles," flickering points of light that impart spiritual warmth and light to the persons receiving them. Others describe the additional souls as robes of light that wrap themselves around the old souls to strengthen and uplift them. The most extreme view holds that when the Sabbath soul arrives, a person needs to "un-shod" his or her normal soul the way people "unshod" their shoes before a holy site, for the extra soul carries with it an extra portion of the sacredness of Shabbat.

In everyday terms, what the rabbis and mystics want to convey is that under the spell of the Sabbath lights and nur-tured by Sabbath serenity, human souls can be enlarged and bodies renewed. The mundane begins to melt away like candle wax as the extra soul, the spiritual dimensions of the day, lifts people out of themselves and onto a higher realm of thinking and feeling. Soon, even appearances change. A leg-end claims that, until his sin, Adam's face beamed with the reflected glow of the primordial light. In the same way, the sages said, the light of a person's face is different on the Sab-bath than it is during the rest of the week. It, too, shines with a touch of celestial radiance. That, Rabbi Simeon bar Yohai taught, is the blessing of the Sabbath and its lights.

After my mother died my father wanted to give me her brass Shabbat candlesticks. "I have no use for them now," he said sadly.

"But don't you know," I countered, "that if there is no woman present a man is obligated to light the candles?" He didn't know that. Although deeply learned in Jewish texts and teachings, my father was of a generation that set clear demarcations between the roles of men and women. He went to synagogue on the Sabbath; his wife lit the candles. Now, with my mother gone, I wanted to keep him engaged in the world of religion and study that had meant so much to him.

"I don't even know the blessing," he said. Like many Jewish women, like Ozzie's mother in the Philip Roth story, my mother would mouth the blessing soundlessly as she stood before the lights with her hands cupped over her eyes. Did she also murmur to God her innermost secrets and personal pleas during those few quiet moments? I suspect she did. Women have always used that time for intimate conversations other people never hear. I told my father the words to the blessing, but I didn't tell him about the whispered words. He would find those himself if he wanted to.

"I'll try to light the candles," he said after some thought, and immediately began doing so. Because my parents lived some distance from me, we rarely spent Shabbat together. It became my job to inform him each week of the exact time for candlelighting—*licht benching*, as he called it in Yiddish. During every phone conversation we had on a Friday afternoon—and there were many—he would recheck the hour to make sure he had it right. He was never late and he never missed a Friday.

Partially paralyzed in his right arm and leg from a stroke he had suffered decades earlier, my father spent much of his time in a wheelchair, cared for by an aide during the last year of his life. At the candlelighting hour the aide would wheel him to the green Formica kitchen counter where my mother had kept the candlesticks and kindled the lights during the forty-two years my parents lived in that home. The aide would light the candles, which were too high for him to reach from his wheelchair, and he would recite the blessing in Hebrew. He didn't say the words silently as most women do, but recited them out loud, almost defiantly. Weighted with age, he was defying the race of time, which he could chronicle clearly with each week's change in the candle-lighting schedule. He was defying the forces that had taken his wife away from him when logic would have dictated that he go first. And he was defying the night that he could feel closing in on him. He said the blessing out loud and took pleasure in the light that also defied the darkness. He took pleasure in the Sabbath that made time stand still for a while and strengthened his soul if not his body.

My father lit the Sabbath candles for three months, until he joined my mother in the world the sages say is all Sabbath. After he died, I took the brass candlesticks home. I don't use them every week; I've got candlesticks of my own that have taken on the patina of tradition during the years of my marriage. But I cherish them, as my mother did. They are my only connection to her mother, who died before I was born. And I use them often enough on holidays, when family and friends visit, and near the anniversaries of my parents' deaths, when I also light a yahrzeit candle in their memory.

After the lights went out for my parents I began the study that became this book. I have observed the Sabbath since childhood—at times less fully than at others. It has been so much a part of the rhythm of my week and the order of my life that I have rarely stopped to analyze why. Certainly I've always loved the Friday evening meal, with its glistening lights and warm, relaxed atmosphere, always felt refreshed by the quiet restfulness of the Sabbath day. But had I been born into a different family or received a different kind of education, would I have chosen these for myself?

I've been to candlelit dinner parties, where the candlelight has cast beauty on other evenings of the week, and I know that there are plenty of ways to relax for a morning or afternoon that don't involve restricting one's activities. In the secular world in which I live much of my life, I am among only a handful of close friends who celebrate the Sabbath. Why do I? Is it the pervasive influence of my parents' long lives that has kept me so caught up in Jewish studies and practice? And if that influence is not the sole reason for my Shabbat involvement—and I know that it is not—can I sort out the intellectual and emotional magnetism the Sabbath lights in all their connotations hold for me apart from habit or sentiment?

I'm not sure why my parents' passing triggered this wish to investigate the power and influence of Shabbat. (Well, Freud began his self-analysis after his father died.) Perhaps it's taking one's place on the front lines of mortality that leads to such examinations. Perhaps it's watching my little grandchildren's eyes become serious and wondering as they stare into the Shabbat flames while their parents and grandparents sanctify the evening. Neither of the two knew my parents, but when I tell them someday about my mother's candlesticks, I also want to tell them about mine, and why for me kindling their lights is one part of an expansive, compelling whole.

This book explores many themes about the Sabbath and its meaning for people's lives today. A more subjective theme has been to uncover the meaning it has held in my own life. Some personal reflections and memories appear in various chapters of the book, and others are pulled together in the discussion on observing the Sabbath. I hope my smaller exploration helps to illumine the larger ones.

One

SPANNING HEAVEN AND EARTH

The Sabbath Command

The midrash tells the story of a pious Jew who owned a remarkable cow. Six days a week the man used the cow in plowing his field. On the seventh day they stopped their work in accordance with the Sabbath command. Sadly, the Jew lost his money and had to sell his cow, which a gentile bought. The cow plowed diligently for her new owner all week, but on the seventh day she lay down and would not work. No matter how hard the man beat the poor animal, she refused to budge. When the man saw how the animal behaved he went to the Jew who had sold her to him and said, "Give me back my money and take back your cow. You guaranteed that she would perform well, but even when I hit her I cannot get her to work."

Having spent the money he received for the cow, the Jew was frightened. But he thought he understood the animal's behavior. "Come with me," he said to the gentile, "and I will get her on her feet."

When he saw the cow, the Jew bent over and whispered in her ear: "Cow, dear cow, you know that when you were in my service, you worked six days and rested on the Sabbath because that is what God commanded me. But now that I have sold you, you are no longer obliged to rest on this day. Please get up and work."

Instantly the cow rose and began to plow. Astounded, the man said to the Jew. "What did you say that made the cow work again? Did you put a spell on her?"

"I am not a wizard and put no spell on her," the Jew answered, and he told the man what he had whispered.

The man was stunned. "Here is a cow that cannot speak nor think, yet she is anxious to acknowledge her Creator and keep the Sabbath command," he said. "Yet here am I, created in God's image, with knowledge and understanding. How can I not acknowledge my Maker?" At once he became a convert and studied much Torah. He became known as Rabbi Johanan ben Torta (Johanan, son of a cow) and his laws and interpretations influenced many later sages.

The rabbis liked to use this tale to impress on people the virtue of observing the Sabbath—a technique that might seem a bit heavy-handed to us today. (The real Rabbi Johanan ben Torta lived in the early second century and may or may not have been a convert. His name, ben Torta, "son of a cow," probably led to the legend, but may actually refer to his place of birth.) Yet the story goes beyond sermonizing. It is also about the power of the Sabbath commandment, which the sages regarded as so profound that an animal might respond to it intuitively and a person change his or her entire life because of it.

One way to begin exploring Shabbat is to look at that commandment within the context of the full ten given at Mount Sinai. Actually, what we call commandments have a different connotation in Hebrew. The Bible refers to them as *devarim* (*davar* in the singular), meaning "words" and also "things." It speaks of *aseret ha'devarim,* the "ten words," which became the source for the term *Decalogue,* adapted from the Greek *deka logoi.* The talmudic sages called them *aseret ha'dibrot,* the "ten utterances," and applied the word *utterance* to divine speech only. Some compared these ten utterances to the ten sayings with which God created the world, as in "Let there be light." The statements at Sinai, this view implies, created a new world order that corresponded to the creation of the universe.

The most popular and commonly used name for those statements in English remains the Ten Commandments, and, indeed, they are commandments, rules to govern the lives of individuals and societies. But the biblical "ten words" offers a different perspective on these rules, a glimpse, perhaps, into their inner meaning. "Words" have a softness that "commandments" lack. "Words" suggest dialogue and connectedness. To use Martin Buber's terms, "words" presupposes an I-Thou relationship between humans and God, a degree of human nearness to the divine, the giver of those words.

The Hebrew *devarim,* "words," as applied to the commandments also evokes a moving passage in the book of Deuteronomy. Moses restates many of the principles and laws he taught the Israelites and then assures them that these instructions are not "beyond reach." They are "not in the heavens" or "beyond the sea," he says. "No, the thing [*ha'davar*] is very close to you, in your mouth and in your heart, to observe it." The thing, the word, the lesson Moses has transmitted is not remote, not meant only for the elite or the very learned. It has been given to all the people so that all can understand and absorb it into their minds and hearts.

So it is with the "ten words." They are presented in the singular in Hebrew and in the second person as if addressed individually to each woman and man: "Honor your father and your mother..." "You shall not murder..." "You shall not covet your neighbor's house..." The assumption is that these rules are also "not in heaven." They speak to everyone, because everyone has the ability to live by them. Or as the rabbis said, the commandments are all in the singular so that each person will feel that he or she, alone in the world, is responsible for studying, performing, and upholding them.

At first blush the Sabbath commandment appears to be of a different ilk than the others. One might expect to find rules against murder or stealing in any legal system—no society could sustain itself without such universal rules, and certainly, similar regulations appear in several ancient codes. One might also expect to find sacred principles, such as those in the first several commandments, stated in the governing laws of a religious community. But centered as it is on ritual and the only one dealing with a holy day, the Sabbath commandment does not seem as immediately essential as the others. In fact, according to some Christian traditions, Jesus abrogated the Jewish Sabbath because he regarded the day as ordained in the Hebrew Bible to be ceremonial and not morally relevant. In Jewish thought, however, the ceremonial and the moral stand side by side in the Sabbath commandment, and far from being extraneous, this commandment is a bridge that holds the rest together.

The Ten Commandments open with the words *your God,* and end with *your neighbor.* The first three concern reverence for God, the last six concern reverence for human life. Fourth in line, the Sabbath command deals with both our relations to God and our relations to one another. In that sense it spans the ideals of all the others; like Jacob's ladder, it spans heaven and earth. "If in the Ten Commandments is enfolded the whole Torah," the poet Hayim Nahman Bialik once said, "then in the Sabbath are probably enfolded all the Ten Commandments."

The commandments appear as a whole in two biblical books, Exodus and Deuteronomy. In Exodus, seven weeks after fleeing from Egypt, the people of Israel encamp at the foot of Mount Sinai. There, amid thunder and smoke and the piercing blare of a horn, God's commandments ring out from above the mountaintop. The Shabbat commandment in Exodus reads:

> *Remember the Sabbath day and keep it holy. Six days you shall labor and do all your work, but the seventh day is a Sabbath of the Eternal your God: you shall not do any work—you, your son or daughter, your male or female slave, or your cattle, or the stranger who is within your settlements. For in six days the Eternal made heaven and earth and sea and all that is in them, and*

*rested on the seventh day; therefore the Eternal blessed
the Sabbath day and hallowed it.*

Almost forty years later, as the Israelites stand poised to
enter and conquer Canaan, Moses recounts to them the
events and laws of those years of wandering in the desert.
His words, in Deuteronomy, include the Ten Commandments, but with some variations, particularly in the Sabbath
command. It reads:

> *Observe the Sabbath day and keep it holy, as the
> Eternal your God has commanded you. Six days you
> shall labor and do all your work, but the seventh day is
> a Sabbath of the Eternal your God; you shall not do any
> work—you, your son or your daughter, your male or
> female slave, your ox or your ass, or any of your cattle,
> or the stranger in your settlements, so that your male
> and female slave may rest as you do. Remember that
> you were a slave in the land of Egypt and the Eternal
> your God freed you from there with a mighty hand and
> an outstretched arm; therefore the Eternal your God has
> commanded you to observe the Sabbath day.*

The two versions of the commandment share basic fea-
tures. Both make refraining from work on the seventh day
of the week a duty that humans owe to God. Both extend
the Sabbath rest to all members of a household, including slaves and even animals (as the cow in the rabbinic story
had learned). In both, religious duty is interwoven with humanitarian concerns; humanitarian duty has its source in a
religious obligation.

But even more than these similarities, the differences between the two versions of the commandment highlight its essential themes. This is the longest of the commandments and the only one among the ten that gives a rationale for its existence, because unlike the others, the reason for this one is not apparent. Why, after all, does the Bible decree a Sabbath day of rest? The explanation varies in the two texts.

The reason given for the Sabbath commandment in Exodus ties the day's rest to the ordering of the universe. The words of the text—"For in six days the Eternal made heaven and earth . . ."—carry us back to the opening of the Bible, to the first chapters in Genesis. There, day-by-day God creates the world and all that is in it. On the seventh day God stops creating, blesses the day, and declares it holy. By refraining from work on the Sabbath, as the commandment dictates, humans imitate God, what the philosophers call *imitatio Dei*. In celebrating Shabbat each week we also re-create the cosmic order, tuning the cadence of our lives to the pattern of work and rest the Bible tells us existed from the beginning of time.

But what does it mean for God to "rest"? Does the Creator of the universe have human needs for food, drink, and rest? Was creation so difficult that God had to take a break afterward? Early Islamic texts attacked Judaism on just those grounds, accusing Jews of holding an anthropomorphic concept of a deity who, like humans, needed to rest. The Bible critic Moshe Weinfeld suggests that the prophet Isaiah may have been so uncomfortable with the idea of the omnipotent God of the vast cosmos resting after hard labor that, almost as if to counter it, he dwells on God's endurance and infinite strength. "The Lord is God from of old," he proclaims, "Creator of the earth from end to end, / He never grows faint or weary, / His wisdom cannot be fathomed." The sages may have been so uncomfortable with the concept of God resting the way ordinary mortals do that they explained the biblical description strictly as a lesson. If Scripture can portray the all-powerful God creating the universe in six days and resting on the seventh, they said, how much more do humans, weak as they are, need to rest on the seventh day.

One can, of course, raise similar questions about the many other human-type images the Bible uses to picture God. How can we say that God "spoke" the commandments? Or descended to Mount Sinai to proclaim them? Or even used words as we know them? Should we think of the divinity as having a voice and a shape? People who regard the biblical descriptions as a literal record of how the Torah was revealed at Mount Sinai believe that God could have been manifested in that way. Others, and I include myself, consider the revelation at Sinai a mystery we can never truly comprehend. The Torah itself presents the event as so mysterious and overwhelming that, as Rashi points out, it relates that the people "saw the thunder... and the sound of the horn." In biblical terms, even the human senses functioned differently at this awesome moment of drama and tension, when people "saw" sounds.

Many of the classical rabbis held that the Israelites heard only the first two commandments and then, trembling with fear, they asked Moses to transmit the rest to them. Maimonides, always a rationalist, maintained that only Moses had the capacity to understand the sounds that emanated from God at Sinai, because he had the superior ability to "hear" God, which others lacked. "It is clear to me that what Moses experienced at the revelation on Mount Sinai was different from that which was experienced by all the other Israelites," Maimonides wrote in his *Guide for the Perplexed*. "It was only Moses who heard the words...and through Moses all the other Israelites learned them when he in intelligible sounds repeated them to the people." God does not speak in human terms, Maimonides is saying, but God communicated the divine will to Moses, and Moses reported God's wishes to the people.

Whatever its precise nature, and however we understand the biblical account, the experience at Sinai and the teachings that grew from it have shaped and sustained Jewish life for millennia. Their place in Jewish tradition and their impact on Jewish history give them authority in their own right in addition to the authority of the biblical narrative. From that point of view, we might also look at the anthropomorphic portrayals of God "speaking" or "resting" as poetic images that continue to inspire us, because they express deep truths.

The image of God resting on the seventh day is especially important, forming as it does the basis for so many of the laws and practices of Shabbat. We can get a better understanding of what that image intends by looking again at the language in the Genesis story of creation. The Hebrew there does not literally mean that God rested after creating the world and everything in it, but that God "ceased" from the divine labors on the seventh day. The word *Shabbat* has the same root as the Hebrew verb for ceased. God's "rest" was ceasing, stepping back as it were from creating.

The sages put it nicely. After finishing the process of creation, they said, God prevented the world, and particularly the seas, from expanding further by declaring "Enough!" (They interpreted one of the names for God in the Bible, El Shaddai, as "the God who said 'Enough!'"—from the Hebrew word *dai*, which means "enough.") By extension, Shabbat is not simply about relaxing or sleeping. It's about declaring "enough" (or enough already): enough technology, enough building, enough fighting against time. For one day a week, humans cease from creative activity, step back, and, like God, bring their everyday world to a standstill. That is the underlying message of the Sabbath commandment in the book of Exodus, the meaning behind resting as God did on the Sabbath day.

Now, although the creation story provides the rationale for the commandment as it appears in Exodus, the story itself does not actually decree that we imitate God's abstention from work. That decree comes in a discussion of the manna that the children of Israel will eat during their forty years of wandering in the wilderness. There, even before receiving the Ten Commandments, the Israelites learn about observing the Sabbath.

Manna was the remarkable white substance the people gathered each morning to grind and bake or boil to their taste. In legend, it had whatever flavor anyone wished it to have—the flavor of bread to some, of honey wafers to others, or of "a stew and a dumpling" in the culinary dreams of one rabbi. In the biblical description, no matter how much or little people gather they discover that they have exactly the right amount to eat. But on the sixth day of the first week in which the manna begins to fall, they find a double portion for each person. Puzzled, the tribal chieftains question Moses. (The midrash has them asking, "Moses, why is this day different from all other days?") He explains that the double portion is to last for two days, because no manna will appear on the seventh day, the "holy Sabbath."

Moses teaches the Israelites that each week they will find two times the usual amount of manna on the sixth day so that they do not violate the Sabbath by going out and collecting food then. (Much later, it would become a custom to have two hallah breads on the Shabbat table in memory of the double portion of manna. Later, also, laws regulating the preparation of food for the Sabbath ahead of time would be based on the manna that anticipated the Sabbath. Other laws concerning how far people may walk on the Sabbath also stem from the manna regulations.) While manna left over from one day to the next ordinarily spoiled, miraculously the manna gathered on the sixth day for the seventh remains fresh.

In this account God stops creating manna on the seventh day just as God stopped creating the universe after six days. But whereas the creation story tells us only that God ceased from work on the seventh day, the manna story indicates that the Israelites—and we—must also cease from work on that day. Here God's rest mandates our rest, and the manna saga serves as a corollary to the creation saga. Rashi makes the connection between the two narratives. When God blessed the Sabbath after creation, he states, "God blessed it with manna, for on all the days of the week a single *omer* [a measure] of manna fell for each person, but on the sixth day a double portion. And God sanctified it with manna, because

the manna did not fall at all on the seventh day." Rashi is saying that more than anything else, the manna illustrates the
meaning behind God's blessing the Sabbath at the end of
creation, the meaning of producing for six days and keeping
the seventh day sacred.

The manna also illustrates another aspect of creation.
Once again it shows God's complete mastery over nature.
However much people have speculated on what the biblical
manna was, whether it resembled a kind of sap secreted by
desert trees or the coriander seed mentioned in the Bible,
the text presents it as a wondrous food that fell in quantities
only according to God's wishes and nurtured the Israelites
through all their years of wandering. The point made is that
God orders nature and provides for people in a manner that
nature cannot. The creation narrative makes the same point.
God creates everything in the universe and then fashions
Shabbat. Enigmatically, it's a day that completes all of creation but it is also a discrete day, entirely outside of nature
and with no ties to anything created earlier.

It is no secret that other ancient peoples had creation
myths that in many respects resemble the biblical description
of the world's beginnings. The best known, the Babylonian
epic Enuma Elish, follows much the same pattern of creation
as the Bible, with the luminaries in the sky and the animals
on earth created before humans. Many of the beliefs in both
works may have been widespread in the Mesopotamian lands
that early Jews inhabited. But those overlapping beliefs do not
diminish the biblical account; they reinforce the uniqueness
of that account in its attitude toward God and humans and
the relationship between them.

One thing that sets the biblical story of creation apart from all others is God's aloneness. As mentioned earlier, other gods have no place in this enterprise. One of the most powerful figures in the *Enuma Elish* is the goddess Tiamat, a personification in part of the primordial waters that fiercely opposed the god of creation. The biblical creation does not even hint of such a goddess. Moreover, where other peoples depicted great battles between sea monsters and gods that led to the formation of the world, the book of Genesis informs us almost nonchalantly that on the fifth day God created "the great sea monsters" along with "all the living creatures of every kind that creep...." The sea monsters have no more independent power than other creatures in this description. All exist only by divine fiat under the control of the one God.

To be sure, biblical psalms tell of God's struggles against fierce forces of nature in creating the universe, especially the raging waters, and some of the prophets compare evildoers to primeval monsters. Such passages indicate that the people of Israel knew and were influenced by the mythological stories popular in their region. Yet even in these references, God always reigns alone and supreme.

A legend relates that with creation completed, one corner of the world still remained dark and unfinished. "Anyone who professes to be a god may come and finish this corner," God announced. From then until this day no one has taken up that challenge, and the corner has become the habitat of demons and evil things. (The Hasidic rabbi, Menahem-Mendl of Kotzk, known as the Kotzker Rebbe, spoke of it as a place for humans to hide in, to get away from the world.)

The legend's moral, of course, is that only God could create the world and its parts.

But the most startling difference between the biblical portrayal of creation and the creation stories of other early peoples is the role humanity plays in these narratives. The scholar Jon Levenson has shown that in the *Enuma Elish* and other Near Eastern poems the gods decide to create humans only in order to free themselves from the drudgery and hard work of running the universe. With people to serve them and replace them in their labor, they can rest after creation. They have little interest, however, in allowing the people any respite. Only in the Torah does the deity's rest at the end of creation become the source for human rest as well. Only in the Torah do humans share in God's Sabbath.

Humans participate in God's rest because in the Bible humans represent the apex of creation. After days of intensive busyness God creates the first man and woman on the sixth day, and they alone among all creatures are fashioned "in the image of God." (Lest we become puffed with pride by this distinction, the sages liked to remind us that the gnats preceded us in the order of creation and have existed on earth far longer than humanity.) The Bible does not mean that humans look like God; the image is spiritual, not physical. Indeed, scholars and other thinkers have written hundreds of thousands of words about the profound implications of being created in God's image. Johanan ben Torta, in the fable above, converted to Judaism when he remembered that unique status the Bible assigns to humans. According to Rashi's interpretation, humans have the gift of insight and creativity, a gift animals lack.

The tenth-century philosopher Saadiah Gaon suggested more abstractly that being created in God's image refers to the blessing God gave the first couple to "fill the earth and master it." The sovereignty over (and custody of) everything on earth that the blessing bestowed on humans echoes God's sovereignty over the entire universe. Humans, alone among the earth's creatures, fashion and plan their world as God fashioned and planned the cosmos.

Levenson and other contemporary scholars tend to agree with Saadiah. The biblical portrait of humans as created in God's image, they say, is a way of conferring royalty on us. Other ancient cultures often portrayed their kings as bearing the likeness of the gods. In fact, kings were often seen as gods themselves or as representations of gods on earth. What is unique—and wonderful—about the biblical description of humans formed in the image of God is that it applies to *every* person, not only kings and queens and their progeny. In the words of the Psalmist, "What are humans that you have been mindful of them.... That you have made them little less than divine and you crown them with glory and majesty." In Jewish tradition, all people have a right to view themselves as royal, because all are "just a little less than divine," endowed with a portion of godliness.

Formed in God's image, we humans keep watch over the world that God created and assigned to our stewardship. We imitate God by ceasing from work and resting on the Sabbath as God ceased from work on the seventh day at the end of creation. In so doing we transcend our humanness and reach for the regal and godly within ourselves. The medieval poet Judah Halevi commented that, in celebrating Shabbat, Jews

are able to rest from work one-seventh of their lives, no matter how rich or poor they are, an opportunity that even royalty does not usually enjoy.

No mention of creation or God resting or the blessing the
Sabbath received appears in the Shabbat commandment in
the book of Deuteronomy. Instead, Moses states: "Remember
that you were a slave in the land of Egypt and the Eternal
your God freed you from there . . . therefore the Eternal your
God has commanded you to observe the Sabbath day." This
explanation appears somewhat removed from the day itself,
not as closely tied to it as the other. How does God's freeing
Israel from Egypt lead to sanctifying the Sabbath?

The answer unfolds in layers. To begin with, the image of
God in this version of the commandment matches the image
of God in the first commandment, which reads: "I the Eternal
am your God who brought you out of the land of Egypt. . . ."
This is a familiar God. This is the God who works through
history, the God whose liberation of the Israelites from Egypt
forms a central theme of the Bible and lies at the core of Jewish
life. In addressing the Israelites shortly before his death, Moses
is speaking to people who witnessed that liberation or heard
about it directly from their parents or other family members.
For them, God as creator may seem remote. God as redeemer is
the God they know. Calling up that aspect of the divine in the
Sabbath commandment stirs in them memories of the slavery they suffered and God's feats in delivering them from it.
Observing the Sabbath God ordained is a way of memorializing
their deliverance and honoring the deity who brought it about.

But in addressing the Israelites Moses is also addressing

generations to come, for as the Passover Haggadah teaches, every one of us must view ourselves as though we personally came out of Egypt. This version of the Sabbath command brings us, too, closer to the God we know most about, the God who freed our ancestors from oppression, and who stands for justice and liberation.

On one level, then, the Sabbath commandment in Deuteronomy is about remembering the Israelites' slavery and showing gratitude to God for redeeming them and their descendants from it. On a deeper level, it is about translating that memory and redemption into treating others with kindness and generosity, especially those who are weak and vulnerable as the Israelites once were.

A midrash relates that when Moses went up to Mount Sinai to receive the Torah from God, the angels objected. "Ruler of the universe," they complained, "You propose to give that precious treasure to a creature of flesh and blood!" Urged by God to respond to them, Moses asked, "What is written in this Torah You are giving me?"

God began with the first commandment, "I the Eternal am your God who brought you out of the land of Egypt." Moses turned to the angels and said, "Have you been down to Egypt? Have you been enslaved to Pharaoh? Why then should you have the Torah?" Moses continued to challenge the angels on each commandment. "Do you do any work that you need to rest?" he asked defiantly when God came to the Sabbath commandment. After hearing Moses' responses the angels admitted their error and showered him with gifts. He had shown them that from their heavenly perches they could not possibly understand the suffering below, and that is why humans both deserved the Torah and needed it to guide them in applying the experiences of slavery and hard work to their lives as free people. It could not remain in heaven.

In the Sabbath commandment, applying Israel's past history to its current life means giving slaves, servants, and resident aliens a day of rest and serenity each week equal to that enjoyed by the master and mistress of a household. To assure that equality the commandment in Deuteronomy spells out, "so that your male and female slave may rest as you do." There is no equivocating here. The Sabbath belongs to all members of the household. For those in charge, remembering Egypt transmutes into remembering how it feels to be mistreated and therefore into being vigilant about treating others humanely. I often quote my father's description of how, in his early years of employment, a poor immigrant boy working in the men's clothing industry, workers labored seven days a week without a break. It wasn't until the 1920s and 1930s that the United States enacted labor laws to ease the workers' burdens, and such laws still don't exist in many parts of the world. Yet four thousand years ago, my father would say, the Bible established a day of rest a week for everyone, including the lowliest of servants and the animals they used in their work.

But now another question crops up: Why does the Bible permit slavery altogether? It was a question raised with some passion in an informal Bible study group I lead for some friends. "How can you speak of slaves resting on the Sabbath like their masters as if that were such a terrific thing?" one member said angrily when we discussed the Sabbath commandment in Deuteronomy. "The whole institution of slavery was immoral. Why didn't the Bible abolish it?"

Yes, why didn't it? What virtue is there in giving slaves a day of rest when nobody should ever be enslaved? This is not the place to undertake a long investigation into the Bible's attitude toward slavery. But the short answer, relevant to the Sabbath law, is that in ancient times slavery was a fact of life, closely woven into the economic and social fabric of society. If, as the rabbis often said, the Torah speaks in the language of human beings, it would have been futile to try to abolish an institution so integral to that world. Unfortunately, today, when the world no longer accepts slavery, millions of people still suffer from it—women sold into prostitution by their families or tricked into it by men trafficking in female trade, starving children and their parents trapped in slavelike conditions to pay off debts—and none has the protection of Sabbath laws.

The Torah surely is uncomfortable with slavery and leans firmly toward mitigating the slaves' lot, although from today's perspective we would want more. Unlike any other early code, it forbids returning runaway slaves to their masters. It holds a slave owner liable for the death penalty if he kills a slave, and if he injures a slave, the slave goes free. Many biblical laws also legislate great leniency toward Hebrew slaves, generally desperately poor people who had sold themselves into servitude as a means of support. "They are My servants," the text says, meaning that Jews owe fealty only to God and may not become slaves to one another. In fact, the first law the Israelites receive after the Ten Commandments concerns releasing Hebrew slaves in their seventh year of labor. That ban on Hebrew slavery lays the moral basis for the eventual abolition of all slavery.

The Sabbath command bolsters that moral basis. It applies to all slaves, both Hebrew and foreign (who may have been acquired as war captives), and makes no distinctions in providing all with Sabbath rest. The Torah stands alone among ancient law codes in concerning itself in this way with slaves' well-being. The Torah stands alone also in its deep concern about "strangers," outsiders who lived among the Israelites but were not of them. Without strong roots in the community, these people could easily have been abused or pressed into slavery, as the Israelites were in Egypt. Therefore, like slaves, they were singled out for consideration on the Sabbath.

Throughout the Torah, reminders of the redemption from Egypt serve as touchstones for ethical behavior. (Someone has said that more than thirty biblical laws relate to the exodus from Egyptian bondage, and almost all of them deal with moral issues.) The Sabbath commandment in Deuteronomy fits into that pattern. Building on the same theme, the prophets never ceased to inform people of the ties between Shabbat and social justice. In one breath, Ezekiel condemns the wealthy who treat strangers badly, wrong orphans and widows, and also profane the Sabbath. And Isaiah equates observing "what is right" and "what is just" with the joy of observing the Sabbath. Classical Jewish thought associates Shabbat with compassion and liberation for all from oppression.

Although not quite so grand, a tiny detail on the Shabbat table Friday night and Saturday afternoon conveys the extreme sensitivity to the feelings of others the day is meant to inspire. Generally, the Shabbat table holds two hallah breads that are covered with a cloth during the kiddush blessing proclaiming the day's sanctity. Why the cover? Because although it is preferable to say the kiddush over wine, it may also be said over bread. So in reciting the kiddush with wine, we cover the hallah breads in order not to "embarrass" them for having lost out on the honor of the blessing. It's a tiny detail, as I say, and not directly related to the Shabbat commandment in Deuteronomy. Yet it is related, because it expresses the spirit of that commandment, the spirit of concern for slaves, animals, and the dependent in society—even for inanimate loaves of bread.

A final layer of meaning in this version of the commandment touches most directly on contemporary life. Simply put: Shabbat affirms our own freedom, not only that of servants and slaves. This may be the most difficult aspect of the Sabbath to assimilate. Freedom? But what about the many restrictions and prohibitions?

The concept of freedom dominates Shabbat despite prohibitions and restrictions, and some might say because of them. The freedom of Shabbat comes from the potential it holds to control time, perhaps the most far-reaching form of freedom anyone can experience.

In the Bible, the Israelites have just barely escaped from Egyptian bondage when they discover the manna in the wilderness. In those early days of liberation, they learn that as a free people they will have one day in seven for complete rest, one day in which time is their own. No slave ever had days like that. As the manna story continues, some people go out on the seventh day against God's will to gather the food, and, of course, find nothing. Bound by their slave mentality, along with their greed, these people cannot conceive of time off. Like the slaves they had been, they go about their work as if nothing has changed. They do not have the capacity to distinguish one day from the next or separate one kind of time from another.

That slave outlook has its counterpart in life today. Oppressed by unrelenting demands, many of us feel incapable of controlling our time. ("Time is my enemy," I lament as deadlines and obligations crush down on me.) Shabbat offers such control. It offers a day when instead of fighting time, we may luxuriate in it. Instead of feeling chained to routine, we may break loose and breathe freely. One of the Hebrew words the Torah uses in connection with the Sabbath rest for both God and humans is *va'yinnafash,* which generally means to be refreshed or restored, but literally has within it the root of the word *nefesh,* or "soul." A medieval mystic explained that when God gave the world the Sabbath, God gave the world its soul.

✦

Recalling the Sabbath of his childhood, Israeli writer Josef Erlich wrote a fictionalized ethnographic account in Yiddish of Shabbat in a Polish shtetl before the Holocaust annihilated that world. His book, *Sabbath,* was first published in 1970 and later translated into Hebrew and then English. In it he describes in loving, minute detail a Shabbat evening and day as experienced by Feivel; his wife, Yachet; and their children—

probably stand-ins for Erlich's own family. Poor, living in a simple house with an earthen floor, Yachet scrimps and barters to have a small piece of meat and other special dishes for *Shabbos*. She and Feivel dress in their *Shabbos* clothes, he in his velvet hat and black silk jacket and she in her long light red dress. When the family sits down to eat lunch on Shabbat, Yachet gives each member some kugel, the noodle pudding with raisins that is their Sabbath treat.

"A *kugel* fit for a king," Yachet says as she spoons the largest portion onto Feivel's plate.

"And you're the queen," Feivel replies.

When the Sabbath ends "two wrinkles" on Feivel's forehead, unseen throughout the holy day, become prominent again, "as on every weekday."

Nostalgic and sometimes sentimental, the book nevertheless captures the sense of both royalty and freedom the Sabbath commandment has given Jews through the ages. The comment of the late-nineteenth-century essayist Ahad Ha'Am that "more than Israel has kept the Sabbath, the Sabbath has kept Israel" has been repeated so often it has become almost a cliché. But clichés have their basis in reality, and the reality is that Jews in every land found in the Sabbath a respite from the poverty and indignity many suffered all week. They dressed in their finest, covered their tables—usually left bare—with a white cloth, and ate the best meal they could manage. Like Feivel and Yachet, they became kings and queens for a day.

It's unlikely that either Feivel and Yachet or their real-life counterparts would have been aware that the feelings of majesty and liberation they enjoyed on Shabbat reflected basic themes of the Sabbath commands. Yet consciously or unconsciously, for them and for all Jews who celebrate Shabbat, the Sabbath commandment in both its versions forms a backdrop for the ideas and emotions that make the day unique.

Modern scholars believe that the book of Deuteronomy was edited or compiled some time after many other parts of the Bible. Its Sabbath commandment stressing equality for every member of a household differs from the Exodus version, they say, because it reflects the humanitarian outlook of Deuteronomy as a whole. Traditional belief, of course, regards Deuteronomy as part of the entire Torah that Moses received at Mount Sinai. According to this belief, the humanitarian explanation given for the Sabbath in Deuteronomy and the cosmic explanation in Exodus do not contradict each other. They complement each other.

"'Remember' and 'Observe' were pronounced in a single utterance," the rabbis said, referring to the opening words of the two versions of the Sabbath commandment—"Remember the Sabbath day" in Exodus; "Observe the Sabbath day" in Deuteronomy. By declaring that God uttered the opening words of both commandments at the same time, the sages wanted to affirm that the two commandments form two sides of the same coin, inseparable in their unity. Later kabbalists incorporated the rabbis' statement in the Lekha Dodi hymn sung in the synagogue on Friday evenings to welcome the Sabbath.

Some sages assigned the word *Remember* to the first set of tablets Moses received on Mount Sinai, before the Israelites fashioned the golden calf, and the word *Observe* to the second set of tablets he received after smashing the tablets in rage at the construction of the calf. Still, they regarded the two words as a single divine command that would have different legal ramifications.

Illustrating the oneness of the two terms, the Talmud tells the legend of Rabbi Simeon bar Yohai, a second-century scholar who with his son Eleazar hid in a cave to escape a death decree against him after he criticized Roman building projects in Palestine. There they lived on the fruits of a miraculous carob tree and drank the water of a well created on their behalf. The two emerged from the cave after twelve years so filled with religious zeal that they had no tolerance for the practical activities they saw about them. This time a heavenly voice banished them back to their cave for twelve months. They finally emerged on the Sabbath eve before sunset and saw an old man carrying two bundles of myrtle.

"What are these for?" they asked him.

"They are in honor of the Sabbath," he answered.

"But one should be enough," they said.

"One is for 'Remember' and one for 'Observe,'" the man replied.

Rabbi Simeon turned to his son. "See how precious these commandments are to Israel," he said. And with that, their spirits revived.

The old man honored Shabbat by decorating his home with the myrtle. His two bundles of the herb, merged into one through their sweet fragrance, represented the two versions of the commandment joined as one. Rabbi Simeon and his son could find peace knowing that in the midst of their worldly pursuits, Jews still celebrated the spiritual pleasures of Shabbat.

The unity of the two commandments that this story

emphasizes extends beyond their first words. The sages saw a bond between their basic motifs—the creation of the world and the redemption of the Israelites from Egypt—that lies at the heart of Jewish belief. The signs and wonders with which God delivered the Israelites from Egyptian slavery, they said, prove that God had the power to create the universe, proving at the same time the very existence of God.

Nahmanides makes the case forcefully. In the Bible, Moses recounts to the people the extraordinary events they have witnessed. "You yourselves saw. . . ." he says, stirring up memories for them (and, through their eyes, for us) of the plagues that decimated Egypt, the parting of the Red Sea, and most wondrous, the revelation at Sinai. Expanding on Moses' words, Nahmanides has him saying, "If ever a doubt arises in your heart concerning . . . the creation of the world by God's will and power, you should remember what your eyes saw at the exodus from Egypt. . . ." Having experienced the miracles, Nahmanides argues, nobody could possibly doubt God's miraculous ability to create the world.

He concludes his argument by saying, "Thus the Sabbath is a remembrance of the exodus from Egypt, and the exodus is a remembrance of the Sabbath." The Sabbath commandment in Deuteronomy calls to mind the liberation of the ancient Israelites and that liberation calls to mind God's power and providence in creating the universe and then setting aside the Sabbath rest.

The medieval philosopher Joseph Albo took those thoughts a step further. Shabbat does not show only the existence of a divine Being who created the world, he says. By celebrating God's rescue of Israel from Egypt, Shabbat also shows that there is a Being who continues to act and control nature even with the world in existence. The two versions of the Sabbath command together, then, affirm God as creator of the world and the creation as ongoing, with God continually involved in the created world.

More than their proofs about divine power, I like the wholeness these commentators and philosophers form between the awesome God of creation and the familiar God of the exodus. I like the link they forge between cosmic history and Jewish history. There's a grandeur in this way of looking at the Bible, a literary and spiritual grandeur in picturing God soaring above nature, pushing back the forces of chaos to form the universe, then pushing back the waters of the Red Sea to birth a new nation. The Shabbat commandment in its two versions commemorates both feats, making that day a symbol of both.

The subjects of creation and exodus come together fully in the Friday evening kiddush blessing. The kiddush opens with the verses from Genesis that begin, "The heaven and the earth were finished, and all their array. . . ." The blessing over the wine follows and then comes a longer passage that speaks of Shabbat first as a "reminder of the work of creation" and afterward as "recalling of the going forth from Egypt." Invoked here one after the other, the commandment in Exodus and the commandment in Deuteronomy complete each other, as though each had ambled out of its place in the biblical text and found its natural partner.

When Bialik spoke of all the Ten Commandments as enfolded within the Sabbath command, he was actually paraphrasing the talmudic rabbis. The third-century Palestinian sage Rabbi Levi had said, "The Sabbath is equal to all the laws." Rabbi Eleazar ben Avina had said more. Interpreting a biblical verse, he pictured God promising, "If you keep the Sabbath, I will count it as though you kept all the laws in the Torah, but if you profane it, I will regard it as though you had profaned all the laws." The rabbis did not truly mean to suggest that observing Shabbat replaces observing all other laws in Judaism. Nor did they mean that it might be as difficult for someone to keep Shabbat as to keep all the Torah's laws. Like the homily about Rabbi Johanan ben Torta and the cow, these sayings underline the importance of Shabbat. They also call attention to the broad expanse of the Sabbath commandment. With its mixture of ritual practice and ethical teaching, its view of all humans as created in God's image and its concern for social justice, it does, indeed, encompass the most fundamental ideals of the Torah.

Two

SACRED SEVENS/
SACRED SIGN

The Shabbat commandment in Exodus begins with the Hebrew word *Zakhor,* "Remember." Its first letter, zayin, is the seventh letter in the Hebrew alphabet.

Like the zayin of the commandment, like the Sabbath itself, sevens appear again and again in Jewish tradition, more than five hundred times in the Bible alone. Their frequency led the midrash to declare "All sevens are beloved." Here is a sampling of Jewish sevens:

The holiest of holy days, Rosh Hashanah and Yom Kippur—the New Year and Day of Atonement—fall at the beginning of the seventh month of the year, Tishrei.

The festivals of Passover and Sukkot in the Bible extend for seven days each. Forty-nine days, or seven times seven, separate Passover from Shavuot, the Feast of Weeks.

In the Bible also, Noah takes seven pairs of clean animals with him into the ark, and seven days after he enters the ark the floodwaters begin. Jacob works seven years for the hand of his beloved Rachel and then another seven after he is tricked into marrying her sister Leah. Jacob's son Joseph correctly interprets Pharaoh's dreams of seven fat cows and seven lean cows to predict seven years of plenty to be followed by seven years of famine in the region. Joshua conquers the city of Jericho by having seven priests with seven trumpets circle it for six days. On the seventh day they march around seven times, sounding their trumpets with a long blast until the walls fall. Samson loses his superhuman strength after Delilah has seven locks of his hair cut off. When the prophet Elisha miraculously brings a boy back to life, the child sneezes seven times as a sign of his revival.

The golden menorah that stood in the Temple in Jerusalem had seven branches.

Rabbi Huna in the Talmud offers this cure for a tertian fever: Take seven prickles from seven palm trees, seven chips from seven beams, seven nails from seven bridges, seven piles of ashes from seven ovens, seven scoops of earth from under seven door sockets, seven kinds of pitch from seven ships, seven handfuls of cumin, and seven hairs from the beard of an old dog and tie them at the nape of the neck with a white twisted thread.

And here are some Shabbat-related sevens:

The creation narrative leading up to the seventh day consists of sentences and paragraphs built around the number seven. For example, the first verse in Genesis has seven words in Hebrew—*Bereshit bara Elohim et ha'shamayim v'et ha'aretz,* "When God began to create the heaven and the earth..." The second verse has fourteen words. The expression "it was good" ("very good" after humans are formed) appears seven times in the description of the six days of creation.

Psalm 92, the psalm read on Shabbat, uses God's name seven times.

Seven Sabbaths of consolation follow Tisha B'Av, the mournful ninth day of the Hebrew month of Av. Synagogue services include reading a prophecy of comfort and hope on each.

Menahem-Mendel of Kotzk, the Kotzker Rebbe, was the seventh rabbi in his Hasidic dynasty. "I am the Sabbath," he told one of his disciples.

What is the meaning behind these and many other sevens that abound in Jewish literature and lore? Do they represent an ever-repeating echo of the Sabbath, the sacred seventh day of creation, or does the day's sacredness actually stem from its being seventh? These were questions I sought to answer when I began this study. The ubiquitousness of the number seven intrigued me and I wanted to know more about its relationship to Shabbat. I also wanted to know whether archaeologists and Bible scholars had found early sources outside the Bible that might offer insights into the origins and influence of the Sabbath in Jewish tradition.

Like so much else about ancient history, the answers I could uncover are murky, yet this much emerged clearly: Shabbat cannot be understood without acknowledging the special place the number seven holds in many ancient cultures. The use of the number seven and its multiples in Jewish tradition cannot be understood without acknowledging their ties to Shabbat.

The number seven had symbolic importance to the Sumerians, Babylonians, Assyrians, and other ancient Near Eastern peoples with whom early Jews came into contact. A Babylonian myth tells of seven gods, for instance, and in the popular epic of Gilgamesh, the hero fails a test that requires him to stay awake for six days and seven nights in order to gain immortality. Instead, he sleeps for seven days, each marked off on the wall of his house.

What symbolism did these ancient sevens convey? Most authorities believe they relate to the number of celestial bodies early peoples could see and often worshiped as gods and goddesses. The sun, the moon, and the planets Saturn, Mercury, Venus, Mars, and Jupiter, seven in all, along with the stars, seemed to many ancients to comprise the universe. The Greek philosopher Pythagoras likened the heavenly spheres to the seven strings of a lyre, and his followers thought they produced a celestial harmony, the music of the spheres. As a symbol of the heavens the number seven came to stand for wholeness and harmony, even perfection.

Although Jewish law forbade worshiping sun or moon, stars or planets, Jews, like their neighbors, continued to associate the number seven with the heavenly bodies. In a vision, the prophet Zechariah sees the seven golden branches of the Temple's menorah and hears an angel say, "Those seven are the eyes of the Eternal, ranging over the whole earth," referring to the celestial bodies that light up the sky. According to the Zohar, "God set seven planets in the firmament, and each firmament contains numerous angels appointed to minister to the Blessed Holy One. . . ." And again, "The Blessed Holy One commanded that seven blessings be pronounced over the Shekhinah on the eve of Passover, and they are her seven maidens, Saturn, Jupiter, Mars, the sun, Venus, Mercury, and the moon. . . ."

Instead of depicting the planets as elements to be worshiped, Zechariah pictures them metaphorically, as the eyes of God, and equates them with the Temple menorah. The Zohar envisions them and other luminaries as worshiping God. Yet both retain the symbolic connection between the planets and the number seven.

A different reason for the specialness of the number seven comes from the fact that it is composed of two other special numbers: four and three. Early peoples spoke of four directions in the world and four winds, perhaps based on the four points of a compass or the four sides of a square. The ancient Egyptians often pictured the universe with a heavenly roof supported by four columns, sometimes represented as four women. The Bible describes four rivers flowing from the Garden of Eden—the Pishon, Gihon, Tigris, and Euphrates. It also introduces four matriarchs of the Jewish people, Sarah, Rebecca, Leah, and Rachel. Three's importance may result from the images of a heaven, earth, and lower world common among many religious groups, or from the basic family unit of mother, father, and child. In the Bible, Abraham, Isaac, and Jacob become Israel's three patriarchs (and together with the four matriarchs make up the seven ancestors of the Jewish people). Three siblings—Moses, Aaron, and Miriam—lead the Israelites in their long journey from Egypt toward the Promised Land. In ancient numerology, four and three, like seven, usually stand for completion and unity.

The first-century Jewish philosopher and Platonist Philo of Alexandria gives yet another symbolic meaning to the number seven. He attributes the number's significance to its position within the series of numbers one to ten, which he calls the "decade." Seven, he shows, is the only number in the decade that is neither produced by multiplication with another larger than one nor produces another in the decade by multiplication. (Five, also, for example, does not result from multiplication by another number in the series larger than one, but when multiplied by two it produces ten. The lowest number seven produces, when multiplied, is fourteen.) Because seven is unrelated to anything around it, he says, it can be compared to the Sovereign of the universe, alone and unique. In this sense it is a symbol of God.

Standing for harmony and divine perfection, seven easily found its place as a sacred number to many groups. Some Bible critics see in the seven-day biblical story of creation a reflection of the significance of the number seven throughout the ancient world. These scholars say that priestly editors who lived during and after the Jewish exile to Babylonia in the sixth century B.C.E. compiled the opening sections of Genesis. Even though these sections come first in the Bible, the critics see them as among the last to have been redacted, and influenced by the environment in which the Jews lived. (As for the Jewish New Year in the seventh month, it may well stem from the seventh day of the week. But scholars also trace its origins to the seven-day fall festival of Sukkot, a holiday not unlike the seven-day agricultural feasts of neighboring nations. The scholars speculate that the day may have split off at some later period into a separate holiday, leading to the unusual seventh-month New Year celebration.)

Undoubtedly, some link exists between the biblical seven-day festivals and those of other religions of the time. Undoubtedly, the many sevens in Jewish tradition have some connection to the popularity of the number seven in other early cultures. But lest it be supposed that the puzzle of the Jewish sevens is neatly solved by these undoubtedlies (even if one accepts the Bible critics' theories), we need to note the loose ends that remain hanging, like fringes on a prayer shawl. Those ends are: Although the biblical description of creation in seven days may relate to the widespread use of the number seven, no other people portrayed the creation of the world as occurring in seven days. Although other societies celebrated seven-day festivals, none consistently divided the week into seven days—the ancient Hebrews invented the week as we know it. And although other people had days when work was forbidden, no other people had a persistent pattern of work and rest, a regular, recurring seventh-day Sabbath for all persons. This remains one of Judaism's great contributions to civilization.

A slew of ideas have been advanced for the origins of Shabbat and with it the beginnings of the seven-day week, aside from the rationales given in the Sabbath commandment. Some talmudic rabbis fancied that Moses invented Shabbat. Seeing the Hebrew slaves at their hard work, he convinced Pharaoh that if they did not receive a day of rest they would die and he would lose their labor. At first Pharaoh conceded, and Moses established the Sabbath as a time of rest and recuperation. Later Pharaoh rescinded that rest day just as he constantly increased the peoples' burdens.

A particularly venomous interpretation of the day comes from Apion, an anti-Semitic ancient Greek grammarian who lived in the first century C.E. He places the source of the Sabbath in the Israelite exodus from Egypt, but he describes the exodus as an Egyptian expulsion of leprous Israelites. After a six-day march in the desert, he says, these people developed tumors in the groin, a disease known in Egypt as *sabbatosis* (which some modern scholars label a venereal disease). When they reached their own land on the seventh day they rested and called the day *sabbaton,* after the Egyptian disease. Their observance of the Sabbath, according to Apion, commemorates that illness.

Some Bible critics have identified the Jewish Sabbath with the days of "ill omen" observed in Mesopotamia on the seventh, fourteenth, twenty-first, and twenty-eighth day of the month, generally corresponding to the four phases of the moon. On these days, believed to be controlled by evil spirits, the king was not permitted to eat roasted meat or baked bread, change his clothes, wear newly laundered garments, or ride in his chariot, and physicians were not permitted to treat patients. Bad luck would ensue for those who broke these rules. Another theory sees a basis for the Sabbath in the Babylonian *shapattu,* a name that sounds like Shabbat. The Babylonians observed this day during the full moon on the fifteenth of the month as a time to appease the gods with sacrifices and festivities.

In her book *ReVisions,* Rabbi Elyse Goldstein cites feminist theorists who suggest that Mesopotamian evil days and the *shapattu* may have been tied in some way to worship of the moon goddess Ishtar. In this theory, people may originally have avoided work one day a month, on the full moon, when they believed the goddess was having her monthly period. Later, such days were extended to the beginning of the moon's four phases. Rabbi Goldstein raises the question of whether in a long forgotten past some association existed between moon worship, the Sabbath, and menstrual taboos. If that association seems far-fetched, so do the other theories. (Apion's, needless to say, is beneath contempt.) The Sabbath does not depend in any manner on the moon, as did the Mesopotamian and Babylonian days—the Bible speaks of "New Moon and Sabbaths" as distinct holy days. Jews observe the Sabbath every seventh day, unconnected to anything in the month or year, and it applies to everyone, not only to kings and physicians. Furthermore, it is not a time of evil or bad luck, but of great joy—what the prophet Isaiah called *oneg Shabbat,* Sabbath delight.

Certainly, our ancestors were aware of their surroundings and affected by them. The prophets' anger at the people for worshiping idols is proof enough that early Jews, like later ones, took up the practices of the nations among whom they lived. A legend has it that the first Hebrew word of the Ten Commandments, *Anokhi,* meaning "I," is actually an Egyptian word. Having toiled as slaves in Egypt for generations, the people knew Egypt's language better than they knew Hebrew. God said, "I will speak to them in Egyptian," and began the commandments with the word *Anokhi.*

It's possible, maybe likely, that Shabbat has some kinship to other Near Eastern days. It may even share an early common source with the Babylonian *shapattu.* But whatever that source or others may have been, the biblical Sabbath made a leap beyond anything that surrounded it. ("It's just like our ornery people," a Bible scholar said to me jokingly. "If everyone else has an evil day, we turn the day around and make it holy.") That leap was enormous, as innovative, perhaps, as the invention of the spinning wheel or the electric light or other things that changed the way people live. This invention changed a day dependent on the whim of the gods into a day imbued with sanctity. It transformed a time rooted in nature, in the turning of the moon, to a time free of all natural ties, free from the constraints of time itself. Above all, it altered the way human beings regarded themselves, giving them the dignity of knowing that their lives are not defined by their labor alone—a lesson many of us are still learning.

"Why did God bless the Sabbath?" the sages asked time and again. Rabbi Berekhiah gave this answer: "Because the Sabbath has no mate. The first day of the week has the second, the third has the fourth, the fifth has the sixth, but the Sabbath has no mate." This was the rabbi's way of affirming that the Sabbath has always been distinct from anything else.

Philo built on that distinctiveness in applying the symbolism of the number seven to Shabbat. "Seven reveals as completed what six has produced," he writes, "and therefore the Sabbath may be quite rightly entitled the birthday of the world." He elaborates on that birthday in a different passage. On the Sabbath, he says, "the heavens and earth and all creatures on the face of the earth celebrate as they rejoice and exult in the harmony of the sacred number seven." Complete and harmonious in itself, the seventh day can be seen as the birthday of the world, the culmination of all of creation.

To sum up the relationship of the number seven to Shabbat, then, it seems fair to say that Shabbat draws on the concepts of wholeness and perfection that many peoples attached to the number seven. At the same time, despite the universal partiality to sevens, Shabbat is so vital to Jewish life and thought that one cannot read a reference to that number or its multiples in the Bible, Talmud, or later literature without immediately associating it with the ultimate seven, the Sabbath day.

When Christians adopted the Sabbath as their own, they divested it of the symbolism of the number seven. In speaking of the Sabbath as the "birthday of the world," Philo also spoke of it as a "festival not of a single city or country, but of the universe." But early Christians, eager to distinguish themselves from the Jewish community, moved away from such a broad view of the day. They regarded the seventh-day Sabbath as a strictly Jewish institution that Moses developed and Jesus displaced. If it had its roots in creation, they held that a new "creation" instituted by Jesus warranted changing the Sabbath to Sunday. They titled Sunday the "Lord's day," and made it a day of prayer and meditation in honor of Jesus' resurrection, which they believed happened on the Sunday after his crucifixion. As church doctrine developed, some theologians justified the Sunday Sabbath by arguing that the biblical commandment of Sabbath rest is meant to be one day in seven, not necessarily the seventh day. In its position as the first of the seven days, Sunday fulfills that mandate. Other church leaders distinguished between what they regarded as the "moral" and the "ceremonial" aspects of the Sabbath commandment. The moral aspect refers to the underlying concept of setting aside a time to rest and worship God. The ceremonial, more transitory, refers to keeping a particular time, the seventh day, for these activities. They could dispense with the ceremonial aspect of the command while retaining the moral by celebrating the Sabbath on Sunday.

There have been a number of Christian denominations, such as the Seventh-day Adventists, who observe Saturday as their Sabbath, and there have been ongoing debates within Christianity about the relationship of Sunday to the Sabbath commandment. For the most part, however, Sunday has remained the day for Christian worship, a day memorializing the resurrection of Jesus.

Islam separated itself from both Christianity and Judaism by choosing Friday as its sacred day of the week, ascribing its celebration, among other things, to the creation of Adam and Eve on the sixth day. Muslims gather for prayer services on Fridays, but do not abstain from work. Islamic tradition regards the Jewish day of rest with its prohibitions against work and the use of money as a punishment for Jewish refusal to accept Friday as the appropriate holy day. God allowed Jews to worship on Saturday, according to this view, but only on condition that they cease from work.

For Jews, of course, the Sabbath is a celebration inextricably linked to the seventh day of the week. (In the late nineteenth century, a few American Reform rabbis called for changing the Jewish Sabbath from Saturday to Sunday to conform to general practice. Their idea never found a significant following.) The sages noted that the "nations of the world" continue to count the days of the week in relation to the Sabbath as Jews do, counting Sunday as the first day, Monday the second, and so on. But still they do not count the seventh as their Sabbath day. Israel, however, "count the

Sabbath exactly as they were commanded." For Israel the seventh day is inherently sacred. According to some mystical traditions, Shabbat existed as a holy day in God's thoughts even before the creation of heaven and earth. By separating their Sabbath from the seventh day, Christians reinforced their attachment to Jesus and Muslims their differentness from Jews. But both religions lost the day's symbolic and emotional attachment to the number seven and with it to the origins of the universe.

In the Bible, in legend, and in later Jewish thought, the rhythm and flow of the sacred seventh day ripples outward, shaping the rhythm and flow of time and events. A favorite tale (later adapted by Christians and Muslims) tells of a miraculous river called Sambatyon that responds to Sabbath time. Behind that river live the ten lost tribes of Israel, exiled from their homeland by the Assyrians and never heard from again. They cannot cross the river to join their people in other lands because all week long it runs fiercely, churning up rocks and sand that make it impassable. On the seventh day the waters become still in keeping with the Sabbath and a great fish comes to rest on the riverbank. But now it is Shabbat, when law forbids the people from fording the river. The dilemma continues year after year, until one day the Messiah will come and the lost tribes will be able to cross the river and return home.

In real time, two biblical institutions grew from the seventh-day Sabbath, spin-offs, as it were, that have affected life in Israel to our own day. The first was the sabbatical year, called in Hebrew *shmitah,* and meant to be observed in the land of Israel every seventh year. The second was the jubilee, or *yovel,* observed on the fiftieth year, at the end of seven cycles of seven years, or forty-nine years.

Hebrew slaves would be freed and debts canceled in the sabbatical year. Farmers would allow their fields to lie fallow and the poor to gather whatever crops grew naturally on the uncultivated land. What the poor did not take remained behind for animals to eat. In the jubilee the shofar sounded to "Proclaim liberty throughout the land for all its inhabitants." All indentured servants gained their freedom, and family land holdings that had been sold reverted to their original owners. Nahmanides linked the seven-times-seven years that led to the jubilee to the seven-times-seven weeks that separate Passover from Shavuot, the festival that commemorates the giving of the Torah at Sinai. Both periods build on the basic sevens to celebrate freedom.

The Hebrews were not the only ancient peoples to set aside fallow years for fields. Other groups had similar practices, and on special occasions kings sometimes remitted debts and released servants. But these releases do not seem to have occurred on a regular basis. For Israel, the regular seven-year and seven-times-seven-year cycles parallel the seventh-day Sabbath and, in turn, influence it.

The Torah makes a clear identification between sabbatical and Sabbath. "Six years you shall sow your land and gather in its yield," the book of Exodus commands, "but in the seventh you shall let it rest...." Immediately following come these words: "Six days you shall do your work, but on the seventh day you shall cease from labor...." The book of Leviticus is even more direct. "When you enter the land that I assign to you, the land shall observe a Sabbath of the Lord," it says, and goes on to speak of the seventh year as a *shabbat shabbaton*, a Sabbath of complete rest—a term used elsewhere only for the Sabbath and the Day of Atonement.

From Shabbat come the humanitarian laws that govern the sabbatical and jubilee years. The concern in these laws for the poor and downtrodden echo the same concerns in the Shabbat commandment. Social justice dictates rest one day in seven for slaves along with their masters, and for animals along with their owners. Social justice dictates respite one year in seven for debtors and the free food of uncultivated lands for people struggling for subsistence. It dictates release after seven cycles for all who have bound themselves into unpaid labor and a return of property to those who have sold their ancestral homes because of overwhelming financial burdens. Matching Shabbat's attempt to give servants equal footing with the people they serve, the jubilee attempts to equalize wealth to an extent, or at least to prevent some people from accumulating it all while others remain impoverished.

From Shabbat also comes a reminder of creation in the sabbatical laws. To early kabbalists the Torah's laws of sabbaticals and jubilees actually held hidden codes about the evolution of the universe. These mystics applied the term *shmitah* to cycles of creation rather than to dealings with the land. They theorized that the earth evolves through seven cosmic cycles, each lasting six thousand years, and each governed by one of seven lower *sefirot*, the emanations of God on earth. In this they built on the pronouncement of the talmudic sage Rabbi Kattina that the world will exist for six thousand years and become desolate in the seventh millennium, its *shmitah* time. In these kabbalists' view a cycle ends in its seventh millennium and the world as it is ceases to exist. Soon, however, the world becomes renewed in another cycle, under the power of another of God's attributes. Our universe, they held, is in the second cycle, dominated by the emanation called Gevurah, or strict justice, a necessary ruler because of the struggle between good and evil in this world. Some kabbalists maintained that after fifty thousand years, at the end of all the cycles, a great jubilee will occur. Then the entire universe will be reabsorbed into the womb of the higher *sefirah*, Binah, also known as "the Mother of the world." Others speculated that a new series of cycles will begin at that time and the process of *shmitah* cycles and jubilees will continue perhaps indefinitely. By delving behind the sabbatical laws, the mystics hoped to uncover the deepest secrets of cosmic history.

Less secretively and in a more conventional manner, the Torah's sabbatical laws relate to the Shabbat theme of creation by emphasizing the divine ownership of the land God created. Commenting on the book of Leviticus, the contemporary scholar Baruch A. Levine suggests that allowing the land in ancient Israel to remain untilled every seven years replenished the soil by reducing the amount of sodium and calcium deposited by irrigation waters. Although that may have been the purpose behind these rules, the Torah doesn't state such practicalities. What we read instead are God's words that "the land is Mine; you are but strangers resident with Me." In biblical terms the Israelites—and, again, by extrapolation, all of us even outside the land of Israel—are only strangers, sojourners, and tenants on land that does not belong to us.

Rabbi Hiyya bar Abba, a third-century Palestinian sage, told this anecdote: He once visited a man from Laodicea, a town in Syria, who entertained him lavishly. The man had an ornate silver tray brought into the room, so heavy that twenty-four servants had to carry it. The tray held an array of delicacies, but also, oddly, two children who stood on either end. One child called out a verse from the book of Psalms, "The earth is the Lord's and the fullness thereof," and the other words of the prophet Haggai, "'Mine is the silver and Mine the gold,' says the God of Hosts."

"What is the meaning of this?" the astounded rabbi asked.

"To remember not to exalt myself," the man answered.

To prevent any tendency toward arrogance because of his good fortune, the man publicly reminded himself of the source of all his wealth. The statement in Leviticus about humans living as residents on God's land has a similar meaning. It is arrogant for any person or family to claim permanent possession of land or resources, for in the long run all are part of nature and all belong to God.

When applied to the land, the creation story in Genesis carries another subtext that speaks to contemporary concerns. With the world newly formed God blesses Adam and Eve and instructs them, "Be fertile and increase, fill the earth and master it...." For years ecologists and others have heaped criticism on the Hebrew Bible because those words seem to imply that humans may use or abuse the world as they wish. But that is not the intention of the text. The rabbis best expressed that intent when they imagined God showing Adam around the Garden of Eden and saying, "See My works, how fine and beautiful they are. Everything I have created has been created for your sake. Think of this, and do not corrupt or destroy My world; for if you corrupt it, there will be no one to set it right after you."

The rabbis want it known that humans have not been handed carte blanche to do whatever they wish with God's world. What we do has consequences for the earth we have been given and the myriad generations that will follow us on it. It is true that the Torah and later authorities give us the right to harness the forces of nature for the benefit of humanity—that is one reason why Judaism has always supported scientific research and technological innovation. Another biblical passage states that God placed Adam in Eden to "till it and tend it," to which the sages added that even in Eden Adam had to work the land in order to eat. Yet that passage makes it evident that Adam not only worked the land, he also tended it. The Torah may give humans mastery over nature, but it also appoints them caretakers of nature, stewards charged with guarding God's creation. Even beyond stewardship, by placing the creation of humans within the broader context of the creation of all other aspects of the world, the Torah shows our unity with those aspects and therefore our responsibility for them.

Those are the broader messages of the sabbatical and jubilee years aside from their application to the land of Israel. They tell us that neither nations nor individuals have final jurisdiction over the world or any of its parts. But that world sustains us and we have a duty to it and all who inhabit it.

How does all this relate to Shabbat? Just as Shabbat themes infuse the sabbatical and jubilee regulations, the ideas behind those periods sharpen and deepen our appreciation of Shabbat. Like the sabbaticals and jubilees, Shabbat is a time of pulling back, letting go, and restraining from interfering with the earth and its fullness. On all other days we are creating, directing, ordering, manipulating, producing, consuming, and often mindlessly sullying our surroundings. On the seventh day, as in the seventh year, we release the world from our grasp and release ourselves from its grasp. In so doing we symbolically acknowledge that we do not—cannot—control everything in that world. We also acknowledge, as the laws of the sabbatical and jubilee do, that it is not ours to control at all times.

The book of Leviticus refers to the sabbatical year as a Sabbath of God, the phrase also used to describe Shabbat in the Sabbath commandment. On both Shabbat and the sabbatical years humans imitate God by ceasing from work and allowing the land and the environment to rest. Put another way, humans and land return to God during these days and years, reconnected, as the kabbalists might have said, to the mother (and father) of the world.

A historical note: Human nature being what it is, the Torah's idealistic sabbatical and jubilee laws had to be modified in practice. Deuteronomy had warned lenders not to refuse loans to the needy when a sabbatical year approached, knowing that the loan would be forgiven. But that is exactly what did happen in time, so that the poor suffered rather than benefited from the law. To encourage lending, the sage Hillel, who lived at the end of the first century B.C.E. and the beginning of the first century C.E., worked out a legal means for bypassing the biblical law. Called the *proshul,* it allowed creditors to declare to a court that a loan would not be subject to the law of remission and thus had to be repaid even in a sabbatical or jubilee year.

The seventh-year sabbatical for the land also had to give way to actual life conditions. Jews did observe the *shmitah* rest for many years in the land of Israel. The Jewish historian Josephus records that Julius Caesar exempted the Judeans from paying taxes to the Romans during their sabbaticals. After the fall of Judea and the destruction of the Second Temple in 70 C.E., however, the Romans pressed the Jews for tax money. (The Roman historian Tacitus complained that the Jews not only "wasted" a seventh of their lives by not working on the Sabbath, they "were also led by the charms of indolence to give over their seventh year to inactivity.") Eventually Rabbi Judah the Prince, one of the great Palestinian sages, found a way to exempt many areas in Palestine from the seventh-year restrictions, and his student, Rabbi Yannai, allowed farmers to plant and harvest some agricultural lands during those years in order to pay their taxes to Rome.

In time, with most Jews living in the diaspora, the question of sabbatical years became moot. It arose again when Zionist groups began to resettle Palestine at the end of the nineteenth century. This time a modern sage, Rabbi Abraham Isaac Kook, who became Ashkenazi Chief Rabbi of Palestine in 1921, recognized that the fledgling cooperatives and other farmlands could not survive if they had to obey the *shmitah* rules. He instituted a legal fiction that involved symbolically "selling" Jewish farmlands to non-Jews—usually Arabs—in sabbatical years while in reality the Jews continued to work their fields. (We use a similar subterfuge on

Passover, when Jews "sell" their unleavened products to non-Jews for the duration of the holiday.)

The system seemed to be operating smoothly, with Israel's chief rabbinates arranging the nominal sale of lands during sabbaticals. Then came the sabbatical year 2000, and fervently Orthodox rabbis insisted that because the country no longer depended economically on agriculture it had to resume a true *shmitah* or have produce grown on Israeli fields declared unkosher. Various Orthodox rabbinic groups finally reached a compromise and the fields were worked, but the issue has not been permanently resolved.

As for the jubilee year, the Talmud has many discussions and regulations concerning the sale of ancestral lands, yet historians have found little information about the jubilee after the destruction of the first Temple in 586 B.C.E.

With the many changes made in the sabbatical and jubilee practices, did these biblical laws serve any real purpose? A small incident symbolizes their accomplishments to me. A friend bought an apartment in old Jerusalem. Reading through the contract, he discovered that ownership of the apartment lasts for forty-nine years, the seven times seven of the jubilee laws. Though legal means exist for reestablishing possession after that, the limitation indicates that the biblical view of land ownership still has resonance in the State of Israel. The jubilee and sabbaticals may have included utopian dreams that could not work among real people and in real society, but they established the principle that land does not belong forever to any individual or group, and we need to safeguard and cherish it, not exploit it endlessly. They also established the principle that poverty should not be limitless and that the wealthy need to share their holdings with the less well off. Long after many of the laws have ceased to function, their ideals still apply (or apply more than ever) to a society whose air has been polluted and waters contaminated by mishandling and where the gap between rich and poor grows ever wider.

~

When I attended high school and college, I was among a small group of students who took standardized tests on Sundays instead of the Saturdays when they were ordinarily given. We were the Sabbath observers, and though today the number of such Sunday test takers has grown considerably, back then there were not many of us. (This was before the days when men nonchalantly wore yarmulkes, skullcaps, in the street—women never wore them at all—before kosher restaurants aspired to gourmet status, before the *New York Times* used the word *shul* in its articles without defining it.) We approached these postponed exams with a mixture of feelings: terror that the exam-givers might punish us for getting an extra day to study by making our test harder than everyone else's; relief, if we dared admit it, that we had that extra day but also a wish to have the exam behind us, as our friends did; embarrassment for being different from those friends; and pride in that difference, considerable pride in maintaining our religious principles no matter the consequences. We knew, of course, that most of our parents and grandparents and generations before them had suffered far greater consequences for upholding their religion than any of us ever had or would, but we felt proud anyway. Keeping the Sabbath so publicly became a mark of our Jewishness, a sign of our commitment.

The Bible makes the seventh-day rest a distinguishing act for Jews. "It is a sign for all time between Me and the people of Israel," the book of Exodus proclaims in words that would later become part of the kiddush prayer chanted before lunch on Shabbat afternoon. If the Sabbath could find no mate among the other days of the week, according to one midrash, another offers a different take on the same theme. Rabbi Simeon bar Yohai imagines the Sabbath pleading before God, "Every other day of the week has a partner, but I have no partner." To which God replies, "The community of Israel shall be your partner."

Israel is Shabbat's partner and vice versa. For the people of Israel, refraining from work on Shabbat serves as a perpetual sign of their adherence to their tradition and to the Jewish community. The Sabbath is one of three major "signs" of treaties between God and humans the Bible cites. The first is the rainbow that appears after Noah's flood, a sign of God's covenant with all of humanity that never again will the world be destroyed by flooding. The other two signify the special tie the people of Israel feel toward their God. One, circumcision, is a sign of the covenant God makes with Abraham that he will be the father of a great people. Abraham is ninety-nine years old when he undergoes the circumcision that binds him and his descendants to God. The other, Shabbat, also symbolizes a covenant, the covenant at Sinai, when the Israelites receive the Torah. From a Jewish standpoint it is the most far-reaching of the covenants.

Unlike the first two treaties, in which God makes promises to humans, the covenant at Sinai is conditional: God will protect and shelter Israel if Israel will fulfill God's commandments. Similarly, as the historian George Foot Moore commented many years ago, circumcision is a sign of the covenant a child receives without his understanding or will, whereas an adult who honors Shabbat acts consciously and deliberately to uphold the pact Israel has made with its God.

Bible scholars have found that in form, the covenant between Israel and God follows ancient Near Eastern treaties between vassals and lords in which the vassal promises exclusive fealty to the lord in return for the lord's protection. In many cases, weaker states drew such treaties with the sovereigns of stronger states. No other people, however, ever made such a treaty with its deity, its divine sovereign. (Within that covenant Jews through the ages have questioned how well God has upheld the divine end of the deal, from Abraham calling God to greater justice in punishing the cities of Sodom and Gomorrah, to the Hasidic rabbi Levi Isaac ben Meir of Berdichev, who put God on trial, to Elie Wiesel and many others who have wondered in anger and pain where God was during the Holocaust. Yet the covenant remains a primal principle of Judaism.)

Along with serving as a sign of the pact at Sinai between Israel and God, the Sabbath became a sign of something even more fundamental. The biblical verse that speaks of it as a sign continues with these words: "For in six days God made heaven and earth, and on the seventh day ceased from work. . . ." In rabbinic thought, the juxtaposition of Shabbat and creation here makes Shabbat a symbol of the creation saga, and honoring it a sign that God created heaven and earth in six days and stopped on the seventh.

An inventive midrash supports this approach. Wondering how the Ten Commandments had been arranged on the tablets Moses received, the sages decided that they paralleled each other, with the first five commandments on one tablet linked in thought to the last five on the other. Thus "Remember the Sabbath day to keep it holy" appeared on one tablet and on the opposite was written, "You shall not bear false witness." This tells us, they said, that "if a person desecrates the Sabbath it is as though she or he had testified that God did not create the world in six days and did not rest on the seventh. But the person who keeps the Sabbath testifies that God did create the world in six days and rest on the seventh."

The fifteenth-century Spanish philosopher Don Isaac Abrabanel summed up rabbinic thought by saying that belief in God's creation of the world is the essence of the Torah, and the Sabbath attests to such belief. It therefore follows that a person who denies the Sabbath denies the seven days of creation, and with that denies all the miracles and commandments in the Torah.

How are we today to understand such statements? Are we expected to take literally the Torah's seven-day creation narrative and maintain that keeping Shabbat is a sign of faith in that narrative? Some people would say so. These people do accept as fact the Torah's day-by-day depiction of creation. Certainly that is the position of creationists, many of whom are fundamentalist Christians, who insist that the theory of evolution be banned from school curricula and the Bible's version of the world's beginnings be the only version taught. But I also know a brilliant Jewish scientist who states that he "absolutely" believes in the Torah's presentation of creation over the course of seven days, although he's comfortable teaching evolution as well. "What God created in days may be unfolding for us over the course of billions of years," he said. "We cannot understand all of God's ways."

Many other scholars and scientists have taken the position that we can keep the literal meaning of the text by interpreting biblical days as different from our own. Some early sages guessed that a day for God might actually consist of a thousand years as we measure time. Nahmanides suggested that the six days of creation refer to "all the days of the world," or six thousand years. The seventh day, Shabbat, alludes to the world to come, a period of everlasting peace. Some contemporary theologians and scientists also try to reconcile the biblical days with various eras of time or stages of evolution.

I don't find such arguments convincing. Plenty of biblical passages refer to days that clearly do not mean years. (When the Bible says that Abraham journeyed three days to bring his son Isaac as a sacrifice to God, it cannot be speaking of thousands or millions of years.) Nevertheless, even without a literal interpretation, the seven-day creation story remains powerful and emotionally compelling. It speaks of an orderly unfolding of the universe, the replacement of chaos and anarchy by a harmonious and balanced cosmos.

An enigmatic passage from the Talmud illustrates the importance of that harmony, what the sages called "the order of creation." It tells of a man whose wife died and left behind a nursing child. The man had no money to pay a wet nurse, but a miracle happened for him. He grew two breasts like those of a woman and he was able to suckle his child himself. The Babylonian sage Rabbi Joseph said, "Come and see, how great is this man that such a miracle has been performed for him." But his disciple Abbaye replied, "On the contrary, how lowly is such a man that for his sake the order of creation had to be changed." As great as the miracle is, in Abbaye's view, the man is lowly because his personal need has disrupted the balance and order of the natural world.

In his book *Just Six Numbers,* the contemporary British astrophysicist Sir Martin Rees demonstrates how intricately interrelated are the forces that make up our universe, all of them governed by basic numbers and physical laws. He shows, for example, that if the ratio between the force of gravity and the expansion of energy were just slightly higher or lower, the universe as we know it would not have come into existence. Or if the universe were not as large as it is, the chain of events crucial for the development of human life would not have happened. It's not essential to accept literally the Genesis picture of creation in seven days to see in that picture a beautiful, metaphorical portrayal of the interdependence and fine-tuning in nature that Rees describes. Or, as Albert Einstein famously said, "The most incomprehensible thing about the universe is that it is comprehensible."

Rees does not believe that such comprehensibility or fine-tuning necessarily assumes the existence of an omnipotent Creator. He speculates that there may be multiverses—many universes—each defined by different numbers and laws, although he cannot say whether they hold or ever will hold life comparable to our own. Jewish belief, on the other hand, regards the balanced "order of creation" as the indisputable work and will of its Creator. As for other universes, from their own perspective the Jewish sages had something to say about them as well. "God went on creating worlds and destroying them until creating this one," Rabbi Abbahu said. "Then God declared, 'This one pleases Me; those did not please Me.'" Rabbi Pinhas explained Abbahu's statement as an elaboration of a verse from Genesis: "And God saw all that had been made, and found it very good." At the end of the sixth day of creation, with humans now formed, God finds *this* newly created world "very good." Shabbat on the seventh day completes that world, an emblem of its goodness and harmony.

The number seven stands for wholeness and balance in many cultures, and for perfection. As the only creation story that takes place over the course of seven days, the biblical account is also the only one that has built into it the concept of the perfection of the created universe, its "very goodness." Certainly, the world as we know it is far from perfect. It is crowded with illness and misery, with natural disasters and human tragedies. But the biblical story of creation is a story of optimism and hope. In portraying the majesty of the universe as it unfolds over the course of six days, the Bible holds out the hope that the perfection and goodness with which the cosmos began can be recaptured. The seventh-day Sabbath testifies to the perfection and the hope. It is a sign of creation and a sign of belonging to a people that sees itself as upholding its covenant with God by striving for perfection once again.

A word about Shabbat and circumcision: The sages often paired these two biblical symbols of God's covenant with

Israel. Jews have been willing to sacrifice their lives for both concepts, they said, and therefore both will endure among the people of Israel forever. On a more positive note, a talmudic passage has the prophet Elijah in heaven appealing to God for rain during a time of drought in Palestine. "Ruler of the universe," he says, "even if Israel had fulfilled no commandments other than those concerning Shabbat and circumcision, these two carry so much weight that you should send down rain because of them." And the rains came.

The rabbis also said, "There can be no seven continuous days without a Sabbath, nor can there be a circumcision without the lapse of a Sabbath." Before being circumcised on the eighth day of his life, a newborn boy lives through the seven-day week. Rabbi Levi elaborated, "It is like the case of a king who enters a province and decrees, 'Let no visitors here see my face until they have first seen the face of my lady.'" The "lady" refers to the Sabbath, which the child needs to experience before entering the covenant through circumcision. The number eight signifies new life in Jewish thought. In the Bible, eight people enter Noah's ark: Noah, his wife, his three sons, and his three daughters-in-law. And in ritual law, after having been declared cleansed of a disease at the end of seven days, people bring sacrifices on the eighth day as a sign of renewal. Accordingly, by experiencing one Shabbat before being circumcised, a child symbolically represents both the end of creation and a new beginning. But how can a newborn experience Shabbat? By being held within the aura of the candles, caressed by their light as the family welcomes the holy day.

Three

HOLINESS IN SPACE
AND TIME

For several weeks in the months of February and March, rabbis tear out their hair trying to devise ways to keep their congregants alert, or at least awake, during Shabbat morning Torah services. Even so, looking around their synagogues, they are bound to see heads nodding with sleep and eyes drooping in boredom. For these are the weeks when the portions of the Torah read aloud concern the mobile sanctuary, the Mishkan, or Tabernacle, the Israelites built in the desert. In the most excruciating detail, the text presents God's instructions to Moses for building the shrine, which will bring the divine presence into the midst of the people. If that weren't enough, it then describes the actual construction, with the same voluminous detail. Altogether, thirteen chapters of Exodus revolve around the sanctuary—chapters, my husband says, only an ancient priest could love.

But here's a confession: I love them, too. Well, like them ... sort of. It's not that I'm intrigued by the cubit measurements of the ark the Tabernacle holds or the number of goats'-hair hangings that cover it. I'm intrigued, instead, by a secret coding within these texts. Wending its way through the myriad building instructions is a pattern of words and paragraphs that links the construction of the Tabernacle to the creation of the world and the Sabbath that concluded it. With this pattern, the completion of the Tabernacle is like the completion of the world, and its sanctity like the sanctity of the Sabbath.

In later years, that relationship got reversed. With the Jews settled in the land of Israel, the Temple in Jerusalem, built by King Solomon, became a permanent replacement for the wilderness shrine. When that was destroyed and then the Second Temple demolished, the Sabbath itself became a sort of portable shrine, its sacred time recalling the sacred space that had once reflected it. Through the centuries and throughout the world, wherever Jews have lived, the Sabbath has remained a spiritual sanctuary; we enter it as we might enter a holy place.

More than anyone else, the philosopher Abraham Joshua Heschel taught people to appreciate the sacredness of time embodied in Shabbat. In his beautiful and poetic meditation, *The Sabbath,* Heschel writes that many early peoples had hallowed things in space, worshiping plants and animals or other parts of nature. But Judaism was the first religion to hallow time by setting aside the Sabbath as a sacred day. "The meaning of the Sabbath is to celebrate time rather than space," he says. "Judaism teaches us to be attached to *holiness in time,* to be attached to sacred events." Instead of soaring church spires, "the Sabbaths," Heschel states, "are our great cathedrals" and Jewish rituals—the Sabbath, the festivals, the sabbatical and jubilee years—create "architecture of time."

Writing during the 1950s, after the Second World War, when science and industry were expanding rapidly, Heschel warned of overdependence on technology and the accumulation of things—a warning that rings just as true today. "Thing is a category that lies heavy on our minds," he wrote, "tyrannizing all our thoughts." And during a period when American Jewish communities were building sprawling, ornate synagogues in newly developed suburbs, he cautioned, "We are all infatuated with the splendor of space, with the grandeur of things of space." The antidote to that infatuation with material things, he said, is to rediscover the spiritual world, to rediscover the Sabbath and thereby celebrate "the coronation of a day in the spiritual wonderland of time."

Under Heschel's influence, and even more so that of his students and followers, the idea that time has greater importance than space in Judaism has become almost a truism, cited constantly as a fact of Jewish life. Like many others, I have quoted that concept in my own writings and lectures. (I studied with Heschel at the Jewish Theological Seminary and got to know his books well, partly because he often read to his students from his works in progress. We grumbled about how hard it was to take notes from his readings, but looking back, he gave us a gift.) As I've delved deeper into the meaning of Shabbat, however, I've come to question the stark dichotomy contemporary rabbis and scholars often make between the sanctity of time and the sanctity of space in Judaism. For one thing, contrary to what people often suppose, Heschel did not negate the importance of places and spaces in Jewish belief. "Time and space are interrelated," he wrote in *The Sabbath*. "To overlook either of them is to be partially blind." In large part he emphasized, and maybe overemphasized, the value of time to combat the widespread "enslavement to things" in space that so troubled him.

Moreover, Jews do celebrate holiness in space as well as holiness in time. In fact, another name for God is Makom, or place, indicating that God is the hub of the universe and the divine presence can be found in every place. Certainly the land of Israel and especially the city of Jerusalem have long been sacred to Jews in their lives, their prayers, and their dreams of redemption. (Heschel himself wrote a book, *Israel: An Echo of Eternity*, in 1969, on the sanctity of those places.) Throughout the first five books of the Bible, the anticipation of that land motivates the people of Israel as they make their long journeys through time. In some ways the entire book of Exodus revolves around issues of space, tracing the Israelites' passage from Egypt, the place of their enslavement; to the desert, the place of their maturation as a people; to Sinai, the place where they encounter God; and finally to the sacred Mishkan, the place they build to symbolize God's spirit in their midst.

Time and space do not compete in these texts or in Jewish life; they complement each other, both equally vital. This is especially true of the Tabernacle narrative, where Shabbat and shrine play off one another in an almost mystical manner.

The story of the Tabernacle begins soon after the revelation at Mount Sinai, when the Israelites receive the Ten Commandments. Returning to the mountaintop, Moses hears God's instructions: "And let them make Me a sanctuary that I may dwell among them. Exactly as I show you—the pattern of the Tabernacle and the pattern of all its furnishings—so shall you make it." God appears as both client and architect here, ordering a physical sanctuary and providing the blueprints whose specifications and execution will fill so many pages of Scripture.

Commentators have noted that the text speaks of God dwelling *among* the people, not *in* the sanctuary, for truly God did not need a home in which to dwell; the people needed God's presence among them. Mishkan, the Tabernacle's Hebrew name, comes from the root *shakhen,* meaning to rest or dwell, and from the same root comes the name Shekhinah, which refers to God's indwelling presence in the universe. In kabbalistic thought, Shekhinah stands for the feminine attribute of God, the one that most interacts with the human world. Taken together, the Mishkan and the images that derive from it symbolized the wish, the yearning, people have always had to narrow the chasm that separates the human from the divine. With the Mishkan, the transcendent, unknowable God could become immanent, a source of holiness within the Israelite camp.

A legend says that after creation, God's Shekhinah moved about here on earth. When Adam and Eve sinned, it withdrew to the first heaven. When Cain sinned by murdering his brother, it withdrew farther, to the second heaven. With the sin of the next generation, it moved even farther upward, to the third heaven. With that of the Flood, it went to the fourth heaven. On and on, with each sinful generation, the divine presence receded more and more, until it hid itself from humans in the seventh and highest heaven. Happily, beginning with Abraham, seven righteous persons brought the Shekhinah out of each firmament and back down to earth. The seventh was Moses, who constructed the sanctuary in which God might dwell among the people of Israel.

God chooses Bezalel, whose name means "in the shadow of God," to be chief craftsman of the shrine. According to another legend, what Moses saw and Bezalel constructed under God's shadow, God's inspiration, stemmed not only from plans. An actual archetype of the Tabernacle existed in heaven, a celestial model for what the people would build on earth.

The Mishkan they built was a large tentlike structure that could be taken apart when the people traveled and reassembled when they encamped. It had three main sections that ascended in holiness from the least holy outer court to the Holy of Holies inner sanctum, which housed the ark, a gold-plated wooden chest. It, in turn, contained the two stone tablets inscribed with the Ten Commandments. The Bible sometimes refers to the shrine as the Tent of Meeting, because in it Moses would meet to speak with God.

Bible critics believe that priestly editors living long after the wilderness period compiled large parts of the Tabernacle narrative and may have based many of their descriptions on Solomon's Temple that later stood in Jerusalem. Scholars have also found that other ancient peoples had similar sanctuaries and temples, but with a crucial difference: In those structures the outer spaces usually led inward toward a holy room that housed the statue of a god. In the Tabernacle, instead of a statue, the ark occupied the innermost holy room, containing within it Israel's most fundamental religious and ethical teachings, the commandments revealed at Sinai.

With Moses on the mountaintop receiving the stone tablets of the commandments, the Israelites fashion a golden calf to worship. A vivid account of the sin of the golden calf intervenes between the chapters in Exodus that instruct Moses on building the Mishkan and those describing its actual construction. This separation between the plans for the shrine and its completion led to a famous controversy between the two great medieval commentators, Rashi and Nahmanides.

According to Rashi the chapters are out of order. (He was not speaking heresy. There is a principle the early sages accepted that events in the Torah do not necessarily follow a chronological sequence. In their words, "there is no earlier or later in the Torah." It is all one truth.) To Rashi's way of thinking, the golden calf episode actually occurred before the command to build the Tabernacle, although the text presents it afterward. He implies by this shift that the Tabernacle served as a concession to the people. Their frenzied worship of the calf proved they still lacked the ability to abandon idols and believe in a single, invisible God. They needed something concrete to represent their deity, something they could see and use. Therefore the command to build the Tabernacle, so they might be reassured that though invisible, God dwells "among them." (Rashi's argument may have been the basis for Heschel's thesis that space is less important than time in Jewish thought.)

Nahmanides disagrees. "The secret of the Tabernacle," he writes, "is that the glory of God that abode on Mount Sinai should abide on it...." Far from a concession to human needs, the Tabernacle is an extension of Sinai, Nahmanides contends. Nor is the text out of sequence, he says in another passage. Moses received the command to make the Mishkan immediately after being given other major laws. The people then sinned with the calf, but when they repented, "God returned to his previous relationship with them and to their early nuptial love...." God forgave and loved Israel again, and deemed this nation deserving of building the shrine. The end result, Nahmanides says, is that "when Moses went into the Tabernacle he would hear God's words spoken to him as he had heard them on Sinai."

For Nahmanides, the Tabernacle is a mark of Israel's importance and a means to nurture its intimacy with God. I find this approach more appealing than Rashi's and truer. It regards the people of Israel as worthy of the sanctuary and the sanctuary as essential to them. It also fits in nicely with Shabbat's place in the Tabernacle saga.

Sabbath regulations appear suddenly in two sections of the story, first at the end of the plans for building the sanctuary and then at the beginning of the building process. In both they seem jarringly out of place. Why inform the Israelites that the Sabbath is a sign of their covenant with God after instructing them in what kind of clothes the priests should wear? Why remind them that Shabbat is holy to God before asking them to contribute gold and silver toward the Tabernacle building fund?

Rashi, Nahmanides, and other commentators agree in this case that the juxtaposition of Shabbat and sanctuary comes to caution Israel that as holy as the Mishkan is, it does not override the holiness of Shabbat. The order to observe the Sabbath at the end of the building plans begins with the words, "Nevertheless, you must keep my Sabbaths...." Rashi interprets this to mean, "Even though you will be eager to do the work, you may not suspend the Sabbath laws for it." This is an important warning, because in their zeal to build God's home among them, the Israelites might easily have neglected Shabbat. Following a similar line of reasoning, the talmudic rabbis derived a system of Sabbath laws from the work involved in building the sanctuary.

Modern scholars have uncovered a more concealed and beguiling reason for the juxtaposition: The appearance of Shabbat in these passages is part of the Torah's hidden design tying the making of the Tabernacle to the making of the world. In this design the Tabernacle comes across, as Nahmanides saw it, neither as a concession nor an afterthought. Even more than an extension of Sinai, however, it is also an extension of cosmic creation. Other ancient peoples also linked creation with building a holy shrine. In various Mesopotamian creation narratives, the gods create the world after slaying sea monsters and other forces of nature. Soon afterward they build a palace for themselves where they might rest in the heavens, with a shrine on earth that replicates it. In the Bible, God does not build a shrine after creation; Shabbat becomes God's "shrine." But when the people do construct a holy sanctuary after revelation, Shabbat serves as the contact between creation and that sanctuary.

The connection between Shabbat, shrine, and cosmos reveals itself in part through a mysterious scheme of sevens within the Tabernacle texts. Some examples:

Before getting the building instructions, Moses waits six days near the mountain. On the seventh he hears the command to appear before God. "And the presence of the Eternal abode on Mount Sinai," the Bible says, "and the cloud hid it for six days. On the seventh day, God called to Moses from the midst of the cloud." Those days of waiting and calling evoke the six days of creation and God's ceasing on the seventh.

On the mountaintop Moses receives seven sets of instructions for the Tabernacle, each beginning, "The Eternal spoke to Moses, saying . . ." The seventh instruction concerns observing Shabbat, with the reminder that "in six days the Eternal made heaven and earth, and on the seventh day ceased from work. . . ."

With the Tabernacle completed, Moses assembles its parts, and the words "just as the Eternal had commanded Moses" repeat like a drumbeat seven times. They correspond to the phrase "And God saw that this was good," which appears (with some variations) seven times in the course of creation. These phrases assure us that the Mishkan, like the world, conforms to God's plans.

Other parallels round out the picture. About creation, we read, "The heaven and the earth were finished. . . ." and again, "On the seventh day God finished the work. . . ." About the Tabernacle we read, "Thus was finished all the work. . . ." and again, "When Moses had finished the work. . . ." In all these examples, the word *finished* comes from the same Hebrew root, the Tabernacle description echoing the creation account.

Most striking, when God completes the work of creation, God blesses the seventh day and sanctifies it. When the Israelites complete the work of the Tabernacle, Moses blesses them and sanctifies the shrine.

To give credit where it's due, long before today's scholars, the sages also noted comparisons between the Tabernacle and creation. The two tablets in the shrine's ark, they said, corresponded to heaven and earth. The Tabernacle's lamp could be compared to the celestial lights, the sun and moon. Man, created on the sixth day, had a counterpart in the man Aaron, the high priest anointed to serve God in the completed sanctuary, and so on. Without picking up all the cosmic clues in the Tabernacle narrative, the rabbis sensed its underlying theme.

Were the clues intentional? I believe so. Indirectly the Torah wants us to regard the Mishkan as another form of creation, an ideal universe filled with God's presence. From this perspective, references to Shabbat interspersed with the building instructions do more than tell us that constructing the Tabernacle does not take priority over observing Shabbat. They tell us that the people must pause in the work of building their mini-world as God paused after the work of building the larger world. They tell us also that in being paired with Shabbat, the Mishkan assumes the aura of Shabbat's holiness and Shabbat receives the glory of being identified with God's resting place. *Ot hi l'olam,* "a sign for eternity," the Torah teaches about Shabbat. The first letters of the Hebrew phrase spell the word *ohel,* which means "tent" or "tabernacle," forever linking Shabbat and shrine, holy time and holy space. The Torah's command "You shall keep My Sabbaths and venerate My Sanctuary" cements the bond between the two.

Tabernacle, Shabbat, and an additional thread pulling them together with creation extend the discussion into our own lives. That thread turns on a word: the Hebrew *la'asot,* meaning "to make," and versions of it. As creation unfolds in the Bible, we read that God makes the firmament, makes the sun and moon and beasts in the field, and finally decides to make man and woman. In all, variations of the word make, *la'asot,* appear in the creation account seven times (as might be expected). They appear nearly two hundred times in the Tabernacle narrative, beginning with God's command to "Make Me a sanctuary..." and continuing with instructions to make the ark, the lamp, the curtains, and everything else. Among the references to Shabbat that surround this sanctuary-making is the directive to the people to "make the Sabbath throughout the ages," meaning to observe and keep it. God makes the world, the Israelites make the mini-world of the Tabernacle, and their descendants ever afterward "make" the Sabbath.

The use of the word *la'asot* here in relation to Shabbat suggests that celebrating the Sabbath does not involve only ceasing from work and resting. It involves also making and doing. Like creation and the construction of the Tabernacle, Shabbat calls for making a new world once a week by transcending the world as it is and stepping into a different realm of existence—the realm of the holy.

~

A memory: I am lying on my bed in the seaside home our family moved to recently. It is Shabbat, and later I will take a long walk on the beach while I await the day's end. Right now I am listening to a record I play softly on my record player with the door shut to keep the sounds from my parents. It's a recording of Gregorian chants, which I play over and over. Never mind that turning on electricity, let alone a record player, is forbidden on Shabbat. Never mind that what I am listening to repeatedly is Catholic liturgical music. I love the quiet, repetitive cadences of these chants. I find them so much more pleasing than the cantor's endless repetition of words in our local synagogue. These days the strongest force pulling me to that synagogue is the rabbi's son, on whom I have a fierce crush. These days I am in search of my own religion, my own soul. I am sixteen.

There is a knock on the door. Despite my precautions, they've heard me. "Francine," my mother says, opening the door slightly. "Daddy doesn't like it when you play that music on *Shabbos*." My parents are pretty liberal with me about Sabbath observance, but the sound of Christian music on this day is more than they can tolerate. In our conventional family, my mother has the thankless task of enforcing discipline. "I don't care," I answer. "Daddy loves shul. For me *Shabbos* is about listening to music. This is beautiful holy music, and I enjoy listening to it." My mother hesitates, about to say something, then closes the door and walks away.

In retrospect, this was not the most earth-shattering adolescent rebellion in the world. In retrospect, and ironically, Gregorian chants do not differ vastly from the singing of psalms in the ancient Temple, and may have originated from that singing or from the chanting of the Torah on the Sabbath. In retrospect, my mother, in her wisdom, decided not to turn this teenage testing into a full-blown battle—there would be other battles about other matters. I'm glad she didn't fight this one; the Gregorian chants eventually slipped out of my life (as did the rabbi's son), leaving behind only the continuing quest for holiness.

The Hebrew word for holy, *kadosh,* is also translated as "separate," "set apart," or "distinctive." Above all else, the source for *kedushah,* or holiness, in Jewish life lies in the biblical teaching, "You shall be holy, for I your God am holy."

Said the rabbis, "It is comparable to the court of the king. What is the court's duty? To imitate the king." Likewise, attaining holiness calls for imitating God. How? "As God is gracious and compassionate, so should you be gracious and compassionate." Imitating God means imitating the highest qualities of goodness and kindness God embodies.

Further, the rabbis added, "As I am holy you should be holy; as I am separated you should be separate." As God is distinctive and separate from everything else in the world, so the Jewish people need to differentiate themselves from other peoples by establishing distinctions and separations in their lives—in the way they worship, the foods they eat, even the manner of their rest.

An aside: Talk of separations or distinctions among Jews makes many people nervous. It calls to mind the even more nervous-making idea of Jewish "chosenness." The ancient Greek historian Cassius Dio wrote with puzzlement and some anger of the people of Judea that they "are distinguished from the rest of mankind in practically every detail of life, and especially by the fact that they do not honor any of the usual gods." More virulent anger, and a lot worse, have been hurled at Jews throughout history, wherever they have stubbornly clung to their beliefs and practices and even when they have not. Jews themselves have often been embarrassed and apologetic about traditional teachings that view their people as having a distinctive relationship with God.

Realistically, however, all religions regard their relationships to the deity as unique. Christianity, after all, acquires its specialness from embracing Jesus as the son of God and the savior of humankind and believing itself embraced in return. Islam regards Allah as the only deity in the world and their prophet Muhammad as his messenger. Judaism does not claim to have exclusive access to God or to be the only recipient of God's love. It does not regard non-Jews as infidels or outside God's grace. (Given the Jewish history of suffering and persecution, many Jews might willingly echo the Yiddish poet Kadia Molodowsky's words to God: "Choose / —another people.") But Jewish tradition is rooted in the belief that the people of Israel made a binding covenant with God at Mount Sinai. Its goal was for them to become a "kingdom of priests and a holy nation" by adhering to the Torah and following in God's path. That is not a bad kind of distinctiveness for a people to aspire toward.

Holiness derives from separations in Jewish thought. Stated more broadly, it derives from making distinctions and drawing boundaries aimed at changing the ordinary into the extraordinary. Contrary to common belief, for example, Jewish dietary laws are not about health or hygiene. They are about holiness, about raising the everyday act of eating above the mundane and giving it meaning beyond itself. Similarly, one can view Saturday as a day like any other day, and most people do. But viewed as Shabbat, it becomes a day set apart from all others, a chosen day, the rabbis said, blessed and given to Israel as a gift from God's treasure house.

"Why is the Sabbath different from any other day of the week?" the wicked Roman governor Tinneius Rufus asked Rabbi Akiva. The Talmud records several disputations between this famous rabbi, who lived in the first and second centuries, and the governor of Judea, where he lived. Nobody can say how accurate these conversations are or if any really took place, but they include ideas the sages want to convey.

"Why are you different from other people?" Akiva responded.

"Because my master, the emperor, has so decreed," Rufus answered, asserting his power by claiming the Roman emperor as its source.

"The Sabbath, too, is different because our Master ordained that it should be so," Akiva retorted.

"How do you know that the day you have chosen actually *is* the Sabbath?" the governor persisted.

"We can prove it by the river Sambatyon" (which rests on the Sabbath), Akiva said. He continued with other proofs until reaching the one he knew would hit home with Rufus. It was based on a legend, and a widespread belief, that on Shabbat the fires in the lower world of Gehenna cease burning, giving sinners a respite from their punishments. "We can prove it," he said, "from your father's grave," implying that the grave is serene on this day, whereas the rest of the week Gehenna's smoke rises from it.

"You have disgraced and shamed my father!" Rufus shouted, enraged at Akiva's inference. Akiva said nothing.

To Akiva and other sages, all of nature bows to the distinctiveness of God's Shabbat, from the mythical river Sambatyon to the flames of Gehenna.

Historically, the Sabbath became especially important to Jews as a holy day after the Babylonian exile in 586 B.C.E. Certainly it had been regarded as a sacred and happy occasion long before that. Although historians know little about how the Israelites marked the Sabbath in earliest biblical times, they know that in later years Israel's kings took part in Sabbath celebrations, business and agricultural work officially ceased on the seventh day, and women as well as men visited with prophets and preachers to listen to their teachings. But more than ever, after the exile Sabbath observance became a distinguishing sign for Jews and a barrier against assimilation into foreign ways in foreign lands. (Not surprisingly, Shabbat attracted numbers of converts from those lands precisely because it provided something different—a day of leisure each week.)

The Sabbath remained an essential part of Jewish life after the exiles returned to Judea and built the Second Temple. When the Romans destroyed that Temple in 70 C.E.—during the lifetime of Akiva and other early sages—Shabbat became a permanent replacement for it. "Rabbi Johanan and Rabbi Eleazar used to say," the Talmud informs us, "so long as the Temple stood, the altar made atonement for Israel. Now a person's table makes atonement for him." While the Temple stood, people brought offerings to the altar to atone for their sins. With the Temple gone, that was no longer possible. Like the Mishkan before it, the Temple had represented an ideal world of holiness, but now the world had to represent the Temple. For the Jewish people, scattered in many places, the home became the center of that world and the Sabbath the center of the home.

With a longing for what had been lost and a genius for re-creating it, the sages symbolically incorporated into Jewish life aspects of the Temple service that still define Shabbat at home.

As the menorah gave light and warmth to the Temple, the Sabbath candles give spiritual light and warmth to the home.

As two columns of bread, twelve loaves altogether, were displayed on the Temple's golden table, two hallah breads stand on the Sabbath table, symbols also of the double portion of manna the Israelites received in the wilderness.

As the priests ritually washed their hands to demonstrate their purity before undertaking their duties, Jews ritually wash their hands before beginning a meal. The symbolic washing also conveys the message that the priesthood does not belong only to an honored class. All Jews have the potential to form a "kingdom of priests."

As the priests offered sacrifices on the Temple altar, many families make meat a part of their Shabbat meal. A container of salt stands on the table to represent the salt used with the sacrifices. Salt sprinkled on the hallah or hallah dipped in salt is also a sign of the hospitality of the day, like the custom of including bread and salt in housewarmings.

As libations of young wine accompanied Temple sacrifices, symbolizing joy and ritual, Jews sanctify the Sabbath over a cup of wine, pronouncing the kiddush blessing that recalls both creation and the exodus from Egypt.

As the Levites sang in the Temple (long before Gregorian

chants began), families and guests sing *zemirot*, songs and hymns, at the Sabbath table.

Lastly, as the Temple symbolized peace along with holiness, the Sabbath meal begins with a song welcoming the angels of peace that accompany people home from the synagogue. At the end of the meal, during the recitation of grace, all knives are removed from the table. This is a reminder that no metal tools were said to have touched the Temple in Jerusalem, for such tools could also be converted into weapons of war. Legend has it that instead of tools a tiny, powerful worm called the *shamir*, created in the twilight before the first Sabbath, cut through the large stones used in building the Temple. Removing the knives emphasizes the peace of the Temple and the peace of Shabbat.

"You shall be holy, for I your God am holy," Scripture had said. With their borrowings from the Temple, the rabbis reinforced Shabbat's holiness. Under their guidance the sacred space that had been the Temple transformed the sacred time of Shabbat and the sacred time of Shabbat transformed the home into sacred space.

The rabbis went further, extending the holiness of Shabbat into other areas and turning the most routine aspects of life into new opportunities for sanctifying the day. In doing this they opened the way for the spirit of the Sabbath to penetrate deep into the lives of ordinary people. "Your Sabbath clothes should not be like your weekday clothes," they said, using as their source Isaiah's words to "call the Sabbath 'delight,' the Lord's holy day 'honored.'" Encouraging people to dress as nicely as possible on Shabbat, they advised those too poor to change clothes to launder what they had and to lower their robes in aristocratic fashion in order to alter their workaday appearance. Rabbi Johanan ben Nappaha called his clothes "my honorers," saying he felt honored to wear them in honoring the Sabbath.

I think of my mother in the final years of her life. Beset by various ailments of old age, she was often homebound, yet she never failed to look her best on Shabbat. Even if she expected no visitors, she would wear one of her prettiest skirts and blouses adorned with some piece of jewelry from the small collection she had accumulated over the years. "After all, it's *Shabbos*," she would say when I visited for a weekend and complimented her on her appearance, and I always felt that for her that simple form of dressing up helped make it *Shabbos*.

In the various Jewish summer camps I attended as a child, campers and counselors dressed all in white on Shabbat eve. I can still picture the blanket of whiteness covering our rough wooden camp benches, as though the heavenly angels had spread their wings over us, crying "holy, holy, holy!"

I continue to dress differently on Shabbat, particularly for shul. Despite the fact that synagogues have become more informal than they were in my youth, I still wear skirts and heels, never pants or sneakers. The clothes set me apart from friends and neighbors I see wearing casual clothes for Saturday morning chores or a run in the park, but as I walk to my synagogue I sometimes spot other women dressed as I, going to theirs. Without knowing each other, we might nod or whisper "Shabbat Shalom." I imagine us part of a secret club, Shabbat clothes our badge of distinction.

"Your walking on the Sabbath should be different from your walking on weekdays," the sages taught, and "your speech on the Sabbath should not be like your speech on the weekdays." A Shabbat walk is more leisurely than others, because one is not rushing off to work or school, the gym or supermarket. I can always recognize observant Jewish men of a certain age taking a Sabbath stroll, aside from their head coverings and such. They place their hands behind them, resting on their backsides, as if to show they have no need to use those hands for productive work this day. As for Shabbat speech, forget about business deals or career worries, the rabbis want to say, this is a chance for unhurried conversations with family members and friends.

Even eating becomes a source of joyous holiness. The Talmud requires people to eat three meals on Shabbat—the festive Friday night and Saturday meals and a smaller third meal before the day ends. In early times most people ate only two meals over the course of an evening and a day, so adding a third had symbolic significance. The kabbalists identified the three meals with the patriarchs Abraham, Isaac, and Jacob. As for food itself, the third-century Babylonian sage Rav proposed that a good Sabbath meal consisted of "a dish of beets, a large fish, and heads of garlic." Considered an aphrodisiac, garlic served an important purpose on the Sabbath eve, when marital sex was recommended to increase the day's gladness. Garlic, folks said, "brings in love and brings out passion."

My father used to recall that in Russia, where he grew up, the family ate meat just once a week, on Shabbat, when they could manage it. Generally, however, chicken, fish, chopped liver, and the like were the usual Sabbath fare in Ashkenazi families like ours, and for many families they remain the foods of choice today. I serve chicken on Shabbat also, but I like to think I have a more sophisticated cuisine than the traditional one, even within the strictures of the dietary laws.

Still, what was it about my mother's roast chicken that I have never been able to duplicate? Was it the onions she put in that browned just enough to become crispy but not burned? Was it the amber color the chicken skin took on as it roasted in the ancient blue pan she kept spotless from week to week? Perhaps it was the mixture of aromas—supplementing the chicken were noodle pudding and carrot tzimmes that included sweet potatoes and prunes, a combination of foods so identified with Jewish family life they seem almost a caricature, yet one that in my mind still conjures up my mother's kitchen and her Friday night chicken. Then again, maybe it was something else.

The Roman emperor Hadrian, an often repeated tale relates, once asked Rabbi Joshua ben Hanania, "Why is Sabbath food so fragrant?" The rabbi answered, "We have a certain spice called Shabbat that we put into it that gives the food its fragrance." The emperor said, "Give us some of it." To which the rabbi replied, "The spice is effective for someone who keeps the Sabbath, but is of no use to someone who does not keep the Sabbath."

Maybe the fragrance in my mother's chicken came from its Sabbath spice, along with the browned onions and side dishes. In truth, it was the best meal she made; she wasn't an outstanding cook, although she could bake great cakes. But she made this dish for Shabbat, and with that condiment blended into its tastes and aromas, it has become in memory unequaled, impossible to replicate, inseparable from the day itself.

The rabbinic discussion of walking, talking, dressing, and eating on the Sabbath made it clear that even the most prosaic aspects of life can contribute to the atmosphere of holiness and differentness on Shabbat. Emerging from this discussion also is the idea that reaching for spiritual heights on Shabbat does not require denying the physical. It does not require fasting, or abstaining from sex, or isolating oneself with soulful music, as I did with my Gregorian chants. Just the opposite. We bring holiness into ordinary life by imbuing the physical—our "enslavement to things," in Heschel's words—with spiritual significance. So a table becomes a Temple altar, and clothing, food, and even sexuality become means of honoring the Sabbath.

A story is told of the great Israel Baal Shem Tov, founder of the Hasidic movement in the eighteenth century. He dreamt one night that an angel carried him to paradise and showed him two vacant seats. "Who are these for?" the Baal Shem asked. "For you," came the answer, "if you make good use of your intelligence, and also for a man whose name and address I am writing down for you."

The angel then took the Baal Shem to the depths of Gehenna and showed him two vacant seats. "Who are these for?" the Baal Shem asked again. "For you," the angel again answered, "if you make no use of your intelligence, and also for a man whose name and address I am writing down for you."

In his dream the Baal Shem visited the person destined to be his companion in paradise. He found the man ignorant of Judaism, except that every Sabbath he made a joyful banquet for all his friends. When asked, the man said he didn't know exactly why he gave the party, but he remembered that in his youth his parents prepared lavish meals on Saturday and sang many songs, therefore he did the same. At first the Baal Shem thought to teach the man about Shabbat, but he stopped himself, knowing that he would spoil the man's Sabbath delight by showing him his religious errors.

Later, when the Baal Shem visited the person slotted to join him in Gehenna, he found the man to be such a strict observer of Judaism that he spent the entire Sabbath tense and anxious lest he break a single rule. The Baal Shem wanted to chide him, but he stopped himself, knowing the man would not understand. From this dream came the Baal Shem's emphasis on joy in religious practice.

The story has many meanings, but nobody should read it as an advertisement to do away with Sabbath rules. Although the Baal Shem began his movement in opposition to what he regarded as an overly legalistic approach to religion among his contemporaries, he was not a religious anarchist. Instead, he aimed to infuse Shabbat, and all of Judaism, with more than rules and regulations. Despite the fact that the second man in his dream obeyed every minutia of law, the man desecrated the Sabbath, because he did not behave differently on it than at any other time of the week. He spent the day tense and anxious about following the rules the way he might have spent a weekday tense and anxious about his work. He added nothing to the sanctity of the day and gained nothing from it, whereas the first man brought joy to the day and to everyone who participated in it with him. Enjoying the sacredness of Shabbat requires fashioning a day so unlike all others that how we act on it contrasts with our actions at any other time of the week.

The kabbalists made much of the concept of the *neshamah yeterah*, the extra Sabbath soul that descends from heaven and enlarges a person's normal soul. That extra soul, they taught, expands consciousness, allowing us to soar above our ordinary selves to a higher level of sensibility. (In legend, the Maharal of Prague, the pious Rabbi Judah Loew ben Bezalel, literally soared on Shabbat, becoming a head taller and thereby earning the nickname, "The Tall Rabbi.") With the extra soul and special food, dress, and other practices, we *make* Shabbat by turning both time and space into holy sites.

The kiddush blessing on Friday evening begins by recounting the completion of the world as Genesis describes it. "The heaven and the earth were finished, and all their array. . . ." In Hebrew "were finished" is *vay'khulu*. Twisting the vowels around, the Talmud changes the word to *vay'kholu*, "they finished." Who are "they"? We, humans. The rabbis claim that anyone who recites this verse on Friday night becomes a partner with God in creation, for by saying these words the person affirms creation and God as creator of the universe. In that sense he or she has participated in the creative process.

But a few verses later lies a further idea about the partnership between God and humans. The idea grows from that much used word *la'asot*, to make, so prominent throughout the creation narrative and the story of the Mishkan. In

English the verse reads clearly enough: "And God blessed the seventh day and declared it holy, for on it God ceased from all the work of creation that God had done." In the biblical Hebrew, however, it seems peculiar, because literally it says that God ceased from all the work God had created to make, *la'asot.* What does this mean? How can God rest from work yet to be made? And if creation ended, what work remained? Enter the partnership concept again. The commentators interpret the *la'asot* here to mean that the work remaining and still to be done is human work. It is the work of sustaining and caring for the created world. How do we understand that work?

Tinneius Rufus and Rabbi Akiva in conversation again: The Roman governor once again tests the rabbi, this time by asking whose deeds are finer, the deeds of God or those of humans. Akiva shocks the Roman by showing him stalks of grain in one hand and loaves of bread in the other. Which is superior? Clearly the bread is. Nature alone, God's creation, is not complete, Akiva teaches Rufus. Human technology and human labor are necessary to transform the grain into bread—the potential in God's created world into the useful. Hence the divine-human partnership. Hence God "created *la'asot.*"

What applies to creation in general applies to Shabbat in particular. The Bible tells us that God created the Sabbath by ceasing from work on the seventh day and sanctifying that time. In ancient lore, Shabbat existed in God's thoughts even before the creation of the world. Nonetheless, Shabbat exists here on earth only when we hallow and celebrate it. In partnership with God we maintain the holiness God introduced into the world, and in doing so we also share in God's holiness. Like the Mishkan with which it was coupled and the Temples it replaced, Shabbat invites the divine presence to dwell among us, but it leaves it to us to ready the dwelling place.

One more thought about *making* Shabbat. In the vernacular, to make Shabbat refers to the shopping, cooking, cleaning, and many other preparations needed to prepare the home for the Sabbath. Traditionally, women have had the major responsibility for this realm of Sabbath making and for creating the atmosphere of holiness that envelops the Sabbath home. The mystics believed that in making Shabbat women become identified with the Shekhinah, whose partnership and union with the masculine attributes of God hold the seeds of salvation. The next chapter takes up that form of partnership.

Four

WOMEN AT THE CENTER

The Mystical Sabbath

My great-grandmother Riva was a formidable woman. Her photo sits on my piano top along with those of other family members, and although creased and faded it dominates the pantheon. The picture was taken soon after she arrived in America at the age of ninety-five from a tiny Russian village called Shipilowitz. Bedecked in her best *Shabbos* dress, she stares out at the world through stern, intelligent eyes. Her flat, dark *sheitel* (the wig she wore as a sign of modesty) fits low on her forehead and has a straight center part. My cousins joke that the *sheitel* set off against her high cheekbones and chiseled jawline gives her the appearance of a Native American chieftain.

How I wish I had known her. Family lore says that even at her advanced age, Riva easily climbed the five flights of stairs that led to the dingy apartment she shared on New York's Lower East Side with my father and his family—his parents and four younger brothers. My grandfather's mother,

Riva was also mother to the ne'er-do-well Uncle Zalman, whom she coddled and protected all her life. It was a long life; she died at the age of 103 (others say 107). In the old country, she had married at fifteen and given birth to five sons and a daughter. Her husband died young along with one son during a flu epidemic, and shortly afterward her daughter also died. Riva reared the rest of her children alone in a big house made of logs on farmland generations of her husband's family had inhabited.

My father wrote about his grandmother in a memoir he composed for our extended family when he himself was in his early nineties. His parents lived on the farm with Riva after they married, and there he and his brothers remained until the family immigrated to America. Riva ruled the roost, directing and dominating her daughter-in-law, my gentle grandmother Goldie, and her son, my grandfather Jacob. But Riva also worked alongside Goldie caring for the children, raising fruits and vegetables, milking the cows, churning butter, and making cheese to be sold in the marketplace. With all that, she became known throughout neighboring villages and towns for her hospitality—the "hostess Riva of Shipilowitz," people called her. Rabbis and other itinerants who traveled about collecting money for various Jewish institutions knew that when they stopped by Riva's home she would welcome them with lunch, dinner, or a glass of tea. Often these wayfarers managed to arrive on a Friday afternoon. Then Riva would invite them to stay over until *Shabbos* ended.

Riva was also known for her learning and her ability to read both Hebrew and Yiddish. She came from a rabbinic family and had a brother who was a famous rabbi in the large city of Minsk. She herself prayed daily in Hebrew from the prayer book. On Friday nights, after lighting the Sabbath candles, she would pore over her worn booklet of *tkhines*, women's prayers of supplication, while her son and oldest grandsons attended shul in a nearby village. She spent Saturday afternoons reading biblical stories and legends from the *Tsena Urena*, a collection of narratives and commentaries in Yiddish designed for women (and uneducated men). Often Riva would read aloud from it to my grandmother and neighboring women who did not know how to read.

The village of Shipilowitz, where the family lived, was in Belorussia, once part of Poland, and later under czarist Russian rule. Among Jews, its inhabitants had become known as *litvaks*, meaning stemming from "Lita," or Lithuania, but referring more to a world outlook than an exact location. It was a rationalistic outlook, with an emphasis on intellect and learning and little interest in the mystical or emotional aspects of Jewish practice. My father could recite long passages from the Torah by heart and quote at ease from the Talmud, but I never heard him tell a Hasidic tale or consciously cite a mystical text. And Riva, with her stern eyes, strong mind, and iron will appears the epitome of what the term *litvak* signifies.

Yet from my father's description of the Sabbath Riva and her family often shared with guests in their big log house, it's clear that, though unrecognized as such, mystical rites and images permeated their *Shabbos* as they do my Shabbat so many years later. When the men in the family chanted the beautiful Lekhah Dodi in their village shul on Friday nights they were saying a kabbalistic hymn that beckons the

Sabbath queen. When, at home, Riva prayed from her booklet of *tkhines,* more than one of her supplications included
mystical references taken from kabbalistic sources. When
my grandfather recited the Shalom Aleikhem song that welcomes the Sabbath angels, he was reading a song composed
by kabbalists. And, dare I say it, when Riva and her husband
and later my grandparents retired to their tiny bedroom after
the *Shabbos* evening meal, they probably knew this was an
auspicious night for lovemaking, not only because the Talmud said so, but because the kabbalists had emphasized it.
Put another way, I would wager that at least some of Riva's
six children and my grandparents' five were conceived on
the Sabbath eve—in kabbalistic terms, each coupling help-
ing to bring harmony to the universe.

Mysticism and spirituality have become so popular today
that even Hollywood stars take courses in kabbalistic ideas.
But it wasn't always that way. For centuries mysticism formed
a hidden, mysterious strain in Judaism, studied only by the
most seasoned and learned scholars. The Hebrew word *kabbalah,* which means "a receiving" or simply "tradition," came
to stand for an esoteric tradition concerning God's relation
to the universe that was often passed on orally and secretly.
Over time, however, kabbalistic ideas began to seep into the
mainstream, and eventually to spread throughout the Jewish
world, affecting the lives of even my determinedly *litvishe*
great-grandmother and her progeny.

One landmark in the development of the Kabbalah was the
compilation of the Zohar. Tradition holds that Rabbi Simeon
bar Yohai, the sage who had hidden with his son in a cave for
twelve years, composed the Zohar. But scholars attribute it to

the late-thirteenth-century Spanish kabbalist Moses de Leon, who intentionally wrote it in an earlier talmudic style to make it seem much older than it is. Another landmark in the history of the Kabbalah was the growth in the sixteenth century of an exuberant school of mysticism and messianism revolving around Rabbi Isaac Luria in the city of Safed in the Galilean region of Palestine. Known as Lurianic or Safed Kabbalah, this mystical movement built on the old ideas and added new ones that won it numerous followers.

Of the many themes common to all strains of the Kabbalah, those dealing with Shabbat are pivotal. In the words of the great scholar of mysticism Gershom Scholem, the "Sabbath is *the* day of the Kabbalah." No discussion of the day would be complete or honest without probing the mystical interpretations that have had a profound influence on the Jewish world and continue to influence the way we think about Shabbat today. Central to those interpretations are the mystics' preoccupation with the feminine—in relation to God, in relation to sexuality, and in relation to the day as a whole.

First some background: Fundamental to all kabbalistic thinking is the notion that God is manifest in the world through the ten *sefirot* mentioned earlier, the ten dimensions of divinity. (Literally, *sefirot* means numbers, although some authorities connect the word to *sappir,* or "sapphire," referring to God's luminosity.) The *sefirot* form a kind of pathway between the hidden, eternal, and transcendent God, whom the mystics called the Ein-Sof, "Without End" or "Infinite," and God's presence as it is experienced in the world. As such, the *sefirot* unfold from the unknowable Godhead, each a cluster of qualities that reveal different attributes of the divine. Through meditation, the contemplation of God's name, or other means, mystics endeavored, and still endeavor, to enter the world of the *sefirot* and unlock some of its mysteries.

The early kabbalists sometimes sketched the order of the *sefirot* in the shape of a man they called Adam Kadmon, the primordial human who symbolically reflects the divine structure. In this portrait, the highest and most concealed *sefirah*, Keter (crown), along with the next two *sefirot*, Hokhmah (wisdom) and Binah (knowledge), form the head and brain of the man. Next come Hesed (loving kindness) and Gevurah or Din (judgment), which make up the right and left arms, respectively. The sixth *sefirah*, Tiferet (beauty), is the trunk of the body. The seventh and eighth, Netsah (triumph) and Hod (glory), are the right and left legs, and Yesod (foundation) is associated with the divine phallus. The final *sefirah*, Malkhut (majesty) or Shekhinah (presence), most interacts with the world as we know it.

Drawing on human life, the kabbalists also visualized the *sefirot* in male and female terms. They regarded Hokhmah as a masculine principle and Binah as a feminine one, labeling them the Divine Father and Mother. From the interactions of these higher *sefirot*, the mystics said, flowed the seven lower ones. Among those, they identified Tiferet and Yesod as masculine and designated the Shekhinah, the seventh lower *sefirah*, as the feminine aspect of God and closest to earth.

Of all the *sefirot*, the Shekhinah has the most meaning in terms of Shabbat. For mainstream talmudic sages, the word

Shekhinah was simply a poetic means of speaking about God's presence. Like the sun, they said, the Shekhinah radiates over the entire world. They also contemplated the Shekhinah's special connection to Israel. "Come and see how beloved Israel is to God," the Talmud states. "In every place to which its people were exiled the Shekhinah went with them. They were exiled to Egypt and the Shekhinah was with them ... to Babylon and the Shekhinah was with them. . . . And when they will be redeemed in the future the Shekhinah will be with them." Wherever the people of Israel go, the passage asserts, God's spirit hovers in their midst.

From the talmudic vision of the Shekhinah accompanying Israel in exile, the kabbalists fashioned a rich, poignant, often radical imagery of it as the feminine side of God that has been separated from its center. In some of their writings they pictured the male and female forces in the universe as originally united in a single divine Being (in much the same way that Plato's *Symposium* imagined a primal androgynous human). But Adam and Eve's sin of eating from the tree of knowledge and Israel's later transgressions split the divine forces, creating disharmony in the cosmos. The feminine Shekhinah was forced into exile, and from her sadness and weeping, she may have lost her eyesight. Humankind, and Israel in particular, have a mission to restore the divine unity of male and female by fulfilling God's commandments with purity and devotion.

Isaac Luria and the sixteenth-century kabbalists regarded the Shekhinah's exile as resulting from a cataclysm that occurred during creation. At that time, they taught, vessels meant to hold God's light burst because of the intensity of energy within them, scattering sparks of divine light into the world. Many of those sparks became trapped by forces of evil, called *kellipot,* that formed from the shards of the broken vessels. Trapped also were the sparks of the Shekhinah. Here, too, through good deeds and sincere dedication, humans can help free the Shekhinah, reunite her with God, and in doing so repair and redeem the universe. Still today, many Orthodox prayer books include in the blessing for donning a tallit, or prayer shawl, the words, "For the sake of the unification of the Blessed Holy One with His Shekhinah."

Kabbalist writings picture the Shekhinah in many ways. They often associate her with light, sustaining both the angels in heaven and the righteous in the world to come. But they also speak of her as the "holy moon" that glows with the reflected light of the sun, because in her position as the lowest *sefirah* she holds no light of her own, shining only with the rays of the upper *sefirot.* They liken the moon's "lessening" as it enters its darker phases to the Shekhinah going into exile. When the world will merit redemption and the universe is healed, they say, the moon will be restored to its full light equal to the light of the sun. Then the Shekhinah will return from exile. At times, the Zohar portrays the Shekhinah as a rainbow, which appears as a sign of protection in the sky. "It is like the king whose son constantly sinned against him," the text says. "But whenever the king went to punish him, the queen consort would appear in beautiful garments of royalty," and the king would cease being angry. Similar to the rainbow that represented God's reconciliation with humanity after Noah's flood, the Shekhinah serves as God's consort who intervenes to protect the people on earth even after they've sinned.

And through a variety of esoteric and intricate interpretations, the kabbalists also identify the Shekhinah with Shabbat, both transmitting God's presence into the world. They characterize Shabbat, like the Shekhinah, as God's consort— the queen, the bride, sometimes the daughter and princess—swathed in beautiful garments of royalty, as beautiful as a rainbow. Again, talmudic sages preceded the kabbalists in expressing their love for Shabbat in such feminine images. In a parable, they described a king who built a beautiful bridal chamber, which he painted and decorated. "What did the chamber lack?" they asked. "A bride to enter it," they answered. So it was with the newly formed world. It lacked the Sabbath until God created the Sabbath bride.

More picturesquely, the Talmud relates that on Friday evenings, in the dusk before the Sabbath approached, Rabbi Hanina ben Dosa would don his best Sabbath robes and do a little dance while he exclaimed, "Let us go forth to welcome the Queen Sabbath." Rabbi Yannai would say, "Come O Bride, Come O Bride."

But again, the kabbalists of the sixteenth century embellished these earlier ideas with daring and imaginative interpretations. Their city of Safed stood on steep hills, and from those hillsides near sunset on Friday afternoons they would walk in procession into the open fields to greet the Sabbath bride. They must have made a dramatic sight, these groups of men (no women included) clad in white, marching together and singing psalms and hymns as they moved along. (The closest scene that comes to mind is of the colorful Hasidic sects in Jerusalem that stream toward the Western Wall for Shabbat evening services, each group wearing its own distinctive clothes.)

Best-known of the hymns the kabbalists sang is the Lekha Dodi, written by Solomon Halevi Alkabez, whose name is spelled out through the first letters of each verse. Over the course of time it became the hymn that my grandfather and father recited on Friday evenings in their little shul in Russia, that I sing in my synagogue, that Jews all over the world say to usher in Shabbat. All over the world, also, Jews turn toward the synagogue entrance during the hymn's last verse and bow slightly as they conclude with Rabbi Yannai's words, "Come, O bride, Come O bride." The turning and bowing have replaced the kabbalists' procession of old. They represent the modern form of going out to meet the Sabbath queen and of beckoning the Shekhinah in from her exile.

The Lekha Dodi hymn has become so popular and so pivotal to the Friday evening Kabbalat Shabbat service welcoming the Sabbath that not many people who sing it know or think about its mystical origins or true meanings. Yet from it we have inherited some of the basic tenets of the kabbalistic Sabbath. In part it expresses a longing for the redemption of Israel and the Shekhinah in its midst.

"Arise, shine, for your light has come," it proclaims, using phrases from the prophet Isaiah. "Awake, awake," it urges the people of Israel in the words of the prophet Deborah. The phrases and words inspire Israel to look forward to a better day, and at the same time they inspire the Shekhinah to rouse herself from her enforced exile.

But Lekha Dodi is also a love song filled with emotion and symbolism. "Come my beloved to greet the bride," its refrain begins, and it ends, "Let us receive the face of the Sabbath." The beloved may be the community of Israel, who in legend had been paired with the Sabbath when she complained that she was the only day of the week without a partner. The beloved may also refer to God, who is alluded to in one verse as the Sabbath's "husband." Or it may be both, God and Israel, accompanying one another to welcome the beloved Sabbath, the beloved Shekhinah.

As symbolic, the song's first verse begins "Observe and Remember were uttered as one," words taken from the Talmud. The sages had tried to reconcile the different openings of the Sabbath command—"Remember" in Exodus and "Observe" in Deuteronomy—by declaring that God had uttered them simultaneously. The kabbalists added a new definition to that concept of unity.

"Why does it say Remember and Observe?" asks Sefer ha-Bahir, an early mystic source. "'Remember' refers to the male and 'Observe' to the female," it answers. In mystical reckoning, "Remember" applies to Tiferet and Yesod, the male aspects of God, and "Observe" to the Shekhinah, the female aspect. On Friday night, the male and female *sefirot* become momentarily whole, as they had once been and would be everlastingly in a future messianic era. On Friday nights, Shabbat, who is also the Shekhinah and bride, reunites with her consort in a mysterious marriage made in heaven.

As they escorted the Sabbath bride, the kabbalists of old hailed that forthcoming marriage in the Lekha Dodi and other hymns. Afterward, they celebrated in their homes with rituals and blessings. Before sitting down to eat, the family would march around the table carrying two bunches of myrtle branches. In ancient Israel, as in other ancient cultures, myrtle symbolized love. Sometimes a wedding canopy would be made of myrtle; sometimes wedding guests would hold myrtle branches while they danced before the bride. (Sometimes they still do.) For the kabbalists, the myrtle recalled the story of Rabbi Simeon bar Yohai and the old man he and his son met on a Friday evening carrying two bundles of myrtle, one for "Remember" and one for "Observe." The myrtle served as a sign of the sacred union that would take place that night.

Other signs appeared throughout the evening. The Shalom Aleikhem poem that the kabbalists composed and we still sing has its source in the talmudic legend that when people return from synagogue on Friday evening two angels accompany them. "Peace be with you," the song bids the "angels of peace." But to the kabbalists these angels, called "ministering angels" in the first verse, were also the servants of the Shekhinah, her escorts as she prepared to enter the royal palace. They viewed the Shabbat dinner, with its traditional *zemirot*, or table songs, as a time to sing to the Sabbath bride and cheer her soul. Accordingly, they wrote many of the most popular table songs we sing today. And they introduced the practice of reading *Eshet Hayil*, the "Woman of Valor" poem from the book of Proverbs that has become part of Shabbat evening among Jewish families in many lands. The "Woman of Valor" praises the diligent housewife for her hard work at home and in business dealings (more about that in a moment). But the mystics interpreted every line as a paean to the Shekhinah, who the Zohar says is "pure" on Friday evening, freed from the evil husks that restrict her during the week.

Finally, after all the hymns, songs, blessings, and rituals, the time arrives for the Shekhinah and her groom to be united. The kabbalists determined that this mating, the culmination of all the evening's rites, takes place at midnight. Now, the Zohar says, the Shekhinah who "is closed and sealed all week" like a rose whose petals cling tightly together, is "opened to receive her husband." Now, in a union of love, Shekhinah and Tiferet become one. Their coupling will infuse the six days of the week with the bounty of their love, and from that coupling will come "holy souls for the world," the souls of the righteous.

Now, also, a parallel act takes place on earth. Before analyzing that, we need to return one more time to the Talmud. There it states that a man has a responsibility to please his wife sexually. In fact, so important do the rabbis regard sex in a marriage that they legislated a minimum schedule for men of various occupations to fulfill their "marital duty." For men of leisure that meant every day. For laborers the requirement was twice a week; for donkey drivers (who traveled about during the week) once a week; for camel drivers (who traveled more extensively) once in thirty days; and for sailors (who were away from home for long stretches) once in six months. But—and this was the category the rabbis cared about most—scholars are expected to meet their sexual responsibilities once a week, on Friday nights.

Using this and other talmudic sources, the kabbalists made Friday night sex for scholars a centerpiece of their Sabbath imaginings. For them, marital sex between a scholar and his wife mirrors that act between God and the Shekhinah. The Zohar explains that scholars "prepare themselves for intercourse, because they know the exalted mystery concerning the time when the consort is united with the King." And when scholars and their wives couple at the same time as the heavenly lovers, their own souls soar to the celestial spheres even while they lie peacefully in their beds. Through their lovemaking they, too, produce "fine children" and "bestow holy souls" upon them.

More important, in the most mystical manner, the couple on earth symbolically becomes the couple on high, the Shekhinah and her groom, and the union below helps complete the union above. In so doing, the earthly couple participates in establishing the cosmic harmony that occurs on Friday nights when the Shekhinah returns temporarily from her exile and becomes one with her spouse. That oneness is so essential that the purpose of marital intercourse on Friday night must be to aid in the divine union of male and female. Intercourse at that time for any other reason, even for the sake of procreation, is improper. Says the Zohar: "'Remember' and 'Observe' are the blessed Holy One and the Shekhinah. Happy is the person who unites them on the Sabbath day. . . ."

Although the kabbalists directed their Sabbath teachings toward scholars, with time their ideas became absorbed into general Jewish thought. On Shabbat, every Jewish woman who celebrates the day has a link to the Shekhinah, the bride and queen, and her observance and acts of love help bring joy and peace to her home. With more time, few people outside kabbalistic circles remembered the details of the mystics' concepts, but their songs and dreams of redemption have remained embedded in the fabric of Jewish life. Did my great grandmother Riva know about the esoteric interpretations of "Remember" and "Observe" or about the mystical significance of marital sex on Friday nights? I doubt it. But she donned her best dress on Shabbat, made her home as beautiful and welcoming for the Sabbath bride and queen as she could, and rejoiced in the spiritual world the kabbalists had brought to life.

As for me, in spite of my litvak background and leanings, I find myself awed by the kabbalistic Shabbat. Here is a great cosmic drama filled with color, fantasy, sexuality, and divine action, a drama in which the audience not only participates, but also affects the outcome. When, in this drama, humans welcome Shabbat into the home, treat it with the respect accorded to royalty, and surround it with happiness and love, they help create balance and peace in the heavens that, in turn, radiate back down to earth. In that sense, participants in Shabbat have the power to span the upper and lower worlds, much as the Sabbath commandment itself does.

Still, I have reservations. Some of my reservations concern the way the kabbalists characterize Shabbat and the Shekhinah almost as if they are real personages. Are these images, in fact, just variations on the goddesses that inhabit other religious imaginations? How should we understand Shabbat as God's consort? How should we understand the female aspect of God cohabiting with the male? Don't such portrayals smack of idolatry, the stuff of foreign religions?

People learned in Kabbalah counter such questions with reminders that kabbalistic theories do not picture an array of gods. They explore the *intra*divine—what takes place within the inner life of the one, indivisible God. The kabbalistic Shekhinah is but one facet of that singular God, just as the other *sefirot* represent various aspects of the deity, channels of energy that flow back and forth within the one God. Looked at another way, the mystics used human language, especially the language of sexuality, to try to uncover the nature of the hidden, complex, and mysterious God who nevertheless acts in the world and shapes human life.

The arguments have merit. Jewish tradition has a long history of describing the relationship between God and Israel in romantic terms. The prophet Hosea used the metaphor of husband and wife when he pictured God reconciling with a wayward Israel. "I will espouse you forever: I will espouse you with righteousness and justice, and with goodness and mercy..." he announced in words that would become part of the liturgy. Later, the rabbis interpreted the most sensual book in the Bible, the Song of Songs, as an allegory of love between God and Israel. For them, its erotic images and lovers' passionate exchanges expressed Israel's intense religious passion for its God.

The kabbalists built on these precedents in their portrayal of the sacred marriage between God and the Shekhinah. They chose the Song of Songs to read on Friday afternoons in preparation for the evening's "nuptials," and, largely because of their choice, many people still read that dialogue of love on Friday afternoons or evenings. But the kabbalists went beyond the prophets and rabbis. By regarding marital relations on Shabbat as a means to help restore unity and harmony to the cosmos, they lifted sexuality out of the realm of the purely physical and into the realm of the spirit. Sex was now tied to the origins and workings of the universe and the desire for redemption.

Most significant, the kabbalists' strong emphasis on the

feminine Shekhinah enhanced our way of thinking about God. The male God whom the prophets pictured as Israel's spouse now had a female side as well. God need not be seen only as father or husband. God could also be mother, sister, daughter, or wife. The kabbalists strove for, and taught all who followed them to strive for unity between the male and female elements of the divine. Shabbat, they showed, offers the best way to achieve that unity temporarily in preparation for permanent unity in a future world.

And yet. Kabbalistic pictures of that female side of God do not gladden a feminist's heart. The female Shekhinah of the mystics is not simply the feminine half of God, equal to God's male attributes. No, the Shekhinah often appears in stereotypical sexual terms as the passive aspect of the deity, a receptacle for male influence. In keeping with this outlook the Zohar describes the Shekhinah as operating in the lower world sometimes as a male force and sometimes as a female. When is it a male force? "When it provides blessings for the world." And when female? "When it brings chastisements on the world"—not an endearing characterization.

Similarly, the Shekhinah does not generate her own light, but merely projects light from the emanations above her. She is the moon, absorbing the glow of the sun, but owning nothing herself. Worse, as the lowest *sefirah,* closest to the material world, the Shekhinah can be overcome by evil forces, which the mystics called *sitra ahra,* or "the other side." As the Zohar describes her, she "tastes the other, bitter side and then her face is dark." Instead of symbolizing a loving mother to humanity she becomes a symbol of divine judgment and punishment.

Moreover, when the kabbalists praise the Shekhinah, or Shabbat, as God's consort and bride, they often mean to highlight God's masculine nature, with the feminine as a subsidiary aspect. The scholar Elliot Wolfson stresses this masculinity, especially in the sacred marriage of God and the Shekhinah so dear to the hearts of the kabbalists. That marriage, he finds, is not meant to be a joining of distinctive female and male principles within the deity. Instead, its ultimate goal, the goal of redemption, is for the female Shekhinah to merge into the all-male Godhead. In the long run, he says, God is an androgynous male with a female element in his makeup, but male nonetheless.

How do we reconcile these contradictory views of the Shekhinah? How do we deal with the disparities between the elevation of the feminine in the kabbalistic Shabbat and the subordination of the feminine in the kabbalistic Shabbat? How should women—and men—respond to a feminine aspect of God that on the one hand symbolizes the love and compassion of the divine presence on earth and on the other stresses female passivity and inferiority?

The questions lead to other, broader ones outside the Kabbalah about women's roles within Judaism, and specifically about their roles in relation to Shabbat. To take one example: By giving women the responsibility of lighting the Sabbath candles, the tradition recognizes their essential roles in upholding the sacredness of the day. For their part, women have always taken special pleasure in lighting those candles, and through that act opening their homes to Shabbat. In fact, Shabbat candlesticks have been a common symbol engraved on women's tombstones, a sign of their high value in the woman's life. With all that, the law requiring women to kindle the Sabbath lights has an edge to it, and a traditional explanation for why that law exists is downright demeaning to women.

The law appears in the Mishnah, the first major code of Jewish law after the Bible, compiled around 200 C.E. "Women die in childbirth for three transgressions," it says, and goes on to list the three as: "not separating from their husbands during menstruation, not setting aside the portion of priests' dough, and not kindling the Sabbath lamp." Sexual separation during menstruation is part of the rules of family purity. Setting aside the priests' dough refers to throwing a piece of dough into the fire while baking bread in memory of the tithe paid to the priests during the time of the Temple. (The portion of dough set aside is called *hallah,* later the name used for the braided Sabbath loaf.) Women's obligation to light the Sabbath lamp, along with the other two "women's commandments," comes from this harsh legal statement about the punishment for not doing so.

Even more disturbing is the rationale for lighting given in the *aggadah,* the nonlegal rabbinic writings. We learn there that all three women's obligations resulted from Eve's disobedience in eating the forbidden fruit. Why must women observe the laws of menstrual separation, the text asks. Because, it answers, Eve shed Adam's blood by bringing death into the world as a result of her sin. Why the precept of the dough offering? Because Eve corrupted Adam (who, separated from the dust of the land, had been sacred, like the priests' tithe). And why kindle the Sabbath lights? Because she "extinguished Adam's soul" by making him mortal.

There it is. Women light the Sabbath candles because the

first woman put out the world's lights by bringing death into it. One of the most universal and emotionally resonant rituals that women perform is traced to a mean-spirited origin. What's a contemporary woman who loves Shabbat and its candlelighting to do?

What women in modern times have done is to reread texts and reexamine history from a different perspective, from a female perspective. In her poem "The Sadness Cage," for example, the Israeli poet Esther Ettinger uses a phrase from the Lekha Dodi song welcoming the Sabbath to urge women to "rise up go forth" and break through the bars that restrict them. And in her poem "The First Time We Made Shabbos Together," the America poet Merle Feld gives the nondescript setting of a couple's first home an air of sanctity. The two sit down at an ugly "second-hand chrome table" in a "third floor walk-up." But when the man makes kiddush under the flickering Shabbat lights, everything changes. The home has become an altar, as the rabbis advised. Then the poet writes, "We will be silent together/We will open our flowers in each other's presence." Through her contemporary experience she has also made the kabbalistic Shabbat of intimacy and love her own.

I need not rehearse in detail here the many other fresh insights with which women have approached both Jewish life and life in general—the investigations into women's history, the rediscovery of long-neglected women's writings, the creation of original rites that express women's feelings, the reconsideration of the language of prayer, the reevaluation of women's roles in society, and more. All these approaches have yielded a fuller understanding of women's lives in the past and changed the landscapes of their lives today.

Applied to the Shabbat lights (to continue that example), such approaches cushion the impact of negative texts by highlighting the positive nature of others. The *aggadah* might present candlelighting as a woman's atonement for Eve's sin, but the Talmud itself offers the possiblity of an alternative explanation. Regarding the verse in Proverbs that reads "The lifebreath of a person is the lamp of God," the Talmud pictures God saying, "The soul that I have placed within you is called a lamp; therefore I commanded you concerning the Sabbath lights." Here the Sabbath lights are identified in a positive way with the soul, the essence of life in every person, not only Adam. By bringing light into the world with the Sabbath candles, a woman celebrates and sustains life. This is a more acceptable explanation for the commandment to kindle Shabbat lights, and one that women today feel comfortable emphasizing.

Women today, and men as well, also emphasize the thoughts and voices of women of yesterday that have been lost or forgotten or silenced in the sea of male laws and legends that make up the bulk of traditional writings about Shabbat. Among the most moving underrated documents of the past are the prayers women recited while baking their Sabbath hallahs, lighting their Sabbath lamps, or at other important moments of their lives. The library of the Jewish Theological Seminary in New York has a touching collection of eighteenth- and nineteenth-century Italian Jewish women's prayers. Surprisingly, most are in Hebrew, indicating that these Sephardi women knew enough Hebrew to at least read prayers. The *tkhines* supplications that my great grandmother and a slew of other Ashkenazi women said were mainly in Yiddish. In her groundbreaking book *Voices of the Matriarchs,*

Chava Weissler analyzes and chronicles such prayers among Ashkenazi women of western and eastern Europe. Men wrote many of the prayers for the women to say, but a number of women also composed *tkhines*.

Here is part of a *tkhine* by an unknown seventeenth-century author written for a woman to say when she puts her Sabbath loaf into the oven: "Lord of all the worlds ... Send an angel to guard the baking, so that everything will be well baked, will rise nicely, and will not burn. ..."

And here is part of a *tkhine* written by an eighteenth-century east European woman, Shifrah bas Joseph, and meant to be said at candlelighting: "... And when the woman kindles the lights, it is fitting for her to kindle with joy and with wholeheartedness, because it is in honor of the Shekhinah and in honor of the Sabbath. ... Thus she will be privileged to have holy children. ... And by this means she gives her husband long life. ..."

These words and those of many other women's prayers and devotions tell us what we already know, that until recent generations women's lives have revolved almost exclusively around domestic matters and been concentrated on the well-being of their husbands and children. But delving behind those words tells us something else: The domestic chores had great meaning, often great spiritual meaning, to the women who engaged in them. There was a time in contemporary life, after large numbers of women had stepped outside their homemaking roles and into professional areas long dominated by men, that many of us looked down on the world of our mothers and grandmothers. We looked down on women whose prayers concerned their baking and cooking or who made their spouses and children the sole focus of their existence. We consciously chose different paths. Now we've moved beyond that attitude. We've begun to reevaluate the home lives of our ancestors and to honor those women.

When the sages spoke of the importance of Sabbath meals in providing the day's delight, they said that "even a humble dish can be a delight" if it is prepared in honor of the Sabbath. "What humble dish, for example?" one rabbi asked. "Fish-hash pie," another answered.

Women knew that the meals they prepared for the Sabbath were essential to the day's spirit. So they prayed for angels to guide them and lavished great efforts on their cooking even if all they could afford was fish-hash pie. They knew that the Sabbath began in their homes when they lit their lamps or candles, although their husbands and sons, and not they, went to shul to welcome the bride. So they uttered their prayers in the light of those lamps or candles and poured out their hearts to their God. They may have been excluded from synagogue activities and formal Torah study, but they could identify with the high priest in the Temple, who lit the great menorah. They could identify the hallahs they baked with the breads displayed in the sanctuary and the portion of dough they threw in the fire with the tithes the priests depended on. Their work, like that of the priests, was sacred work.

Through her cooking and baking and her Shabbat hospitality, my great-grandmother, "the hostess Riva of Shipilowitz," converted the ordinary into the holy. Although I may not want her life for myself (or for my daughter or granddaughter), I can revere it on its own terms and reclaim it as a rich and lasting part of my heritage.

Women today are also reclaiming other parts of the past. The Talmud, for example, relates this story: A certain woman would go every Friday evening to hear the great sage Rabbi Meir teach and preach. One Friday she came home so late that her Sabbath lamp had burned down. "Where have you been?" her husband asked furiously. "I was sitting and listening to Rabbi Meir preach," she answered.

"I swear I won't let you back into this house until you spit in that preacher's eye," the husband thundered.

The woman stayed away from home for a few weeks and the incident reached Rabbi Meir. When he next saw her, with some neighbors, he pretended to be suffering from eye trouble. "Does anyone here know how to heal eyes with a charm?" he asked. Urged by her friends, the woman stepped forward. Then, frightened, she admitted that she didn't really know how to heal.

"Spit in my eye seven times and I'll be cured," the rabbi said.

The woman spat. "Go and tell your husband," he said, "you told me to spit once, but I spat seven times." The woman did as the rabbi said, and the couple was reconciled.

By no stretch of the imagination can this be construed as a feminist story. Its message is the importance of establishing peace between husband and wife even at the cost of a rabbi's dignity. According to some scholars, a more insidious message may be its warning about the dangers to family life in allowing a woman to study Torah. But as I read it, it holds

a different concealed message: the very fact of women studying. The story accepts without comment the woman's weekly
attendance at the rabbi's study sessions as though there were
nothing unusual about that. This indicates that even in the
ancient past women had some access to Jewish learning, although we know that few had the religious training many
men received. Probably that learning took place on Shabbat,
the only leisure time most women enjoyed. In this case also,
and maybe others, the woman seems far more devoted to
study and perhaps far more learned than her husband, who
stayed home every week while she attended Shabbat lectures.
And all this indicates that women's roles have always been
more complex and fuller than what they have seemed on the
surface. The story tantalizes because it hints at those complexities while revealing little about them. But it is the kind
of story that contemporary women are revisiting as we seek
to uncover the hidden dimensions of earlier women's lives.

In many homes on Shabbat evening, men pay tribute to
their wives by singing *Eshet Hayil,* the "Woman of Valor"
hymn, most of them unaware of its mystical connotations. In
some homes, women and men sing the hymn to each other,
because both have shared in Sabbath preparations and per-
formance, and in some, the woman responds to the man's
singing by reciting a psalm to him. The words to the "Woman
of Valor" appear in Chapter 31 of the book of Proverbs as an
acrostic of the Hebrew alphabet. Like so much else about
women's history, this poem has a checkered past. For centuries equating a woman with the valiant wife in the poem
was considered the highest praise anyone could give her.

After all, the biblical woman of valor "rises while it is still night" to provide food and clothing for her family, acquires land, plants vineyards, conducts business, "gives generously to the poor," and "never eats the bread of idleness"—all while her husband "sits among the elders of the land." To this day, it's a sure bet that in eulogizing a woman, most rabbis will refer to her at some point as a woman of valor. ("When I die," my sister-in-law says, "make sure nobody calls me a woman of valor. It's such a cliché.")

More than a cliché, contemporary women began to see the poem as a male fantasy of what an ideal wife should be: a superwoman who devotes herself completely to her family and remains in the background while her husband "becomes prominent in the gates." More than one woman struggling to break out of traditional bounds insisted that this unattainable portrait with its emphasis on domesticity be dropped from her Shabbat evening dinner.

Again, however, as women have reassessed the past, many of us have regained admiration for the multifaceted woman of valor whose abilities range from household management to financial acumen to philanthropic giving. She is my great-grandmother Riva, milking cows, caring for children, growing vegetables, and opening her home to needy strangers; she is my grandmother Goldie, churning butter, making cheese, and rising before dawn, as my father wrote, to bargain with farmers and fishermen for products that she and her husband will sell in town. She is my mother, lighting her Shabbat candles with her last stores of energy. She is contemporary woman, married or single, with or without a partner, strong, determined, accomplished in many areas, finding ways to balance the numerous competing parts of her life, both the private and public, the religious and secular.

She is the Shekhinah. "Many daughters have done valiantly, but you excel them all," the kabbalists sang from the poem, and related those words to the presence of the Shekhinah among the people of Israel. The kabbalists identified the biblical woman of valor with the Shekhinah, and by reciting the poem on Friday evenings they led others to identify the Shekhinah with the Jewish woman of valor, the Jewish everywoman who honored and hallowed the evening.

How do we reconcile the many contradictory views the kabbalists presented of the Shekhinah? We don't. They exist in tandem. But we can sort out the positive images and validate them, just as we have come to validate the lives and activities of real women of the past. The interpretation of the "Woman of Valor" poem as praise for the Shekhinah is such a positive picture, a portrait of the Shekhinah in terms of glory and love.

There are other views of the Shekhinah that women today can affirm. Some feminists see the Shekhinah so affirmatively that they use the name Shekhinah to refer to God in prayers and blessings, as in the feminine *berukha at Shekhinah*, "Blessed are you, Shekhinah." Such usage doesn't satisfy me, partly because to my mind it smacks of goddess worship, and partly because an all-female representation of God serves no better purpose than an all-male one. The God of the universe transcends a single gender. But I join in celebrating the strong and active feminine attributes of that one God. If in kabbalistic thought, for example, the Shekhinah glows only with the light of the *sefirot* above her, it is also true that those higher *sefirot* assert their influence on the world by shining through her. She is the ultimate conduit for conveying the divine will on earth. If she is closest to the material world and can be corrupted by it, as some kabbalistic writings indicate, her closeness to that world can also help change and improve it.

The mystics described the Shekhinah metaphorically in many ways—as the moon and the rainbow, as the Sabbath queen and consort, as the community of Israel. One of their most pleasing likenesses grows out of equating the Shekhinah with the peace that Shabbat brings. The Friday evening prayer service includes a blessing for the sukkah, or canopy, of peace spread over Israel. The Zohar interprets that blessing to mean that when people honor the Sabbath on Friday evening, a canopy of peace descends from heaven. This canopy of peace "is the Sabbath, and when it comes down, all evil spirits ... hide themselves. ..." Therefore, the text continues, "we should invite that canopy to spread itself over us and to rest on us and to shield us as a mother shields her children, so that we should feel secure on every side."

The Sabbath is a canopy of peace that envelops the world. But, the text adds a little later, the canopy is also the "Matron of the world" (another term for Shekhinah), who carries within her "the souls which are the celestial lamp." As the canopy of peace, the Shekhinah holds the extra Sabbath souls that emerge from on high to add light and strength to the people below. The Zohar goes on to say that just as the Shekhinah brings light into the world with those souls, the "matron" on earth kindles the Sabbath lights, and in that way she attaches herself "to her rightful place," alongside the Shekhinah.

Here Shekhinah and Shabbat appear interlocked as a

canopy, a tent that encloses the earth in peace and illuminates it with the additional Shabbat souls that emanate from heaven. Here, also, we find the best reason for why women light the Shabbat candles—not as a punishment but because the women represent the Shekhinah on earth; they, too, spread a canopy of peace through the lights they kindle. Like the "Woman of Valor" poem, these portraits of the Shekhinah may use traditional female imagery, but in these contexts, those images deepen our appreciation of the day and place the feminine at the heart of Shabbat, where it belongs.

Five

OF LABOR AND LAWS

Five women, a dead father, some sticks of wood, and a broken fence form the raw materials for a midrash whose twists and turns lead now into a discussion of the laws that govern the Sabbath.

To begin with the women: They were five sisters, often regarded as the first persons in history to stand up for female rights. Their names were Mahlah, Tirzah, Hoglah, Milcah, and Noah, and their story appears in Chapters 27 and 36 of the book of Numbers. Their father, Zelophehad, had died leaving no sons to inherit his property. Because in biblical law women did not inherit from their fathers, these women appealed to Moses for the right to do so. They not only received that right, but also set a precedent in Jewish law for a daughter to inherit when there are no sons. Later, the sages of the Talmud were much taken with the biblical account of these women, whom they spoke of as both wise and righteous, and they wondered what kind of man had fathered them. A brief description by the daughters set them on an imaginative trail.

In their appeal to Moses, the daughters had said that

their father "died for his own sin" and had not taken part in a rebellion that occurred among the Israelites in the wilderness. They may have meant that he died of natural causes, but the sages puzzled over what sin Zelophehad could have committed that caused his death. Rabbi Akiva found the answer in another wilderness incident: The Bible relates that one day the people came across an Israelite man gathering wood on the Sabbath. They brought him to Moses, who, not knowing how to handle Sabbath violations, appealed to God for instruction. He received word that the community must stone the man to death. (Such a severe punishment may have been a response to the man's so openly profaning the Sabbath and thus publicly undermining this most basic of all institutions.) Said Rabbi Akiva, "The wood gatherer was Zelophehad."

What led Akiva to identify the sinful wood gatherer with Zelophehad, father of the five righteous sisters? Perhaps it was his name, which may refer to a caper tree. *Tzalaf* in Hebrew means "caper"; *had* means "sharp." Zelophehad may mean "sharp caper," indicating that the wood the man gathered was the wood of a caper tree. The caper tree has thin dry branches that make fine kindling wood. It's likely that the man was gathering the branches to kindle a fire on the Sabbath, a practice the Torah specifically forbids. In Akiva's view, Zelophehad, whose name refers to a caper, was Scripture's wood gatherer.

Not everyone agreed. Rabbi Judah ben Bathyra said, "Akiva, in either case you will have to account for your interpretation. If you are right, the Torah protected the man [by omitting his name], yet you revealed him. If you are wrong [and Zelophehad was not the wood gatherer], you have slandered a good man." Akiva did not back down, and tradition has ever since linked Zelophehad with the wood gatherer.

Unrelated to the biblical incident, the Talmud tells the tale of a pious man who, strolling around his property, found a break in the fence surrounding it. He was about to fix the fence when he remembered that this was the Sabbath day. Although leaving the fence unmended made his property vulnerable to thieves, he refrained from doing the necessary repair work. Thereupon a miracle occurred. A caper tree grew in the opening of the fence, sealing it. Compounding the miracle, the man and his family lived off the income of the caper for the rest of their lives.

A seemingly unrelated tale, but in kabbalistic thought, the soul of the Sabbath observer was none other than that of Zelophehad, who had died for the sin of violating the Sabbath. Zelophehad's soul could not rest until it had transmigrated into the body of the pious man. Then Zelophehad and that unnamed man were joined, and the caper tree, the original source of Sabbath violation, became the reward for Sabbath keeping.

As for Zelophehad's splendid daughters, they inherited their father's portion in the land of Israel, and their names are still associated with areas in modern Israel where caper trees grow. For the sages, however, these women did not simply raise issues of inheritance; their story also opened a window on the basic issue of Sabbath regulations.

It could be said that rules and regulations make up the prosaic aspects of Shabbat. In this they contrast with the more spiritual or "poetic" aspects explored so far—the underlying themes of the Sabbath commandment, the symbolism of the day, and the qualities of mysticism and holiness that cling to it. Yet Judaism is a religion of practices, of doing, not just of spirit. The laws form the framework for Shabbat practices. They may seem at times excessively detailed and demanding; their very existence may appear to contradict the sense of joy and relaxation that should mark the Sabbath. Yet for those who live by them, the rules and their details build into an intricate structure within which the pleasures of the day can flourish. Without that structure the rest would crumble.

The odd thing about Sabbath rules is how few specifics can be found in the Torah itself. There is the Sabbath commandment to remember and observe the day by refraining from work along with several reminders of that command in different words. There is the passage that forbids kindling a fire on Shabbat and another that extends Sabbath rest to plowing and harvesting. There is the story of the wood gatherer and the description of the manna that fell in a double portion on the sixth day so that the Israelites would not leave their places to gather it on the seventh. There are warnings from various prophets against hauling burdens and engaging in commercial activity on Shabbat. And that's about it.

So few guidelines for observing the day appear in the Bible that when confronted with the Sabbath wood gatherer Moses had to turn to God for instructions on how to handle the situation. Even the nature of the wood gatherer's sin is unclear, for nowhere does the Bible prohibit gathering wood on Shabbat. The text's ambiguity led to disagreements among the rabbis. Rabbi Judah said in Samuel's name that the man's offense was carrying the wood on the Sabbath. Rabbi Aha ben Joseph said it was tying the sticks together, as one might do in harvesting sheaves of wheat. The presumption has remained that the man was gathering the wood for use in kindling a fire, but the text does not spell that out.

Why is the text so vague? Because on the whole the Torah presents basic rules that convey its ethical and theological teachings. The oral law interprets and expounds on those rules. In traditional Jewish belief, all of the written law in the Torah and all of the oral law, which was written down later, were revealed to Moses on Mount Sinai. Most modern scholars regard the oral law as having developed over time, as rabbis and sages sought to understand and explain the Scriptures and to respond to new questions that arose. In terms of the Sabbath, almost the entire talmudic tractates of Shabbat and Eruvin are devoted to expanding on the small number of rules given in the Bible. The result, as the rabbis themselves said, was the creation of "mountains hanging by a hair"—a large body of regulations supported by a thin strand of biblical directives.

The sages' interpretations begin with the most fundamental matter of God's ceasing from work on the seventh day, the paradigm for human rest on the Sabbath. The text in Genesis, which Jews recite at the beginning of the Friday evening kiddush, presents a quandary. "On the seventh day God finished the work of creation, and ceased on the seventh day from all the work that had been done," it says. But how is it that God finishes work on the *seventh* day, Shabbat, the very day we emulate as a time of total divine rest? Wasn't creation completed on the sixth day? Today's biblical critics have no problem with this passage. They say that it results from a scribal error and should, in fact, read, "On the *sixth* day God finished the work. ..." That is the wording that appears in the Septuagint, the earliest Greek translation of the Bible, and several other early Bibles, which may have used a different text as their source than does our traditional one.

The ancient rabbis were not likely to describe a biblical text as having a scribal error. Nor would they compromise on the teaching that God had ceased from work by the seventh day. Why, even the demons, Rabbi Judah the Prince said, proved that creation ended before Shabbat. An old tradition held that along with the creeping things and the beasts of the earth created on the sixth day, God also created the souls of demons. But before the Holy One could fashion the demons' bodies, the Sabbath descended. Thus demons have remained bodiless, spirits only, and an example to the people of Israel to stop all their work when the Sabbath arrives.

What then is the meaning of the puzzling verse about God finishing work on the seventh day? What more could God possibly have made?

Serenity, tranquillity, peace, and quiet. Creation did not end until God ceased from work and rested on the seventh day, some sages said, and in doing so created *menuhah,* the deep spiritual tranquillity that is the Sabbath rest.

Another opinion: Rabbi Judah the Prince asked Rabbi Ishmael ben Yose ben Halafta: "Did you learn from your father the meaning of the verse, 'On the seventh day God finished the work ...'?" Said he to him, "It is like the blacksmith who strikes his hammer on the anvil, raising it by day and bringing it down after nightfall." In the moment between the time the blacksmith raises his hammer and lowers it, nighttime may fall. So it was with creation. God concluded the work of creation at the end of the sixth day, and in that moment of completion, Shabbat began. Mortals, said Rabbi Simeon bar Yohai, must know their exact minutes and hours, but God, who has total control over all minutes and hours can "enter Shabbat by a hair's breadth." That is why the text says, "On the seventh day. . . ." In that hair's breadth, God finished creating.

These two attempts to solve the problem of God finishing creation on the seventh day in the biblical text make a similar point: Shabbat was as much a part of the scheme of creation as was each day's work Although all aspects of the world were finished at the end of the sixth day, the world became whole and perfect only on the seventh day, when the hammer fell, as it were, and God's rest brought *menuhah* into being. As different as the seventh day became from those that preceded it, it still had tight links to them. It was the crown of creation, but it was also its climax and completion.

The tightness between the six days of creation and the seventh day of rest carries an important lesson: Twinned with the necessity to rest one day a week is the duty to work on the other days—a duty the rabbis considered part of the Sabbath commandment. "Six days you shall labor and do all your work, but the seventh day is a Sabbath of the Eternal your God," the commandment states. "Six days you shall labor . . ." they said, teaches that "just as the Torah was given as a covenant, so was work given as a covenant." They found proof for that idea in the story of Adam's creation.

"Even Adam tasted nothing before he worked," Rabbi Simeon ben Eleazar, a second-century sage, said, citing two biblical verses to prove his point: First the text says, "And the Eternal took the man and placed him in the Garden of Eden, to till it and tend it." Only afterward does it say, "Of every tree of the garden you are free to eat." Even in Eden, Adam had to labor to till the land before being allowed to eat of it.

Moreover, Dostai ben Yannai, another second-century rabbi, argued that a person who does not work during the six days of the week might end up violating the seventh. How so? "Suppose a man sits idle all week and on the Sabbath eve discovers he has nothing to eat. He might go and fall in with a troop of bandits. Then he would be seized and taken in chains and put to work on the Sabbath. All this because he would not work on the six days!" With a little imagination and a lot of zeal, Rabbi Dostai could foretell dire calamity befalling someone who, like my great-uncle Zalman, fritters away the workweek.

Less imaginatively, but more significantly, the third-century scholar Rabban Gamaliel said, "All study of Torah that is not combined with work in the end will become futile and be the cause of sin," which led Maimonides to declare centuries later that "whoever decides to study Torah and not to work ... profanes the name of God." In keeping with that outlook, Maimonides worked as a physician while devoting himself to Jewish law and philosophy. Some of the earlier sages and Torah scholars did menial work, becoming woodchoppers, tailors, and sandal makers.

More than any saying, the legend of Rabbi Simeon bar Yohai, partially told in Chapter 1, bears out the importance of human labor in the scheme of the universe. While hiding in their cave for twelve years to escape Roman authorities, Rabbi Simeon and his son Eleazar spent all their time studying Torah. They stopped only to pray three times a day.

When they finally left the cave, they saw a farmer plowing his fields. "These people give up eternal life to engage in temporal life," they exclaimed, enraged that people should toil at ordinary tasks instead of devoting themselves fully to the Torah. Whatever they looked at burned up from the fire in their eyes and the fervor of their feelings.

Then a voice from heaven called out, "Have you emerged in order to destroy My world? Return to your cave!"

The men remained in their cave until they received divine permission to leave it permanently. Torah study, the path to eternal life, these scholars learned, needs to be balanced by the work of earthly life, the daily work of maintaining the world.

Only at the end of that daily work does the Sabbath come with the opposite message of *not* doing, *not* working, *not* producing. Shabbat bears witness that God created a world so well ordered that it could survive even after divine labor ceased. And it testifies that in imitation of God and in tribute to God humans can also cease from creating one day a week and the world will not fall apart. The Sabbath laws provide the parameters for this weekly pause in creating and producing.

🌿

The body of rules and teachings that comprise Jewish law is known as *halakhah*, which literally means "the way." Within the halakhah, the sages spoke of two kinds of Sabbath laws, in keeping with the opening word of the two versions of the Sabbath commandment—our old friends "Remember" and "Observe." In rabbinic thought, "Remember" denotes the positive rules, the "dos" that give the day its uniqueness and joy, such as resting, dressing differently, eating more lavishly, reciting the kiddush blessing that sanctifies Shabbat, and performing the havdalah service that ends it. Nahmanides regarded "Remember" also as the source for the Hebrew terms used for the days of the week. As mentioned earlier, in Hebrew only Shabbat has a name of its own; the other names reveal the day's relation to it. Thus, Sunday is called the "first day toward the Sabbath," Monday, the "second day," and on through the six days. With these numbered days, Nahmanides says, people "remember" Shabbat all week long.

"Observe" signifies the negative Sabbath rules, the "don'ts" designed to prevent the day from being ordinary. I once heard the Israeli Talmud scholar Adin Steinsaltz speak of the many negative Shabbat rules as a form of setting necessary limits on our activities, much the way a parent sets limits on a child's activities. "Shabbat begins," he said, "first of all by saying 'don't,' by setting limits. You have your time of working all week, and then something comes like an iron curtain and says Stop! The person who can't stop working is the same as the one who can't start. Both are enslaved."

Rabbi Steinsaltz went on to say that everything in the world must have some sort of end. "Heaven and earth have an end," he said. "Life has an end. For something to have meaning, it needs limits. That is why browsing the Internet with its infinite amount of information is like having no information at all." It is too diffuse and undifferentiated, too free and unending.

"Being able to say 'no' on Shabbat," the rabbi added, is, paradoxically, "a beginning, not an end." He meant that the negative Shabbat rules that restrict ordinary activity clear a path to something new, a beginning to a different kind of time. "Shabbat is negative in one way, but in another way it is the source of everything," he said.

Parenthetically, the negative laws of Shabbat are also the basis for affirming women's right to say the kiddush blessing as men do. In Jewish law, women are exempt from fulfilling positive commands that must be performed at a fixed time, such as praying at set hours. The rabbis may have reasoned that with child care and other domestic chores women could not be held to time-bound rituals. (Today, many women devoted to Jewish practice argue that exemption from such rituals actually narrows their opportunities for religious expression. Drawing on a growing body of Jewish women's scholarship, they are finding ways to reinterpret this general rule in order to increase their religious participation.) One might have assumed that legally women do not need to say or hear the kiddush blessing, because the obligation to do so is a positive ruling, under the category of "Remember." But the negative laws of "Observe"—the "don'ts" of Shabbat—apply to women as well as to men. Said the sages, "Whoever has to 'Observe' has to 'Remember' also." Women therefore have a duty to sanctify the Sabbath as men do. That means that a woman, like a man, must say the kiddush aloud along with others—in more liberal interpretations, she may lead it—as all begin the Sabbath meal.

Standing for the "don'ts," the word *Observe* in the Sabbath commandment represents the many limitations on work that characterize Shabbat. The Hebrew word for work in the Sabbath command is *melakhah*, which has the same root as the word *malakh*, meaning an angel or messenger. Like fulfilling a mission or delivering a message, *melakhah* connotes something that has a goal or purpose, and that is how the rabbis would define work in relation to the Sabbath. But their definition has a history.

The Mishnah lists thirty-nine categories of work forbidden on the Sabbath. It is a legal list, but to me it has the feel of a child's poem, with its chantlike cadence and count of "forty less one" categories. This is how it goes:

> *The main labors are forty less one. Sowing, plowing, reaping, binding sheaves, threshing, winnowing, sorting grain, grinding, sifting, kneading, baking, shearing wool, washing it, beating it, dyeing it, spinning, weaving, making two loops, weaving two threads, separating threads, tying a knot, untying a knot, sewing, tearing, hunting, slaughtering, skinning, tanning, scraping, marking out, cutting [and shaping], writing, erasing, building, demolishing [to improve a space or build again], extinguishing a fire, kindling a fire, striking with a hammer, carrying from one domain to another. These are the main labors—forty less one.*

Redacted about three hundred years after the Mishnah, the Talmud includes voluminous discussions and interpretations of all the Mishnah's rulings—known as the Gemara. Among the rules discussed at length is the "forty less one" list. Considering the scarcity of biblical laws about the Sabbath, later talmudic sages wondered how the earlier scholars had arrived at their thirty-nine prohibitions. Perhaps, they thought, the thirty-nine forms of forbidden labor correspond to thirty-nine citations of the word *melakhah* in the Torah. No, that wasn't it, they decided. They finally found their answer in the model for so many other lessons about holiness—the Mishkan, the Israelites' portable desert sanctuary. The Sabbath rules interspersed in the Bible with instructions for building the Tabernacle indicated, they said, that the labors needed to construct the shrine were the very ones to be avoided on Shabbat. "They sowed, therefore you must not sow," the Talmud says. "They reaped, therefore you must not reap. They lifted up the boards from the ground to the wagon, therefore you must not carry from a public to a private domain." Making Shabbat became for the rabbis the converse of making the Tabernacle, and once again space and time interacted to form that holy day.

The Talmud finds an allusion to the thirty-nine prohibited labors in Moses' words as he begins his instructions for building the shrine. *Eileh ha'devarim*, "these are the things" the Eternal has commanded, he says. The numerical value of the Hebrew letters in those words is thirty-nine. To the talmudic mind, that meant the thirty-nine forms of work required for constructing the Tabernacle, hence the thirty-nine forms banned on Shabbat. A mystical interpretation attributes the number thirty-nine to the thirty-nine lashes brought upon the world by the first couple's sin of eating from the Tree of Knowledge: ten lashes for Adam, ten for Eve, ten for the serpent, and nine for the ground itself.

In reality, the Mishnah's "forty less one" categories of taboo labors summarize fundamental concerns of civilization—preparing food, clothing, and shelter along with writing and transportation. By limiting these pursuits, Shabbat calls a halt to the routines of everyday living. Although the Mishnah's categories center on agriculture, religious authorities have applied them to all aspects of society.

The sages of the Mishnah called the broad thirty-nine forbidden labors *avot*, fathers, and from these they and later rabbis derived more detailed prohibitions, labeled *toladot*, offspring or derivatives. Had Sigmund Freud cared to delve into talmudic thinking, he might have been intrigued by the relationships between the parents and offspring in these categories of work. For example, one might suppose that a ruling against sharpening a pencil on Shabbat would come under the heading of writing. After all, pencil sharpening has direct connections to writing. Not so in talmudic literature. Sharpening a pencil falls into the category of cutting, for the rabbis defined cutting as any activity that changes the size or shape of an object to make it more suitable for human use. Sharpening does just that to a pencil. Squeezing the juice from an orange is a forbidden form of threshing. Why threshing? That category includes not only separating a grain from its husk, but also separating any natural liquid or solid product from its natural container. Hence juice from an orange.

Complex and exacting, the dozens of secondary laws derived from the primary thirty-nine categories have an internal logic that associates them one to another and to the broad categories they fall under. They also have a deeper logic, an underlying rationale exhibited in the rabbis' definition of *melakhah* as purposeful work. That is, the prohibitions against work on Shabbat have little to do with how difficult a work is or how much time or energy it requires. They have everything to do with work that has a positive purpose—creative, intentional work that changes the physical environment in a way that makes it more useful to people.

More specifically, the *melakhah* the sages outlawed derived from what they called *melekhet mahshevet*, roughly meaning "workmanship" or purposeful design. Like so much else about Shabbat, the term comes from the Tabernacle story, this time from the role of Bezalel, the shrine's chief craftsman. The Torah tells us that God singled out Bezalel and inspired him to design in gold, silver, copper, and wood—in every kind of "*melekhet mahshevet*," every kind of creative craft.

In line with this description, purposeful workmanship or creative activity became the criteria the rabbis used for labors they forbade on the Sabbath—the very type of labors meant to be performed on other days. But strangely, the prohibition against positive, constructive activities has the consequence of permitting destructive ones.

"Anyone who performs an act of destruction is not liable," the Talmud states, indicating that simply destroying or defacing something does not violate the Sabbath. Thus the rules forbid erasing, one of the thirty-nine categories of labors, only if a person erases for the positive purpose of writing again or preparing a clean space for writing. Simply erasing does not count as a creative act. Thus, also, at least in theory, a person could destroy a table or a building on Shabbat without profaning the day. In reality, many qualifications rein in destructive acts that might interfere with the Sabbath spirit. Still, the common thread in the Sabbath laws is their ban against creating, not destroying. The pious man in the

Talmudic legend, who may have had Zelophehad's soul, received his caper tree reward because he did not commit the positive transgression of repairing his fence.

My favorite Sabbath rule for understanding the philosophy behind all of them comes from the thirty-eighth category of the Mishnah's list, called "the final hammer blow." Resonant of the talmudic image of God completing the world "like the blacksmith who strikes his hammer on the anvil," it deals with putting the finishing touches on a product or improving it. One such finishing touch that appears under the "offspring" prohibitions is putting shoelaces into a new pair of shoes. Because the shoes have never been worn and cannot be worn without their laces, inserting the laces "completes" them. A stretch? Maybe. Yet a person who threads laces into a new pair of shoes creates something that did not exist before: shoes that can be used. And that is as much an act of will and creation as painting a picture or planting a garden.

Closely related to the concept of creating in determining a taboo Sabbath act is the principle of intentionality. Jewish law regards someone as a Sabbath violator only if she or he intentionally breaks the law. Generally, it does not hold a person responsible for committing a forbidden act on Shabbat accidentally or without meaning to. The Talmud records a telling incident about intent. The law bans cooking, like baking, on the Sabbath. But it does permit food that had been cooked before Shabbat to be kept warm in a stove or oven that had also been lit before Shabbat. Accordingly, the Talmud relates that in early days a person who forgot to remove a pot from the stove before Shabbat and thereby unintentionally allowed the food in it to cook during Shabbat had permission to eat that food. But someone who deliberately left a pot with partially cooked food in the stove on Shabbat was forbidden to eat that food after it cooked through. What happened?

"The numbers of people who intentionally left their food cooking grew," the Talmud says, "but they pleaded, 'It was an accident; we forgot to remove the dish from the stove.'" So the sages retracted their lenient ruling and held those who "forgot" responsible for their actions. Ah, the universal impulse to skirt laws—and right under the noses of those authorities!

Cooking, by the way, is an example of how the Shabbat rules, with their emphasis on creativeness and intentionality, shaped customs and practices still followed today. Observant families complete all cooking for Shabbat before sundown on Friday. To keep the food warm they may leave the oven or stovetop burners on a low flame until the Sabbath ends. They cover the stovetop with a metal sheet called a *blech*, designed also to cover the controls so as to prevent them from being adjusted. (This funny-sounding name is Yiddish for "tin.") A kettle with boiled water for tea or coffee and pots with warm food may be kept on the *blech* throughout the day for Sabbath use. (Shabbat differs from such festivals as Passover and Sukkot when one may cook food for use on that day.)

Of more interest, the prohibitions surrounding Sabbath cooking gave rise to one of the most popular Saturday lunch dishes and a staple of Jewish cooking: the one-pot meal called *cholent* and its Sephardi equivalent, *dafina* or *hamin*, cooked on Friday and left in the oven overnight for the Saturday meal. Traditional cholent usually combines meat, beans, potatoes, and barley, sometimes with the addition of kishke (stuffed derma) or *knaidlach* (various dumplings) as people wish. Some cooking experts relate the dish to the French *cassoulet* (a more elegant combination of goose, sausage, and beans), and its name to the French words *chault,* meaning "hot," and *lent,* "slow." But the origins of this stew probably date to talmudic times or earlier. The heavy feeling it leaves behind—perfect for lulling the mind and body into a Shabbat afternoon nap—is legendary.

Many women in the shtetls of eastern Europe carried their cooked *cholents* to a communal baker's oven for overnight warming. In some places the women attached colorful braided yarns to their *cholent* pots for identification; in other places, the baker would give people numbers with metal tags. On their way home from synagogue on Shabbat, the men and boys in the family would retrieve the *cholent* from the bakery for the main meal of the day. In Josef Erlich's ethnographic book *Sabbath,* Yachet, the housewife, goes out herself on an icy cold day to carry her *cholent* home. As she opens the door on her return, the mixture of foods in the pot fills the room with its savory aroma, and the warmth the dish exudes brings Sabbath warmth to this poor shtetl family. "A great *cholent,*" Yachet says proudly, the food a metaphor for the day itself.

I confess that *cholent* is not part of my Sabbath heritage. My mother never made it, nor do I, although I do have vague memories of eating it in my grandparents' home, and not much liking the bulky combination of beans and potatoes. The main Saturday meal in my parents' house usually consisted of foods that were cold or at room temperature: chopped liver my mother had made with her hand chopper in a wooden bowl on Friday; sliced tomatoes and cucumbers; noodle pudding, perhaps; gefilte fish sometimes; and most usually cold chicken with ketchup and hallah, accompanied by potato chips. For dessert, however, we always had home-made cake with hot tea.

The custom of having something hot on Shabbat after-noon recalls the fight between the ancient Pharisees and Sadducees over the proper interpretation of the biblical in-junction against kindling a flame on Shabbat. A warm dish on Shabbat attests to the victory of the Pharisees, who per-mitted lighting a fire before Shabbat that would provide the comfort of light and heat throughout the Sabbath day.

But for me, potato chips, which my mother allowed at no other time, stood out as the highlight of Saturday lunches. That chicken-ketchup–potato chips combination became so fixed in my mind that to this day I cannot eat cold chicken alone or in a sandwich without ketchup and potato chips, and this threesome often appears on my Shabbat day table as well. Thus do traditions get started.

Back to Sabbath laws. Along with cooking, two other areas of Shabbat rulings probably have the greatest impact on the life of observant Jews today, and have aroused the greatest con-troversy. The first concerns carrying, the last of the thirty-nine forbidden labors. The rules prohibit carrying from a private to a public domain and vice versa, which calls for some explanation.

The ban against carrying on Shabbat has deep roots in the

Bible. The prophet Jeremiah warned the people of his day to "Guard yourselves for your own sake against carrying burdens on the Sabbath day, and bringing them through the gates of Jerusalem...." The burdens Jeremiah and other prophets preached against may have been used for commercial purposes, but typical of the sages, they embellished the prophets' warnings by extending the prohibitions far beyond commerce. To limit carrying, they designated various kinds of spaces where people may or may not carry an object on Shabbat. The most important are private and public domains. A private domain generally connotes one's home or garden, or in more technical terms an enclosed area no less than fifteen inches square bounded by walls no less than three feet high. A public domain means a street or road, or technically an open space not less than about twenty-eight feet wide.

The basic rules are that objects may be carried within a private domain, but they may not be carried between private and public domains or moved more than about seven feet in a public area. I grew up in a neighborhood where people tied their handkerchiefs around their wrists to avoid carrying them in the open on Shabbat. A handkerchief placed in a pocket constitutes carrying because that is the usual method of transporting objects. A handkerchief tied around the wrist or neck gets transformed into personal attire, an object worn, not carried.

These distinctions may sound petty to some, but strictly observant people take such matters extremely seriously. So seriously that the laws against carrying have often been a strain, especially on parents with young children. Because the law forbids carrying a child or even pushing a baby carriage in a public domain on Shabbat, parents (read mothers) in Orthodox communities often find themselves prisoners in their homes, unable to go outside with their children.

But there is an escape hatch: the *eruv*. An eruv (literally "blending") constitutes a kind of legal fiction the ancient rabbis devised to modify their own stringent rules against carrying. It symbolically changes a public space into a large private one by way of a series of cords and wires that encircle the public area, often incorporating existing utility poles and lines. An eruv allows for baby carriages and wheelchairs to be used on Shabbat, and for people to carry outside their homes as they would inside. In one of the numerous talmudic disputes between Rabbi Akiva and Tinneius Rufus, Akiva teaches the Roman governor that only God has no need for an eruv, for "since the whole world belongs to the Holy One, He may carry things on the Sabbath anywhere in the world." For mere mortals, on the other hand, the eruv can be a godsend.

A talmudic story tells of how two women who had been fighting made peace when they set up an eruv together in their courtyard, allowing them to carry from one home to the next. I can understand that. I find the concept of an eruv pleasing, aside from its religious legalities. There's something pleasing about the idea of converting large, cold spaces into intimate areas, even if the intimacy exists only on a symbolic level. There's something charming, actually, in the notion that big cities can be turned into private homes by wrapping strings around them, as if wrapping up a huge gift (the gift of the Sabbath?). To be sure, plenty of people have been less pleased than I by the eruv, in theory or reality. Bitter fights have erupted in various localities when people have broached the subject. The fights have most often been between Jew and Jew.

In some communities, secular Jews or those from liberal denominations have opposed the eruv for fear that its presence would attract many more Orthodox Jews and change the nature of the neighborhood. Calvin Trillin wrote an article in the *New Yorker* magazine describing anti-eruv Jews in a London suburb angrily labeling the eruv a "magic schlepping circle" that they regarded as "an insanely legalistic bit of medieval hairsplitting."

In some communities, Jews have joined with non-Jews in raising church-state issues—is an eruv a religious symbol, like a cross, and should it therefore be banned from public property? (The answer has usually been no; it is not in itself a religious symbol, and its presence does not intrude on most people's lives.) Some of the fiercest debates have been among Orthodox groups themselves, when one faction of rabbis wants to create an eruv and another insists that according to strict Jewish law the area does not lend itself to an eruv. Although the eruv has yet to become a burning feminist issue, in the midst of such battles most women have backed its use, arguing that they lose out on the joy of Shabbat by being confined to their homes with their children all day.

Every city in Israel has an eruv, and despite debates the eruv solution has spread to Jewish communities throughout the world. A number of those communities have eruv websites on the Internet with information about creating an eruv. The ancient sages might have liked that.

The use of electricity on Shabbat has been another subject of major controversy. The prohibition against kindling a fire is one of the few stated in the Bible, and appears among the forbidden thirty-nine labors of the Mishnah. But is turning on electricity a form of kindling a fire? Obviously pressing a light switch entails less work than building a fire, but again, the amount of exertion involved in a task does not determine its status in the law. Purposefulness and creativeness do. Accordingly, Orthodox authorities across the board have banned any form of creating light or heat on the Sabbath, deeming them extensions of kindling a fire. Most do permit timers that automatically turn lights, clocks, ovens, or other electrical appliances on and off at preset times.

Some scholars in the Conservative movement argue that electricity is not the same as fire, and they permit switching lights on and off, although on different grounds they prohibit many activities that use electricity, such as running a washing machine. But the greatest disputes in regard to electricity have concerned riding on Shabbat. Unlike the Reform movement, the Conservative movement regards Jewish law as binding upon its members. At the same time, it believes the law has always responded to the changing needs of the times and must continue to do so. In 1950 that principle led the Committee on Jewish Law and Standards of the Rabbinical Assembly, the Conservative movement's legal body, to rule by majority opinion that people may ride to synagogue on the Sabbath. Although a substantial minority of committee members disagreed, the opinion held that the indirect combustion for power used in driving a car does not fall under the prohibition against kindling a light. The main thrust of the argument, however, was that people who needed to ride to get to a synagogue gained more religiously from doing so than from not riding on Shabbat and missing out on religious services.

The ruling came at a time when large numbers of Jews had moved from inner cities to suburbs, where many did not live within walking distance of synagogues. Still, it sent its own electric sparks flying. Everyone misunderstood. Many Conservative Jews didn't realize, or forgot, or didn't want to remember, that the ruling permitted driving on Shabbat only to attend synagogue services and for no other purpose. Orthodox authorities persistently attacked the ruling as a license to Conservative Jews to violate the Sabbath. After more than half a century, this Conservative opinion still remains fuzzy for many members of the movement, and a bone of contention between Conservative and Orthodox leaders.

With all the laws the ancients enacted—the "Remembers" and "Observes," the "dos" and "don'ts," the legal fictions and nonfictions—they still worried about slippery slopes. Suppose you finger some coins in your home on Shabbat, might you not be tempted to carry them outside and buy yourself an ice cream cone or a newspaper? Suppose you sit near a business acquaintance in synagogue and begin discussing work-related matters, might you not be tempted to make a deal, violating the very essence of the moment? To safeguard the day from these and a thousand other situations that might lure people to profane it, the rabbis created what they called "fences" around the laws. One class of fences, known as *muktzeh* ("excluded"), pertains to objects that should not be handled on Shabbat, like money or pencils or work tools. Another group, called *shevut* ("rest," from the same root as Shabbat), concerns making the Sabbath rest as complete as possible by avoiding acts that are not forbidden in themselves but could destroy the spirit of the day, such as planning a shopping spree or packing a suitcase. Along similar lines are regulations designed to avoid behavior that resembles week-day behavior, as in watching television, even if the set has been turned on automatically or before Shabbat.

If the piles upon piles of laws and fences can seem daunt-ing and out of reach for many people, for others they create an ideal to reach for—placing Shabbat as far as possible beyond the everyday. A prominent woman of early times named Yalta, one of the few women the Talmud cites, said that for everything divine law forbids, it provides something of equal value. For people who live the Sabbath every week, at whatever their level of observance, the positive laws of "Remember" and the negatives of "Observe" together pre-serve the day and keep it whole.

And always, at the heart of the law lies its ethical intent. Maimonides lays down rules about not discussing busi-ness on Shabbat or even talking about weekday matters. Nevertheless, he adds, "one may discuss the betrothal of a young girl, arrange for a boy to be taught book learning or a trade, visit the sick, or comfort people in mourning." Week-day matters that affect those in need remain matters for Sab-bath attention also.

The Mishnah includes a debate about whether a man may carry arms on the Sabbath. The majority of sages forbid it, since carrying is banned on Shabbat. Rabbi Eliezer disagrees. Arms are not a burden one carries but an ornament to be worn as part of one's clothing, he argues. The sages reply caus-tically: Armaments are not ornaments; they are a disgrace for a man to carry. For does not the prophet Isaiah hold out the dream of a time when "nation will not lift up sword against nation..."? Shabbat peace embodies the vision of a peaceful world. To carry arms on this day denigrates that vision.

In the Mishnah, again, a discussion revolves around the propriety of easing the pain of a wound by rubbing oil on it on Shabbat. The sages seem to agree to the activity if the oil is a commonplace one. But no one except the children of kings may use rose oil, they say, because that is a kind of oil only royalty uses regularly. Says Rabbi Simon, "all Israel are the children of royalty." No class distinctions exist on Shabbat.

Shabbat rules treat all Israel like children of royalty, entitled to elevate their bodies and souls above the daily toil. The Shabbat rules also include exceptions, for laws without exceptions shut out morality and conscience.

A circumcision may take place on Shabbat, because like Shabbat itself it must come at a fixed time, the eighth day of a boy's life. Yom Kippur may fall on Shabbat and its fast observed, although it is forbidden to fast and diminish the day's joy on a regular Sabbath. Yom Kippur does not outweigh Shabbat in holiness or honor, as people often suppose, but this special time of atonement and soul-searching need not be deferred because of the Sabbath.

The most far-reaching exceptions to the Sabbath laws involve saving a life, *pikuah nefesh* in Hebrew. Our laws exist to "live by them, but not to die because of them," the rabbis said. Consequently, when a life is at stake or appears to be in danger all Sabbath regulations must be set aside. This ruling has a background. In the second century B.C.E., the Maccabees led a rebellion against the attempts of the Syrian

king, Antiochus IV Epiphanes, to abolish Jewish practice in
Palestine. The Hanukkah festival celebrates their victory. But
early in the battle, a pious group of soldiers were slaughtered
when they refused to fight on the Sabbath. The other war-
riors decided that they must defend themselves on Shabbat
or the enemy "will soon wipe us off the face of the earth."

The pious men's unwillingness to fight had precedents
in earlier Jewish history. The Greek writer Agatharchides
described a military defeat in Jerusalem in the fourth century B.C.E. that occurred because "the inhabitants, instead of
protecting their city, persevered in their folly" of not fighting
on the Sabbath. The Maccabees' decision to take up arms on
Shabbat forever changed that attitude.

The New Testament notes several disputes between Jesus
and the Pharisees about Shabbat observance. In one incident
Jesus' disciples pick ears of corn on the Sabbath and eat them,
and the rabbis rebuke him for breaking the Sabbath law. In
another, Jesus heals a man with a withered arm on Shabbat,
and again gets into a debate with the rabbis. Jesus argues his
case by giving examples of other occasions when worthy
causes outweighed the law, but his most often quoted response
to rabbinic complaints is, "The Sabbath was made for man, and
not man for the Sabbath." In that statement he actually echoes
the teachings of Rabbi Simeon ben Menasya—"The Sabbath
is given to you, but you are not surrendered to the Sabbath."

From the Pharisees' point of view, neither of the incidents
with Jesus posed a threat to human life. The disciples were
not starving when they picked corn on Shabbat and the man
with the withered arm had a chronic illness that did not have
to be healed on the Sabbath. From an early Christian point of

view, as stated in the Gospel of Matthew, "it is allowed to do good on the Sabbath" even if that means disregarding the law. Moreover, Jesus had a right to disregard the law, because "the Son of Man is lord of the Sabbath." These differences have never been resolved.

In recognized danger to human life and health the talmudic masters, descendants of the Pharisees, bent over backward to be lenient about the Sabbath laws. One small example speaks for the whole.

The Talmud states that the needs of a woman giving birth override the Sabbath. In the course of discussing that idea, one rabbi mentions a separate ruling that if a woman in labor asks for a lamp, a neighbor may light a lamp and carry it to her. The question then arises about why this ruling about the light should be singled out in the talmudic teaching. After all, a general principle has been established that the Sabbath may be violated for a woman in labor.

The answer is that this permission to light a lamp on the Sabbath refers especially to a blind woman who is in labor.

A blind woman? Why would a blind woman need to have a light lit for her?

But that is exactly the point. Since the woman cannot see, you might suppose that it is forbidden to light the lamp for her on the Sabbath. But no, the passage comes to teach us that even if the woman giving birth is blind, you must light a lamp for her if she requests it. Why? Because she will feel secure knowing that the lamp has been lit and that light is available if necessary to anyone assisting her. We learn from this passage that easing a woman's mind in such a situation equals saving a life. It takes precedence over all the laws of Shabbat.

The Sabbath laws and their exceptions consistently lean toward compassion and concern for every human being, even the weakest members of society, even a blind woman in labor. In the end, the minutiae of the law—that mass of detail that can be so exasperating to absorb and challenging to practice—is also its strength. The details carry the law into every aspect of living, every facet of being, overlooking no person or situation, neglecting nothing.

In his essay, "Halakhah and Aggadah," Bialik contrasts the halakhah with its vast body of rules and regulations to the lore, legends, and poetry of Jewish life, the aggadah. People tend to view halakhah, he says, as "grim," "narrow," and forbidding, whereas they see aggadah as "buoyant," "flexible," and easily accessible. Yet in reality the two profoundly interact to give depth and vibrancy to the tradition.

The pages of the talmudic tractates of Shabbat and Eruvin, Bialik points out, abound with discussions and relentless details about the thirty-nine forbidden labors, with only a "pitifully small" amount of legend and narrative. "What a sorry expense of ingenuity over every jot and tittle!" he exclaims. Yet, he goes on, when he thinks about the sages at their work, he sees them as "artists of life," no less artistic than the craftsmen who built the world's great cathedrals. Although they worked as individuals across generations, each with his own abilities, the spirit of the Sabbath drew them together, inspiring them as one.

"And what is the result of all this strenuous labor of halakhah?" Bialik asks. "A day that is wholly aggadah." From the mountains of rules, Shabbat emerges, an enchanted day.

Six

THE SABBATH JEW AND THE
SABBATH GENTILE

Reflections on Observing Shabbat

Memory again. I am walking with a group of school friends, on our way home from an *oneg Shabbat* gathering, our weekly Saturday afternoon social get-together. This is the Borough Park of my youth, a middle-class Jewish neighborhood in Brooklyn that would later become an enclave for fervently Orthodox Hasidic Jews. My friends and I attend a small Hebrew elementary school for girls, where Jewish studies combine with secular ones and our lives center on Jewish practice. As we stroll along leisurely, laughing, arms linked, I spot at a slight distance from us a shadow behind a tree. No, it's not a shadow; it's a woman carrying something. What is she carrying? I see it now. She's carrying a bag of groceries in one arm and she has the finger of her other hand to her lips, motioning me to silence. Who is this strange woman? Now I see her more clearly. Good heavens! It's Aunt Molly, my mother's unmarried sister who lives with my family. She's been shopping again on *Shabbos*. I will die of embarrassment if my friends see her with her groceries. So will she; that's why she's hiding behind the tree. I distract my friends before they notice her, and rush them along as she slips out from behind the tree and takes an alternate route home.

When Isaiah taught Israel that Shabbat should be an *oneg*, a delight, he actually did so in the context of an appeal to the people of his time. "If you refrain from trampling the Sabbath, / From pursuing your affairs on My holy day, / If you call the Sabbath 'delight', / The Lord's holy day 'honored'..." he said, God would reward them. His words suggest that people did trample Shabbat, pursue their business affairs, and neglect to honor the Sabbath. Indeed, much of what scholars have learned about how early Jews kept the Sabbath comes from the words of prophets admonishing them to do better. Jeremiah, who lived before and during the Babylonian exile, warned against carrying burdens to and from Jerusalem on Shabbat, an indication that people had carried commercial goods in and out of the city. His contemporary, Ezekiel, chastised bluntly in God's name, "You have despised My holy things and profaned My Sabbaths."

In short, Aunt Molly was not the first Jew to violate the Sabbath.

As cherished a place as the seventh day holds in Jewish belief and imagination, from ancient times through today, tensions have existed between its spiritual ideals and the demands of its laws, the liberation it offers and the limitations it imposes. Ironically, at moments of greatest persecutions and stresses for the Jewish community, Jews have clung to Sabbath observance and other religious practices, often at the cost of their lives. At other times, they have been more lax in their observance, the greatest laxities occurring in the modern age, when Jews have also enjoyed the greatest freedoms they ever had within society as a whole.

The tensions surrounding Shabbat observance appear in the earliest biblical stories. In Exodus, some Israelites try to gather manna on the seventh day although expressly forbidden to do so. In Numbers, Moses and the people punish the unnamed wood gatherer for desecrating the Sabbath. The pulls and tugs between observing and not observing Sabbath strictures became more intense in later biblical times, after the Israelites settled in their own land and established the kingdoms of Israel and Judah. When, in the seventh century B.C.E., King Manasseh of Judah promoted the worship of pagan gods, the prophets responded by putting greater emphasis than ever before on the importance of Sabbath observance, holding it up as the finest symbol of Israel's uniqueness and a bulwark against foreign practices.

By the time the Jews were exiled to Babylonia, the major prophets—Isaiah, Jeremiah, and Ezekiel—had raised Shabbat to such a high plane that they linked the fate of the nation as a whole, not only that of individuals, to its observance. To a great extent they blamed the destruction of the Temple and the dispersal of the Jews on their disregard of Shabbat, and they held out the hope that by keeping the day, the nation would be redeemed in the future. If you "hallow the Sabbath day and do no work on it," Jeremiah told the exiles, "then through the gates of this city shall enter kings who sit upon the throne of David.... And this city shall be inhabited for all time."

Shabbat did become a distinctive mark of Jewishness for the exiles. But for many who returned to Palestine after the exile ended in 538 B.C.E., the lure of commerce preempted Sabbath observance as it had before and would again in the future. About a hundred years later, when the political leader Nehemiah arrived in Jerusalem to help rebuild the city, he was shocked to find "men in Judah treading winepresses on the Sabbath and others bringing heaps of grain...." Moreover, he discovered that non-Jews in the area brought "fish and all sorts of wares and sold them to the Judahites in Jerusalem." Nehemiah rebuked the people and reminded them that "This is just what your ancestors did, and for it God brought all this misfortune on this city...." To combat such behavior, he had the gates to Jerusalem shut on Shabbat and stationed guards to prevent merchants from entering, warning them that if they try, "I will lay hands upon you!"

It's hard to know whether Nehemiah's strong-arm tactics prevented all Sabbath desecration, but the tradition credits him and the scribe Ezra with reviving religious devotion among the Jews in Palestine. Certainly by the talmudic age, in the last centuries before the Common Era and first several centuries after it, Sabbath observance had become deeply ingrained in Jewish life. Now the Roman satirist Persius writes disparagingly of how the Sabbath lamps of the Jews "ranged round the greasy windowsills have spat forth their thick clouds of smoke," ignoring the fact that Rome's own citizens have incorporated Sabbath lamps into their weekly customs. Now the classic sages formulate basic laws for the

Shabbat celebration. Scholars point out that the sages did not invent the rules, but they standardized practices that had developed through the years. Still, under their guidance, Sabbath observance took on the forms that would be followed for centuries, the forms we know today.

After the Romans destroyed the Second Temple in 70 C.E., Shabbat became a prime symbol of Jewish unity and identity both inside Palestine and in the diaspora communities outside it. "The Sabbath adds holiness to Israel," the sages said. "Why is the shop of So-and-so closed? Because he keeps the Sabbath. Why does So-and-so abstain from work? Because he keeps the Sabbath." By keeping the Sabbath wherever they lived, Jews demonstrated to the world their loyalty to their faith.

To reinforce Sabbath keeping, the rabbis told entertaining parables and stories, like the tale of the cow that refused to work on Shabbat. Probably the most popular rabbinic legend concerns Joseph Who Honors the Sabbath. (So popular that I learned it as a schoolchild; my daughter learned a slightly different version in her day school; and I have no doubt my grandchildren will learn it in some form or other in theirs.) This Joseph acquired his name by scrimping and saving all week to buy the best foods he could to honor Shabbat. Now Joseph had a rich neighbor who learned from astrologers that all his wealth would soon fall into Joseph's hands. Frightened, the man sold everything he owned and with the money bought a precious jewel, which he protected by knotting it into the turban around his head. Alas, as the man crossed a bridge, a heavy wind sent his turban hurtling into the sea, where a huge fish swallowed it.

A fisherman caught the fish and hauled it to the market on the Sabbath eve. "Who will buy such a large fish at this time?" he asked. "Take it to Joseph Who Honors the Sabbath," people said. Joseph quickly bought the fish, and when he slit it open, behold, there was the precious jewel! He later sold the jewel for a great deal of money and lived out his life in wealth and comfort. And the moral: One day Joseph met an old man who said to him, "For the person who lends to the Sabbath, the Sabbath repays him," meaning that a person who honors the Sabbath will be rewarded with honor.

The sages did not teach that Sabbath observance always results in monetary reward, but they did suggest that Sabbath observance brings blessings that may not always be anticipated. Under their tutelage, Jews in many places and times lived the Sabbath fully and proudly, often despite dire conditions.

Jump ahead several centuries to Spain in 1486. We are at the trial of Juana Martínez of Alcazar, a *conversa,* feminine for *converso* or New Christian, the term for a Jew who has converted to Christianity, often under duress. The Inquisition has accused Juana of practicing "judaizing" rituals and she is confessing her crimes, hoping to be spared from being burned at the stake like so many other *conversos.* "I sinned in that I observed some Sabbaths and wore clean clothes on some of them," she admits. She goes on to say that she also "lit clean candles on Friday nights" and "prepared cooked food on Friday for the Sabbath." Where did she, supposedly a good Catholic woman, learn these practices? "I saw my mother do all these things," she tells the court. Her mother soon confesses to the same crimes. Both women will be condemned for betraying their adopted Christian religion and secretly practicing the faith of their ancestors.

Throughout the Middle Ages that faith remained at the crux of Jewish life. To be sure, some individuals disobeyed the laws and others converted out of Judaism, but on the whole, tight-knit and committed Jewish communities headed by rabbis kept to the cycle of the Jewish year and the pattern of the Jewish week. In western and central European countries, many Ashkenazic Jews martyred themselves during the Crusades, beginning in the eleventh century, rather than relinquish their religious beliefs. In Islamic lands, Judaism flourished for several hundred years, especially in Spain, where Sephardic Jews built a rich culture and practiced their traditions freely. The Spanish situation deteriorated after radical Muslims gained control, improved again under Christian rule, but fell into an abyss in 1391, when rioters murdered thousands of Jews and forcibly baptized thousands of others. With these baptisms, pressure on all Spanish Jews to convert heightened, and the number of New Christians on the Iberian Peninsula grew enormously. In the fifteenth century the long arm of the Inquisitor began to reach into the lives of these converts to snatch those crypto-Jews who secretly maintained their Jewish practices or were accused of doing so. The Inquisition continued its work long after Spain expelled the Jews themselves in 1492.

Jewish women like Juana Martínez ranked high on the Inquisitor's lists. Prosecutors knew that many of the most important Jewish rituals took place in the home, and the home had always been the woman's domain. The Israeli scholar Renée Levine Melammed studied the lives of crypto-Jewish women of Castile, including records of their trials before the Inquisition. In her book *Heretics or Daughters of Israel?*, she argues that because men's roles had revolved around the synagogue and community life, men had fewer outlets for secretly practicing Judaism than did women. At trials, prosecutors sometimes accused men of "allowing" their wives to perform Jewish rituals, whereas they accused women of actively doing so. (That's not to say that men did not suffer the Inquisitor's pryings and punishments. Men were charged with such crimes as organizing prayer services or performing circumcisions. But the more visible home practices made the women particularly vulnerable.)

The Sabbath held top priority for crypto-Jewish women. Like Juana's mother, who taught her daughter the Shabbat rites, generations of women continued some form of Sabbath observance long after they had officially converted. Often servants testified before the Inquisition's tribunals that their mistresses prepared special Sabbath breads and, following the Jewish custom, burned a piece of dough before baking the bread. They gave accounts of women cleaning their homes on Friday in preparation for the Jewish Sabbath, and women and men wearing clean clothes and dressing up on Saturdays instead of Sundays. Accusers invariably pointed a damning finger at the lights the mistress lit on Friday evenings, using clean wicks, and allowing the flames to burn down. One of the most incriminating charges against the crypto-Jewish women alleged that they cooked on Friday for Saturday and did no cooking on Saturday. The cooking referred to was *dafina*, the Sephardic stew usually made with lamb and chickpeas and left to heat overnight for the Sabbath day meal. The dish was a giveaway because a Christian had no reason to prepare such food in advance (although in later years the Spanish cuisine incorporated versions of this stew).

Centuries after the Inquisition, there are Catholic families in Spanish and Latin American countries who, for no apparent reason, clean their houses on Fridays and light candles on Friday evenings, sometimes in jars or in their basements. They most likely inherited these customs from *converso* ancestors who observed the Sabbath in secret, struggling against all odds not to abandon it. Over the years, numbers of descendants of crypto-Jews have resurfaced and reclaimed their Jewish heritage.

In one of the *conversa* trials, a woman named Elvira spoke of lending out her servant to various Jewish families to serve as a *goy shel Shabbat* and light the fire for them on the Sabbath. The term referred to a gentile who performs chores forbidden to Jews on the Sabbath, or in common Ashkenazic parlance, a *Shabbos goy*. (Elvis Presley spoke about being, during his teen years, the *Shabbos goy* for an Orthodox rabbi and other Orthodox families who lived near his Memphis apartment.) From earliest times, as Jews spread out in many lands and guidelines for Shabbat observance grew, questions arose about whether non-Jews may perform tasks for Jews on Shabbat. No doubt ever existed that non-Jews could do their own work on the Sabbath—Jewish law does not obligate them to observe the seventh-day rest. But what about work for Jews? Did it not disgrace the holiness of the Sabbath and

Judaism itself to have non-Jews labor for Jews while they observed the day by resting?

The sages believed it did. The Mishnah states categorically, "If a gentile lights a lamp [on the Sabbath], a Jew might make use of the light, but if it is done for the sake of the Jew, it is forbidden" [the Jew may not make use of the light]. Likewise, if the gentile "made a gangplank for descending [when disembarking from a ship] a Jew may descend after him, but if for the Jew's sake, it is prohibited." The Talmud goes far beyond these specific examples, establishing a fundamental principle that guided later Jewish communities: Jews may not ask gentiles to perform work for them on the Sabbath, but if a gentile performs the work for himself or herself, the Jew may enjoy its benefit.

There have always been exceptions to this rule, however. My great-grandmother Riva and my grandmother Goldie awoke before dawn every day except Saturday to milk the cows on their family farm in Russia. "On *Shabbos,*" my father wrote in his memoirs, "we would engage a local farmer's daughter as a milkmaid, paying her in advance the equivalent of 25 cents for a day's work." Hiring a non-Jew to milk the cows became one exception to the rule against employing a gentile to work while the Jew observes the Sabbath. It fell into the category of relieving animals in pain, a duty that cannot wait until Sabbath's end.

Another exception was having a gentile light a fire in a Jewish home in cold weather. This exception developed in France and Germany, where winters could be bitter. Some rabbinic authorities never agreed to it. The outstanding legal expert in thirteenth-century Germany, Rabbi Meir of

Rothenburg, wrote that his housekeeper insisted on heating his home on winter days against his wishes, and the only way he could prevent her was to make a lock for the furnace. "Every Friday I lock it and leave it locked until Saturday night," he said. A similar story is told of the leading thirteenth-century Spanish rabbi Solomon ben Abraham Adret. Even so, the practice of allowing a non-Jew to light a fire in a Jewish home became so widespread and routine that most rabbis accepted it. Often the same person did the lighting for several families or an entire neighborhood. That is how the *conversa* Elvira came to lend her servant to Jewish families to kindle their fires on the Sabbath.

As might be expected, along with exceptions, there have also been people who misused the concept of the Sabbath gentile. I found in an anthology on Jewish preaching an eighteenth-century British rabbi, Hirschel Levin, railing about the "profaning of the Sabbath by having a gentile woman light a fire to heat water for tea or coffee." Apparently, instead of limiting fire lighting on Shabbat to warming the home, people extended it to heating water for beverages and probably also to warming foods or cooking—all of which would be forbidden for a Jew and forbidden to request of a non-Jew.

On a different tack, the Yiddish writer I. L. Peretz portrayed the Sabbath gentile as a symbol of the fears Jews had of their non-Jewish neighbors. His short story "The Shabbes Goy" tells satirically of how the rabbi of the mythical town of Chelm repeatedly makes excuses for the community's *Shabbes goy,* who gratuitously attacks and bloodies one of the townspeople, Yankele. Finally the rabbi decides that to prevent further attacks, rather than punish the *Shabbos goy*, the townspeople should banish Yankele and raise the gentile's wages—"Perhaps he'll have compassion!" A bitter commentary on Jewish timidity under the stresses of diaspora life.

But aside from exclusions, abuses, or fears in regard to the Sabbath gentile, the fact of Jews living among non-Jews forced rabbis around the world to answer scores of queries. For example, may a Jew give clothes before the Sabbath to a non-Jew to launder, knowing that the non-Jew might work on the clothes during the Sabbath? The answer is yes, as long as the non-Jew freely decides when the work should be done. But a Jew may not give out laundry just before the Sabbath and ask to have it returned immediately afterward, for in that case it would be impossible for the non-Jew to complete the laundering without working on the Sabbath and the Jew would directly benefit from that person's Sabbath labor.

If a Jew is building a new house, may gentiles work on the house on the Sabbath? Generally no. Not only should a Jew not benefit directly from the Sabbath labor of non-Jews, but also no labor on behalf of a Jew should be done in public on the Sabbath, giving the impression that the Jew has hired the laborers to work on Shabbat.

On and on the queries stretch, their subtleties myriad. In more recent times, new kinds of questions have arisen as technology has replaced some of the needs for gentile help on the Sabbath. Now rabbis have had to decide about the use of devices that automatically turn lights or ovens on and off on Shabbat or automated Sabbath elevators that stop on every floor of a building so that occupants do not have to create an electric current by pressing buttons. The responses of authorities to these and tens of thousands of other questions form the vast rabbinic literature known as *responsa*. This literature began in talmudic times and continues to the present, among every branch of Judaism. It covers questions on all areas of Jewish life, not only Sabbath observance. But inquiries to rabbinic authorities about the Sabbath, including Sabbath relations with gentiles, make up a vital part of it.

A contemporary example comes from the response Rabbi Moshe Feinstein, a leading twentieth-century Orthodox scholar, gave to volunteer ambulance workers. Members of Hatzolah, a Jewish emergency medical service, inquired whether a volunteer may drive back to his home base on the Sabbath after delivering a patient to the hospital.

The rabbi begins his response with the assurance that Hatzolah members may violate the Sabbath by driving in an ambulance and using every life-saving measure necessary on behalf of a patient, for saving a life outweighs all laws. He recommends, however, that the ambulance have a non-Jewish driver to minimize a Jewish volunteer's Sabbath desecration. But if waiting for such a driver entails even the slightest delay in responding to a call, the Hatzolah member should drive the ambulance himself. And what about returning home? With saving a life no longer the issue, must the volunteer wait until the Sabbath ends in order to drive home?

Again the rabbi suggests using a non-Jewish driver. If that is not possible, he concludes after quoting many earlier authorities that Hatzolah volunteers may return home when their assignment ends, although that might involve breaking

Sabbath laws. His rationale comes from a principle of Jewish law known as "permitting the end because of the beginning." In this case that means Hatzolah volunteers may transgress at the end of their task lest the inconvenience of taking a Sabbath call discourages them to begin with from making themselves available on that day. Rabbi Feinstein has no problem with using gentile help on Shabbat or with breaking the law in this situation, although he writes that some Hasidic rabbis opposed allowing the volunteers to drive home. For him, the most important goal is to aid patients.

Of all the queries rabbis have received from Jews seeking to observe the Sabbath as meticulously as possible wherever they lived, the most moving came from people suffering the anguish of the Holocaust. These inquiries never concerned the use of paid gentile labor to ease Sabbath restrictions. Instead, they dealt with the unpaid forced labor Jews had to perform for gentiles and the dangers that ensued from trying to uphold even the most minimum Sabbath requirements. On a continuum with the *conversos,* Jews trapped in the grip of the Shoah clung to their religion, especially what they could of Shabbat observance.

Ephraim Oshry, a rabbi from the ghetto of Kovno, Lithuania, published several volumes of *responsa* after the war based on questions he said had been brought to him from 1941 to 1944, during the Nazi occupation of the Kovno ghetto. One question came from the rabbi's student Reb Ya'akov at a time when starvation had overcome many ghetto inhabitants. The student had an opportunity to do his slave labor in the ghetto kitchen rather than in a more physically grueling construction project. But in the kitchen he would have to cook on Shabbat. Would such cooking be permitted under these circumstances, and was he permitted to eat from the soup he made? Referring to many sources in his response, the rabbi gave the reasons why, working under duress as the student was, he had a right to transgress the Sabbath by cooking and to eat the food he cooked—not least of the reasons being the necessity to save his life. For Reb Ya'akov and others in those dread times, holding on to the Sabbath was a way of holding on to their humanity.

❦

In the course of an exhaustive study of the Sabbath gentile, the Israeli scholar Jacob Katz discovered that, paradoxically, as the numbers of Jews observing the Sabbath diminished in modern times, the numbers of questions about Sabbath observance posed to rabbis expanded. Along the lines of the Hatzolah volunteers, questioners today probe increasingly refined areas of observance. It is as though people who keep the traditions want to hug them ever closer to themselves, to protect them from abandonment by encircling them with more and more precise ways of practicing.

They have good reason. The self-sufficient Jewish communities dominated by tradition that had once made up the entire Jewish world have dwindled away. When the Enlightenment that swept through Europe in the mid-eighteenth century opened the way for Jews to enter the larger society, most flew readily into those open spaces. For many, Shabbat rituals fell by the wayside, along with much else in Jewish practice. Jews no longer needed to hire gentiles to light the

fires or do other Sabbath chores. They became their own
Shabbos goyim, while Sabbath observers turned into a
minority.

The story is told of the Hasidic rebbe Levi-Yitzhak of
Berdichev. On his way to services on the Sabbath he meets a
young man, a product of the Enlightenment, who pulls out a
pipe and lights it. The rebbe stops to remind him that this is
Shabbat.

"I haven't forgotten that," the man responds.

"Then you must not know the law that forbids us to
smoke on Shabbat?"

"I know the law," the man snaps back.

The rebbe lifts his hands to the heavens and addresses
the Ruler of the Universe. "Did you hear that?" he asks. "It is
true this young man violates the Shabbat commandment.
But you see, nothing will induce him to tell a lie."

Like Rebbe Levi-Yitzhak, leaders concerned about Sabbath observance had to think creatively to find a silver lining
in the rampant desertion of tradition after the Enlightenment and the emancipation Jews enjoyed in many countries.

Attitudes toward observance differed in various parts of
the world. Western Europe gave birth in the early 1800s to
the German Reform movement, which aimed at making
Judaism more palatable by moving closer to Protestant practices in its synagogues (now called "temples") and eliminating most religious ceremonies. Reform Judaism did continue
to celebrate the Sabbath, but with a revised prayer book,
fewer rites, and, in some places, Sunday instead of Saturday
services. Change came more slowly to eastern European
countries. Like my great-grandmother Riva and the rest of

my family, most Jews in Russia, Poland, and other eastern lands remained in villages and shtetls, where Shabbat endured as the high point of the week and children held fast to the old customs.

But by the late 1800s, cracks had begun to show in shtetl life as the Haskalah, the Jewish enlightenment movement— an offshoot of the European—cut through even those cohesive communities. Modern schools shifted away from the exclusive study of Torah and Talmud, and through Hebrew and Yiddish translations introduced young people to secular literature. At the same time, Jewish writers began to reach wide audiences with stories and poems that reflected a growing ambivalence toward traditional practices.

In his autobiographical novel *From the Fair,* Sholom Aleichem humorously describes his character Sholom's first Sabbath transgression. While the whole town is asleep on a Shabbat afternoon, young Sholom discovers a piece of chalk in his pocket. Looking at the walls of the neighborhood houses and the wooden fences of the courtyards, he cannot resist the impulse first to draw, then to write on them. But just as he finishes writing a Russian rhyme, he feels two fingers pinching his ears—Uncle Pinny has caught him. Soon, word of his Sabbath desecration spreads throughout the town. His school principal almost expels him, and his teachers anoint him with a new name. Whenever they summon him to a class blackboard, they call him either "artist" or "author," stretching the latter into two long syllables, as in "Au-thor!" Of course, he will retain that name for the rest of his life.

The author who perhaps most epitomized the currents of

change and doubt that streamed through eastern Europe and spread beyond that region was Bialik. The great poet who sang of the sun vanishing behind the treetops on the Sabbath eve, who saw the beauty beneath the burden of Sabbath laws, who moved to Palestine and worked tirelessly to prevent Sabbath violations, did not himself observe Shabbat, at least not in private. Bialik confessed to a friend that he smoked at home on Shabbat. He told another that he distinguished between public observance of the day, which he considered critical to Jewish life, and private observance, which he felt individuals could determine themselves. He was a man at war with himself, steeped in Jewish learning yet lacking the faith that suffused his parents' lives. He devoted himself to Jewish culture, but could not fully accept religious practices. He exalted the Sabbath, but didn't always keep it.

In varying ways, Bialik's internal conflicts characterized the masses of Jews who left eastern Europe and journeyed to America and, in lesser numbers, other countries. My father arrived in the United States in 1911 at the age of fifteen. My grandfather, who came a few years earlier, had already found work as a sponger in a clothing shop. Because my grandfather refused to work on Shabbat, and even though he worked on Sundays instead, he received only a pittance of the other workers' pay. When my father and his brothers began to work, they made compromises their father would not. In his memoirs, my father wrote, about his own father: "My father's greatest ambition was for his sons to be educated and to follow in the religion of their ancestors. What a disappointment it was for him to see them violate the Sabbath. He was sick at heart over it."

Many immigrants like my father transgressed the Sabbath out of economic necessity. Signs on factory doors read: "If you don't work on Saturday, don't bother to come in on Monday." So men and women who in the old country would never have dreamed of working on Shabbat did so in the golden land of opportunity. Later, when economic pressures eased, my father returned to Sabbath observance. His brothers did not. Other considerations had pulled them and their families further away from the traditional Sabbath rest and they were not about to turn back. Along with the majority of immigrants and children of immigrants, they had fallen in step with the American way of life. Along with the majority, they worked or shopped or ran errands on Saturday and relaxed on Sunday, America's rest day.

My father's description of his father's pain when his sons violated Shabbat has a counterpart in a poem by the Israeli poet Yehuda Amichai that reveals another path away from the Sabbath. In "A Song of Falsehoods on Sabbath Eve," the poet writes of a summer Sabbath eve, when the air is filled with "the odor of food and prayer" and "the sound of the wings of the Sabbath angels." At this time, in his childhood, he begins to lie to his father: "I went to a different synagogue." Whether in America or Israel, England or South Africa, new generations of Jews chose not to go to their parents' synagogue, or any synagogue at all. They chose the secular over the religious life, and left the habitat of their fathers and mothers behind them.

And for some the split from Sabbath observance resulted from rage at the Jewish past and dreams of a Utopian future. In Tillie Olsen's story "Tell Me a Riddle," a dying immigrant woman, a revolutionary from Russia, fumes at knowing that her daughter Hannah lights Sabbath candles. "Does she look back at the dark centuries? Candles bought instead of bread . . . ," the woman says bitterly. "Religion that stifled and said: in Paradise, woman, you will be the footstool of your husband. . . ."

Many factors came together in the modern world to make people remember the Sabbath day for one reason or another, but not particularly for observance.

There is, however, another side to the story. Around 1792, a woman named Rachel Lazarus wrote home, in Yiddish, to her parents in Germany that she and her family are moving from Petersburg, Virginia, to Charleston, South Carolina, which has a larger Jewish population. They hate it that all the Jewish shops in Petersburg are open on the Sabbath except their own, and they are seeking a place to raise their children more Jewishly. In the 1890s, a Jewish immigrant peddles his wares in Northfield, Minnesota. In Lithuania he had been a *shochet* (a ritual slaughterer), and now he puts his skills to good use. When he cannot get home in time for the Sabbath, he stays in the home of a friendly farmer. He arrives early enough before Shabbat to slaughter a chicken and cook it along with other Sabbath foods in kosher utensils he has brought with him. He observes Shabbat until Saturday evening, when a child in the family goes outside to watch for three stars, and returns to tell him that he may smoke now. The Sabbath has ended.

In spite of change, self-doubts, emancipation, assimilation, and outright rejection of Shabbat, there have always been Jews who lovingly kept the day. The sages had said that the things for which Jews were willing to sacrifice their lives would remain with them forever. The Sabbath is one of those things. Jews have given up their lives to uphold it—in ancient Rome and medieval Europe, under the tortures of the Inquisition and the abominations of the Nazis. And it survives.

In Orthodox communities like that of my childhood and those that still exist in many places, Shabbat fits neatly into every person's life. People like my aunt Molly who break it stand out as exceptions. But Shabbat also has meaning to plenty of people outside Orthodox circles. Greater economic security today coupled with a wish for spiritual nourishment have led many people, like the daughter in Tillie Olsen's story, to rediscover Sabbath rituals a previous generation had discarded.

Growing numbers of Conservative Jews have moved closer to traditional ways of keeping the day. The Reform movement has welcomed Shabbat, along with many other Jewish rites, in a manner far beyond and far richer than the revised rituals its founders had introduced. In Israel, with its largely secular population, the entire country seems to come to a halt on Friday afternoon until Shabbat ends on Saturday night. Stores close early, the streets become still, and even nonobservant families share Friday night dinner at home. Some of the most secular Israeli lawmakers I know oppose allowing commerce on Shabbat, because they love the quiet, spiritual atmosphere of the day.

An American woman said to me, "I don't observe all the laws, but I 'observe' Shabbat. In one way or another every caring Jew observes Shabbat."

In one way or another, and the ways may differ greatly, most Jews have maintained some attachment to the Sabbath, some awareness of the day's presence and acknowledgment of its significance.

A dialogue group I belong to made Shabbat the topic of discussion one evening. This is a group of women from across the Jewish religious spectrum that meets regularly to exchange commonalities and differences. Every woman, from the least devout to the most, spoke warmly of her attachment to the Sabbath. Every one told of how lighting Sabbath candles stirred profound emotions for her—the most observant kindling the lights at the prescribed moment; others waiting until family or guests had gathered for dinner. Some women from the more liberal movements felt strongly about attending synagogue services every Saturday morning, although they might not observe the Sabbath in the afternoon. Some more traditional women liked to sleep late on Saturday morning, leaving synagogue services to the men in their families. None would consider not observing in the afternoon.

People observe selectively, a man said to me recalling his father, who worked on the Sabbath but would never write or hold a pencil on it. Rabbi Mordecai Kaplan, founder of the Reconstructionist movement, described Shabbat as a time to "discover within ourselves unsuspected powers of the spirit" and encouraged its observance. Yet he confided in his journals that he did some of his own writing on Shabbat, although "only when unseen." He argued, as Bialik had, that a "secret transgression" was far less serious than a public one. The German-Jewish philosopher Franz Rosenzweig, who found his way back to Judaism after almost abandoning it, decided at first that he would write letters to friends on Shabbat but would do no business correspondence. One Shabbat a friend asked him to jot down notes concerning a discussion they were having, on the assumption that Rosenzweig would not mind such writing. Rosenzweig realized then, he said, that he could not draw fine distinctions between kinds of writing. After much inner struggle, he gave up all writing on Shabbat.

People observe selectively. A friend remembers with affection how, when her children were young, the family would gather around the television set on Friday nights after a traditional dinner to watch their favorite programs. It was the only time they had all week to relax together. Another woman speaks of taking long walks with friends on Shabbat and setting aside time to think or talk about Jewish matters on that day, even if she spends the rest of the day working.

People observe differently and often not in traditional ways. Nonetheless, as the rabbis said, Shabbat will remain with the Jewish people forever. It will remain forever, because in a world that rapidly grows more technological and impersonal it reminds us each week of our humanness. And it will remain forever, because more than any other aspect of Jewish life and history, Shabbat is stamped indelibly on Jewish consciousness.

In the Prologue to this book I raised the question of why I, who live as comfortably in the secular world as in the religious, continue to keep Shabbat much as I have since childhood. This is the place to gather some of the strands of personal thought spread throughout into a more cohesive whole. What does Shabbat mean to me?

When I posed a similar question to the chancellor of the Jewish Theological Seminary, Ismar Schorsch, he used the word *tzimtzum*. That seems a good word with which to introduce my own thoughts. *Tzimtzum* is a term the kabbalists devised to explain how God, whose infinite Being filled all eternity, could have created a finite world that did not become instantly reabsorbed into that infinity. The answer they gave was self-contraction, God's voluntary withdrawal or stepping aside, so to speak, to make room for the created world. *Tzimtzum* is that withdrawal. What has God's self-contraction to do with my Shabbat? "Before you can create you have to contract," Dr. Schorsch said.

Shabbat is about contracting, pulling back for a day from the infinite cacophony, competition, and commotion of the world around us. Commenting on the words of the Fourth Commandment, "Six days you shall labor and do all your work," the sages asked, "But is it possible for human beings to do all their work in six days?" They answered, "The verse means rest on the Sabbath *as if* all your work were done." In the busyness of life, work can be endless, but when I light candles on Friday evenings to welcome the Sabbath, I often feel I've also built a wall of flame around my home, shutting off the outside and creating an inner realm of calm and quiet. Within that realm I don't have to think about the work I haven't completed, the meetings I haven't attended, or the messages I haven't returned. (In truth, I cannot always stop thinking of such things, the rabbis notwithstanding, but at least I have a context for trying.) Within that realm I can simply *be,* not striving to become, produce, or achieve. I can live fully in the present without having to attend to yesterday's pressures or tomorrow's demands. Withdrawing from the tumult, I make room for time itself.

But calm and quiet are not everything. More compelling, Shabbat's air of sacredness draws me to it. There's an intriguing puzzle about the sanctity of Shabbat. We create that sanctity through the things we do—lighting candles, saying blessings, singing songs—and through the things we don't do, the *not* cooking or cleaning or shopping. But once created, Shabbat's holiness takes on a reality of its own, the intrinsic holiness the rabbis claimed it had from before the world began. Time becomes sacred, as Heschel taught us, and so does space. When Moses saw the bush that burned but was not consumed, he heard the words, "Remove your sandals from your feet, for the place on which you stand is holy ground." An ordinary place had become holy because of God's presence near it. On Shabbat, I feel the ordinary space of my home mysteriously altered into something that surpasses ordinariness. I know I had a part in making it that way, with Sabbath preparations and rituals, and I can't speak with certainty about God's presence in it, but it is altered, and I feel the day's peace and spirit envelop me, as if they existed independent of me. Other holidays bring gladness and sensations of their own. Shabbat brings holiness into my life every seventh day, and because it does I am aware of the holiness in the universe the other six.

Then there is the matter of commandedness. As the fourth of the Ten Commandments, Shabbat embodies as the others do the commanding voice at Sinai, the divine sounds the Bible tells us the Israelites heard as they stood at the foot of the mountain and received the Torah. I cannot explain that moment of revelation in the hidden past, but I know that its words and sounds have reverberated through the ages, penetrating the collective Jewish soul. I feel commanded by the moment, but even more so by the meaning it has held throughout Jewish history. Observing Shabbat, I relive the rhythm of the universe from its inception, as the Torah has pictured it and Jewish belief and teachings have made real. Observing Shabbat I pay tribute to ideals of freedom and equality inherent in that day from its ancient beginnings. Observing Shabbat, I align myself with the community of Israel, which holds the seventh day sacred as a sign of its covenant with God. How could I not honor this day?

The story of Franz Rosenzweig's return to Judaism has been told many times. An emancipated intellectual, Rosenzweig had decided to convert to Christianity. Because he wanted to approach his conversion as a Jew and not simply a dropout from Judaism, he attended synagogue on the Yom Kippur before he was to be baptized, in October 1913. He left that service a different person. Giving up all thought of conversion, he devoted his life after that to Jewish study and philosophy. In his writings, he urged readers interested in broadening their Jewish practice to "begin modestly," and to recognize that there may be things they "cannot yet" accept, but may want to accept at a future time. Tradition has it that when asked whether he himself observed certain practices, instead of "no," he would optimistically answer "not yet." And he did continually take on more religious commitments.

"Not yet" has become a good measuring rod for people who wish to find their place on the spectrum between observing and not observing Shabbat. For some, following as many rules as possible turns the day into a true oasis of serenity, untouched by the workaday world. (But even the most fervently Orthodox have "not yets" they haven't reached.) Others may not wish to assume full Shabbat responsibilities. They may want to "begin modestly" as Rosenzweig advised, perhaps with lighting candles or having family dinners on Friday evenings or using part of Saturday to focus on Jewish teachings, and moving on at their own pace to what they feel they can accept.

Long before Rosenzweig, Maimonides gave a parable about religion that can be applied to Shabbat. It goes this way: "The ruler is in his palace, and all his subjects are partly within the city and partly outside the city. Of those within the city, some have turned their backs on the ruler's habitation. . . . Others seek to reach the ruler's habitation, turn toward it, and desire to enter it . . . but until now have not seen the wall of the habitation. Some of those who seek to reach it have come up to the habitation and walk around it searching for its gate. Some of them have entered the gate and walk about in the antechambers. Some of them have entered the inner court . . . and have come to be with the king. . . ."

People have different ways of approaching the palace in time that is Shabbat. Some may want to look at it from a distance, others to go no farther than its antechambers. And some may gain the most satisfaction from walking through and entering.

Seven

THE LOVELIEST OF DAYS

Living Shabbat

"With what may we light the Sabbath lamp and with what may we not light it?" These are the words with which the second chapter of the tractate Shabbat in the Mishnah begins an investigation, before candles existed, into the materials that may and may not be used for the wick and oil of a Sabbath lamp. The text continues: "We may not light with a wick made of cedar fiber or uncombed flax or raw silk or willow bast or desert fiber or sea moss. And we may not light it with pitch or liquid wax, not with castor oil or oil that must be destroyed by burning, not with fat from a sheep's tail nor with tallow...."

Essentially, the sages are teaching that wicks that flicker or burn unevenly or generally do not provide clear flames may not be used for Sabbath lights. Likewise, oil that burns or has an unpleasant odor or does not flow easily into the wick may not be used. An unsteady flame might cause someone to tilt the Sabbath lamp to improve the light, a forbidden act akin to kindling on Shabbat. But what the sages really want to convey is that Shabbat, which the liturgy calls the "loveliest of days," *hemdat yamim,* must begin in the loveliest of ways, with a pure and steadfast light.

The Gemara defines and expands on the many strange-sounding wicks and oils the Mishnah outlaws, moving, as always, into arguments, tangential issues, and unrelated anecdotes, but in the process also expanding on how to welcome Shabbat. We learn in the course of the discussions that the substances prohibited for the Sabbath lamp may be used to make a fire before the Sabbath, to provide warmth and light. The prohibitions extend only to the lamp, which symbolizes the day's arrival and receives a blessing.

We listen in on a debate among the rabbis: Suppose a person cannot afford to buy oil for both Hanukkah lights and Sabbath lights, which takes precedence? Sabbath lights, says Rava, because of the peace they bring to the home. Sabbath lights and wine for kiddush? Again, Sabbath lights; again, because of the peace that accompanies them.

We come upon a dreadful anecdote. A woman who hates her daughter-in-law tells the young woman to anoint herself with balsam oil, which has a nice fragrance. The obedient daughter-in-law does as told. The mother-in-law then tells her to light the Sabbath lamp. The daughter-in-law lights the lamp, whereupon the flame leaps out and consumes her. Why include this story? It demonstrates why balsam oil may not be used to light the Sabbath lamp—it is too volatile and explosive. The incident also teaches another lesson about peace at home. Hatred within a family can lead to fiery explosions and tragedy that even the Sabbath lamp, a symbol of peace, cannot prevent.

Finally, in the midst of the analyzing, arguing, and telling we return to the Mishnah and a ruling by Rabbi Tarfon: "We may kindle only with olive oil." Some of the sages disagree. What about Jews in Babylonia, they ask, or Media, Alexandria, and other places that do not have easy access to olive oil? The law as it evolves from this disagreement will permit the use of several other oils, but olive oil will remain the preferred fuel for lighting the Sabbath lamp. Olive oil, easily absorbed by a wick, produces the best flame, uniform and smokeless. More relevant, olive oil has a strong association with the land of Israel, where olives grow in abundance, and with the Temple in Jerusalem, whose priests used it for lighting the great menorah. Shabbat and the land, Shabbat and the Temple, never far apart.

But why recount any of this discussion today, when almost everyone uses candles, not oil, for kindling Sabbath lights? For this reason: Still today, at many Friday evening services welcoming the Sabbath, congregants study the Mishnah listings of forbidden wicks and oils as they did in early days. Orthodox services usually include extended texts on the subject, Conservative and some Reform use selected passages. The study today serves the same purpose it did earlier: to highlight Sabbath joy and the lights that represent that joy, whether they glow from wicks soaked in oil or from the wicks of candles. (There's some irony here. In early times, as in many traditional families still, men went to synagogue and women stayed home. This meant that while the men studied the technicalities of kindling the Sabbath lamp, women had the pleasure of actually performing the deed.)

There is an old custom of dividing the Mishnah of Shabbat into three sections and studying one section before each of the three Sabbath meals. The talmudic expert David Weiss Halivni, writing of his experiences in a Nazi slave labor camp during the Holocaust, tells of teaching this and the other sections of the tractate from memory to his fellow inmates during their few rare free moments. For them the words were not only about light, they were also about life.

In most congregations, the passages studied end with a statement attributed to Rabbi Hanina, he who danced out to greet the Sabbath queen, exciting the kabbalists' imaginations. Citing a verse from Isaiah, "And all your children shall be disciples of God, and great will be the peace of your children," the rabbi said, "Do not read your children [*banayikh*] but your builders [*bonayikh*]." Candlelighting at home and study and prayer in the synagogue build the peace and gladness that will mark the Sabbath day.

Long before that day begins, preparations for it get under way. Mystics and sages have compared the Sabbath to the central branch of the Temple's seven-branched menorah. The holy day's radiance touches the three days that precede it and the three that follow the way the menorah's central branch casts its glow on the six branches that face it, three by three. "Remember" and "Observe," the rabbis said, in still another explanation of those commandment words, teach us to remember the Sabbath until three days after it has passed and observe it—in this case, watch for it—even three days before it arrives. In that sense, my great-uncle Zalman wasn't altogether wrong in framing his week around Shabbat. He just seemed unable to acknowledge that one could work for six days and still keep the seventh in mind.

The sages Hillel and Shammai approached Shabbat preparations differently. Shammai's students said of him that every day of the week he would eat in honor of Shabbat. If he found a fine morsel, he would say, "This will be for the Sabbath." But when he found an even better treat, he would eat the first and save the second for the Sabbath table. Shammai would also begin to collect firewood for the Sabbath on the previous Sunday, declaring, "Prepare every day for the Sabbath." Hillel prepared ahead of time for Shabbat as well, but he had a different slogan: "Praised be the Eternal day by day," a phrase from the Psalms. By this he meant that the days of the week leading to and from Shabbat have their own dignity and should be lived for themselves as well as for Shabbat. Nahmanides says that Hillel trusted God to provide him with a better portion for Shabbat than for the other days of the week while he gave each day its due.

Certainly the Talmud presents a wealth of miracle stories about people who had little and found much awaiting them on the Sabbath. My favorite concerns Rabbi Hanina's wife. We never learn her name, but this spunky woman had to cope with the couple's crippling poverty while her husband focused on more ethereal matters. Too proud to admit to the family's lack of food, she pretended on Fridays that she had food in the oven by placing pots or other substances in it that would create smoke. In that way, her neighbors would assume she was cooking for Shabbat. One Friday a nosy neighbor who knew of the family's destitution grew suspicious and knocked at the door. Humiliated at the thought of being found out, Hanina's wife hid in the bedroom. But a miracle happened. When the neighbor entered the kitchen she saw the oven filled with baking hallah breads. "Hurry," she called out, "bring the bread shovel or the bread will burn." Without batting an eye, Hanina's wife replied calmly, "I just went to get it."

One commentary claims that Hanina's wife really had gone to fetch the bread shovel, because this pious family had grown accustomed to receiving miracles.

Most poor people through the centuries couldn't count on miracles to provide their Sabbath meals, and many faced great hardship in trying to set this day apart. Aside from their own desires, they felt community pressure, as did Rabbi Hanina's wife, to prepare special meals for Shabbat. The Talmud offers contradictory approaches to Shabbat for people in need. On the one hand, Rabbi Johanan taught in the name of Rabbi Eleazar that God would repay a person who borrows money in order to celebrate Shabbat properly. On the other hand, Rabbi Akiva stated, in a frequently quoted saying, "Better to treat your Sabbath like a weekday than be dependent on other people." Rabbi Akiva did not suggest that people should work on the Sabbath as they would on a weekday. He meant that a person who could not afford Sabbath luxuries should do without rather than borrow or take charity to obtain them.

Rabbi Akiva's down-to-earth words probably resonate more with most of us today than do Rabbi Johanan's starry-eyed ones. Yet in Akiva's day and wherever Jews have lived,

Jewish communities provided funds or food to bring Sabbath joy into the lives of people who could not afford it themselves, and nobody criticized those who accepted such charity. The Talmud discusses at great length how to distribute money from the community charity box so that no person will go hungry on Shabbat. And when my great-grandmother Riva invited passersby to the family home for the Sabbath, she saw to it that they ate as well as the family, even when money was scarce. "Mother and grandmother served these poor strangers as though they were paying customers at a hotel we owned," my father wrote.

As a schoolchild I was expected to bring some money to class every Friday for the *tzedaka,* or charity, box. Today, when philanthropy has become highly institutionalized, the *tzedaka* box is less prominent than it once was in Jewish homes and classrooms. But such boxes still exist—some beautifully crafted—and children can still learn to put aside coins or small bills for charity on Fridays in honor of the Sabbath. Rabbi Akiva was right in insisting that people be as self-sufficient as possible, even for Shabbat. Rabbi Johanan was right in believing that the needy also deserve to receive help from elsewhere, especially for Shabbat.

With each passing day, Sabbath preparations become increasingly intense. I order chicken, or occasionally meat, for Friday night's dinner on Wednesday or Thursday, and often spend Thursday evening cooking in advance for Shabbat, especially during the short winter Fridays. I buy other groceries and baked goods early Friday morning, and I always buy flowers for our Shabbat table. One of my most vivid childhood memories of Shabbat preparation is of my mother, who had no household help, washing and waxing the floors of our apartment every Friday morning. In those days we had a long black linoleum hallway that would shine like new when she finished her work. To protect her gleaming floors, she would cover them with newspapers, which she removed just before Shabbat. On occasion, when I mention this memory in lectures, people around the room smile and nod their heads—their mothers or grandmothers did the same thing. I found it a strange practice as a child, because the newspapers would become messy and slippery during the course of the day. But probably my mother learned it from her mother, imported from the shtetls of eastern Europe. This was their way of making their homes glow in time for Shabbat.

The Talmud relates that some of the most prominent sages performed menial pre-Shabbat chores, although undoubtedly their wives handled the main preparations. Rav Abba would buy meat from thirteen butchers and urge his household staff to "be energetic and hurry" to cook it. (The number thirteen denotes many, not necessarily a real quantity.) Rav Abbahu would sit on an ivory stool—a sign of his wealth—yet carry out the lowly task of fanning the flames of the fire prepared for the Sabbath. Rav Safra would singe the head of an animal being readied for the Sabbath meal, to rid it of hairs or feathers. Rav Hisda would cut up the beets. Rabba and Rav Joseph would chop wood, and so on. These scholars wanted to teach that giving proper honor to Shabbat calls for hands-on involvement in its preparation, irrespective of one's station in life.

In kabbalistic thought, the beauty and plenitude of the Friday evening table will bring blessings throughout the six weekdays, so special care needs to be given to that first Shabbat meal. Moreover, Friday's home preparations reflect preparations on high for welcoming the Shekhinah in from her weeklong exile among the forces of evil. The home symbolically becomes a bridal chamber, cleaned, adorned, and ready for the Shabbat bride. Meanwhile, in the heavenly realms, the extra Sabbath souls prepare in a frenzy of activity for their descent to earth, where they will enhance the ordinary weekday souls of those who participate in Shabbat.

Erev Shabbat, the term for Friday evening, applies also to the entire day. Throughout Friday, and often beginning on Thursday, people all over the world end their telephone or Internet exchanges with wishes for a "Shabbat Shalom." Maimonides declared that "it is forbidden to set a banquet or a drinking party for Friday afternoon ... in order to enter the Sabbath with an appetite for food." Accordingly, many Sabbath observers try to avoid business lunches or parties, or any substantial lunch on Friday, so that they can fully enjoy the first Sabbath meal. At home, people set the table as far in advance as they can, usually with their best tableware. Soon, the countdown begins to candlelighting time, eighteen minutes before sunset, those extra minutes designed by the rabbis to "increase the holy by adding to it from the non-holy."

The sages tried to stretch the day out as much as possible. Said Rabbi Yose, "May my lot be among those who welcome the Sabbath in Tiberias and end it in Sepphoris." The Jews of Tiberias, situated in a valley, began Shabbat slightly early. The Jews of Sepphoris, located on a mountaintop, ended it slightly late. Rabbi Yose would have liked to have it both ways. And what should people do if they have been lost on the road or sea and don't know when Shabbat begins, or even which day to keep as Shabbat? Count off six days and observe the seventh, saying the kiddush at the beginning and havdalah at the end, so they retain the feel of Shabbat in their lives.

When the Second Temple stood, six blasts of the shofar announced the approach of the Sabbath to the Jewish community. The first blast signaled the farmers to stop their plowing, digging, or other work in the fields. The second directed the merchants in the towns to place the shutters on their windows and close their shops. The third meant that all cooking must end and the time had come to light the Sabbath lamp. Soon after, three more blasts proclaimed the official beginning of the Sabbath.

Without the shofar to tell me when to stop work, I rely on my Jewish calendar with its lists of candlelighting times around the world. One of the pleasures I get from following the appropriate hour to light candles is a heightened awareness of the changing seasons and the shifting light that accompanies them. I used to cringe on the Friday in June when I lit the candles a few minutes earlier than I had the week before. For most people summer was just beginning, but I knew the summer solstice had passed and the long days of summer would gradually diminish as I lit my candles a little sooner each week. But that's changed over time. I sense something exciting now about the days inching into night, the night taking over until daytime becomes just a sliver of light between two walls of blackness. My candles track the abbreviated days, and then suddenly, almost unnoticed, I light them a little later one week, and the cycle begins again. Rabbi Hanina's wife may have had her miraculous hallahs, but to me this is the real miracle, this rolling time, this disappearing and emerging light, this weekly tapping into the beat of the universe by kindling a flame.

I find it easy to say the blessing over the lights on every Sabbath of the year, easy to add my own words of gratitude for the many miracles that surround my life.

A legal fiction underlies the blessing ceremony. Generally, a blessing comes before an act—we say the blessing over bread before we eat it, for example. But once a woman recites the blessing over candles, she has accepted the Sabbath into her home and may no longer kindle lights. So she lights the candles and covers her eyes, first circling the flames with her hands to draw their radiance inward. ("My old grandmother, in her lace bonnet, waved spells over the Sabbath candle," wrote the Russian writer Isaac Babel.) The woman says the blessing with her eyes covered, as if she does not see the candles, then she uncovers them to face the shining lights. Folklore has it that someone with weak eyes can heal them after that by staring intensely into those lights.

A few rules about the candles: They must be lit in the same room in which the Sabbath dinner will take place and be allowed to burn down, not be blown out. And they should last at least as long as the meal, to spread their glow and tranquillity throughout. They may not be moved after they are lit, for they fall into the category of tools of labor that must not be handled on Shabbat. People can light any number of candles they wish, and some light a candle for each child in the family. But custom calls for at least two candles, to stand for "Remember" and "Observe." Traditionally, men light candles in women's absence, as my father did after my mother died. In our egalitarian age, however, the men in a family may alternate with the women in candlelighting. Still, most women I know have guarded this ceremony for themselves, out of love for the moment and identification with the generations of women who came before them and kindled the lights.

ɛ

In the heavens, legend says, with creation finished, God seated the Sabbath angel upon a throne, and all the other angels gathered around to dance and sing praises to it. Even Adam miraculously rose to heaven to join in the angelic chorus. In another version of the legend Adam had a special reason to sing to the Sabbath. After he and Eve sinned and were banished from paradise on the Sabbath eve, the angels mocked him. Although he repented of his sin, he still feared he would be sent to burn in the fires of Gehenna. The Sabbath appeared before God and pleaded, "Ruler of the Universe. No creature was slain during the six days of creation. If you now slay Adam, what will become of the blessing and holiness of Shabbat?" God spared Adam, and in gratitude the first man began to compose a special hymn in honor of the Sabbath. The Sabbath stopped him, saying, "Do you sing a hymn to me? Let us rather sing a hymn together to the Blessed Holy One." So they both sang, "It is good to give thanks to God. . . ." Later, King David would include their hymn in his book of Psalms.

Adam's song is the ninety-second psalm, whose first verse opens with the legend's words of praise, "It is good to give thanks to God, / to sing hymns to Your name, O Most High. . . ."

Worshipers chant it in the synagogue on the Sabbath eve and again the next day, one of a series of psalms recited.

Traditionally, Shabbat evening services begin at sunset, varying in time from week to week just as candle lighting varies. Years ago the Reform and Conservative movements instituted late, after dinner, Friday evening services, which gave people who worked late an opportunity to attend. Many Reform congregations have kept that practice. Some Conservative ones have changed to a set time before dinner, around six P.M., and others have returned to the traditional time schedule that depends on Shabbat's beginning. The change reflects the changing status of Jews, many of whom have more flexibility today than in the past to leave work early and attend services if they wish.

The Kabbalat Shabbat welcoming and accepting the Sabbath makes up the centerpiece of the evening's prayers. It is omitted only during festival weeks, in deference to those holidays. Until the kabbalists introduced it in the sixteenth century, the Sabbath evening service did not differ much from weekday evening services. Once introduced, Kabbalat Shabbat spread throughout the Jewish world, loved as one of the most beautiful of all synagogue services.

The section opens with six psalms that sing of God the creator enthroned in glory and reigning over heaven and earth. (Sephardi synagogues include only one of these hymns, Psalm 29.) They represent the six days of the week, six days of creation, or, according to some, the six shofar blasts that announced Shabbat in Temple times. Some Bible critics see a connection between these hymns and the stories of other early peoples that pictured the gods resting on thrones in their temples after they completed creation. There may truly be traces in these songs of those early influences, but if so, the psalmist turned ancient myths into powerful poetry, not to be taken literally.

The jewel of the unit, the Lekha Dodi hymn, follows the six psalms, almost like a seventh. I have heard it sung in many different melodies, all of them lovely. Though the Sabbath was fashioned last, it proclaims, that holy day existed in God's thoughts before any other part of creation. Using biblical and talmudic references, the hymn dwells on love and sorrow and a longing for a better time. It ends as it began, an ode to the adored Sabbath queen, whom congregants turn to greet.

"A Song for the Sabbath," Adam's hymn, concludes the Kabbalat Shabbat section of the service, with the short ninety-third psalm attached to it. In legend, Adam composed that hymn also, on the day he was created and before he sinned. Oddly, the Sabbath song, Psalm 92, never mentions Shabbat. Its association with the seventh day goes back to Temple rites, when the Levites sang a different hymn every day of the week to accompany the sacrifices offered on the altar. They sang this psalm on the Sabbath. Scholars have found a parallel to the Temple singing on Shabbat among manuscript fragments of the Dead Sea Scrolls, probably composed by religious sects between the second century B.C.E. and the first century C.E. Called "Songs of the Sabbath Sacrifice," these hymns apply to the first thirteen Sabbaths of the year. In them, priestly angels sing praises to God, much the way Adam and the Sabbath angel do in the legend of the Sabbath song.

One major feature distinguishes the evening service that follows the Kabbalat Shabbat from the everyday one. The ordinary Amidah includes nineteen blessings. (The Amidah is a silent group of prayers said at every service while standing, as though before God.) On Shabbat it has only seven. The central core of thirteen blessings has been replaced by one special Sabbath benediction. The excluded prayers are all petitions for healing, long life, forgiveness, and other individual and community needs. On Shabbat we are supposed to live as if such cares don't exist, so we do not even bring them up in prayer. The Hasidim taught that one may not weep on the joyful Sabbath, but it is acceptable to weep for joy.

For the same reason, formal mourning is not permitted on the Sabbath. Mourners who have experienced a death recently and have been sitting shiva may come to services on Friday evening, usually entering the synagogue after the singing of Lekha Dodi. The congregation welcomes them with the ritual words used during the shiva period, "May God comfort you together with all the other mourners of Zion and Jerusalem." Then they participate in the services along with everyone else.

The kabbalists gave a different interpretation to the seven blessings of the Amidah prayer. For them, these benedictions correspond to the *sheva berakhot,* the seven nuptial blessings traditionally said before and after a wedding ceremony. The seven Amidah blessings anticipate the mystical wedding ceremony that will take place later, uniting the Shabbat bride and her groom, the female and male emanations of the divine being.

As everyone knows, two angels accompany people home from the synagogue. There they do a quick checkup of Shabbat preparations. If the candles are lit and the table set, the good angel says, "May it be this way next Shabbat," and the bad angel must answer, "Amen." If the home has not been readied for the Sabbath, the bad angel says, "May it be this way next Shabbat," and the good angel must answer, "Amen."

In the home, family and guests sing "Shalom Aleikhem" to welcome the angels and then bid them farewell, ignoring the possibility that one of them may be up to no good. Everything is doubled this night: Two angels, two lighted candles, two loaves of hallah breads, two souls expanding our minds, and the two Sabbath commandments at the source of it all. And everything will take place at the table, the Sabbath altar. As divided as Jews are on so many issues, there's something remarkable about the unity Shabbat brings, with the same ceremonies and rituals appearing everywhere. Well, almost everywhere. Visiting a family in Paris one Shabbat evening, my husband and I discovered two long French breads instead of hallahs on the table. "These are so much better," our host said without apology. They were delicious.

The ceremonies at dinner follow one another in dance-like sequence, each aimed at making the evening different from all others. First, parents bless their children, asking that their daughters be like the foremothers, Sarah, Rebecca, Rachel, and Leah, and their sons like Ephraim and Manasseh, children of the biblical Joseph. (Some families bless the children later, after kiddush.) The blessing for sons originated in the Bible, with Jacob's words to his grandsons: "By you shall Israel invoke blessings, saying: God make you like Ephraim and Manasseh." The priestly benediction that follows for both daughters and sons also comes from the Bible, in passages the priests said during Temple services. Beginning with the priests' words "May God bless you and keep you," parents pray that God's grace and light shine upon the lives of their children. Some parents add their own blessings to these standard ones, and in some families, children bless their parents in return.

I've always regretted that because neither my husband's parents nor mine practiced the custom of blessing their children, it did not become part of our own Shabbat practice with our daughter (who, however, blesses her children each week). I imagine children feel especially loved when blessed at the Shabbat table.

The kiddush now sanctifies the Sabbath over a cup of wine. (The kiddush is also said earlier, at the end of the synagogue service. It was added to that service for the benefit of people who could not afford wine at home, and remained part of it.) The word *kiddush*, like *kadosh*, refers to holiness or separateness; the kiddush formally separates Shabbat from the week's workdays.

The ancient Greeks worshiped the god of wine, Dionysus, and held wild Dionysian festivals in which revelers would "become" the god on some level. The Romans did the same, with their god Bacchus. In the Christian sacrament of the Eucharist wine symbolizes the blood of Jesus. Although some Jewish sources also associate wine with blood, mainstream Judaism does not generally give wine such mystical powers. Early Jews used it in libations to accompany Temple sacrifices, but also as a symbol on the altar of the bounty of grapes that grew in the land of Israel. The sages found it natural, then, to consecrate the Sabbath over a cup of wine, another reminder of the Temple and the land. "Remember the Sabbath day to keep it holy," they said. "Remember it over wine." The holiness resides in the Sabbath, not the wine.

The leader of the kiddush, either man or woman, holds a brimming cup of wine in hand (the rabbis also specified "brimming," to stand for the expansive pleasures of the day). Kabbalistic practice calls for placing the cup in the palm of the right hand with fingers pointing upward, like rose petals. The cup with wine recalls the Shekhinah, often associated with the image of a rose. In some homes, everybody sips from the main cup at the end of the ceremony. In others, wine from that cup is poured into individual cups for all. In our home, each person has a small silver cup in place filled with wine, except for the grape juice in my little grandchildren's cups. All the customs are acceptable.

The same can be said for sitting or standing during kiddush—people vary in their practices. (We generally sit; sometimes we stand.) And any kind of kosher wine can be used, preferably red. We frequently invite guests for Shabbat dinner, as do many people, and even the most sophisticated, Jews and non-Jews, seem to prefer old-fashioned sweet wine for kiddush over a fine, dry one. For some reason, the sweetness seems more fitting for religious ceremony. (Shabbat dinner, I might add, is a unique Jewish contribution to the dinner party, and a much sought after invitation.)

The kiddush opens with the passages from Genesis that recall the first Shabbat at the end of creation. The blessing for wine, the "fruit of the vine," comes next, followed by the third section mentioning both creation and the exodus from Egypt. In traditional prayer books this paragraph also speaks of Israel's chosenness. To pick up on an earlier discussion

about the subject: The liturgy does not make blanket pro-
nouncements about chosenness. It always ties that idea to a
particular command or obligation. In the kiddush, Israel's
election is linked to its acceptance of Shabbat, a sign of its
covenant with God. In Saturday morning prayers, chosenness refers to the giving of the Torah, the covenant itself. For
Israel, to be chosen also means to choose. Jews chose the
covenant and the responsibilities that go with it.

Immediately after kiddush, ritual calls for people to wash
their hands in a prescribed manner and say a silent blessing.
The covering over the hallah is removed, the blessing over
bread recited, and all assembled receive hallah pieces with salt.
In keeping with the Shabbat theme of peace, some people
tear the hallah rather than cut it with a knife. We use a knife
because hallah knives and hallah coverings, like kiddush cups,
have become craft objects, and I like having beautiful ritual
objects on the Sabbath table. Custom dictates that people do
not speak between hand washing and their first bite of hallah
as a way of emphasizing the connectedness of all the ceremonies. We explain that custom beforehand to guests, who usually
accept the silence as part of the evening's sacred atmosphere.
But someone always forgets, and that's all right also.

The Roman emperor Augustus wrote in a letter to the
future emperor Tiberius, "Not even a Jew fasts so scrupu-
lously on his Sabbaths as I have done today...." Fasting on
the Sabbath? That practice is forbidden. So where did Augustus and several ancient Greeks and Romans who also wrote
about it get that idea? The usual explanation is that they con-
fused the Sabbath with the Day of Atonement. But some
scholars suggest that there were groups of ascetics in ancient

times, and even later, for whom Shabbat "delight" meant fasting and praying all day, Yom Kippur–style. Fortunately, they didn't represent the majority opinion. The rabbis considered Shabbat meals a major part of the day's joy, and so they have remained. In many homes today Shabbat meals are also the only time family members manage to gather to eat together.

For the first several years of our marriage, my husband and I had Friday evening dinner every week with either his parents or mine. My mother-in-law made gefilte fish with sugar, a reflection of her Galician heritage. My mother made spicy gefilte fish, in keeping with our family's *litvishe* background. It took me a while to get used to the sugary fish, but in time I came to love both kinds. I especially loved not having to make anything.

Traditionally, families add to the festive Shabbat feeling by singing *zemirot* throughout the evening, choosing a variety of songs and tunes, most old, some contemporary. Dining concludes with *birkat hamazon,* the after meal grace generally recited quietly and hurriedly during the week, but sung aloud leisurely now.

As Shabbat evening ends, the scent of melted wax mingles with the fragrance of foods eaten. "With what may we light the Sabbath lamp?" The sages answered their own question with laws and teachings about wicks and oils, but also about wine, good food, blessings, ceremonies, and happiness. The lingering aroma of candle wax, the last vestige of Shabbat candles, seems to capture it all.

It has been said that Jews invented linear time. Other early peoples measured time in circular fashion, imagining it only as a great wheel, with the pattern of seasons and years repeating themselves endlessly, each much like the previous one and the next to come. In the Jewish view, time moves forward, ever onward. Biblical events happen in historical time, each event unique, one leading to the next, as the exodus leads to the giving of the Torah. In reality, however, the dichotomy between cyclical and linear time in Jewish life is not absolute. Within their linear framework Jews also recognize the circular nature of time, celebrating the cycle of holidays in their seasons year after year. More conspicuously, Jews read the Torah publicly in cyclical fashion. After the last chapter of Deuteronomy is chanted in the synagogue on the holiday of Simhat Torah, a reader immediately begins again with the first chapter of Genesis. ("By the time Simhat Torah rolls around, God forgets..." Yehuda Amichai wrote in a poem.) The Torah plots its narrative on a line, its stories and teachings unfolding one after the next. But we read the text in a never-ending cycle.

The key time and place for that public reading is on Shabbat morning in shul, with smaller sections read at other times. Although prayer services precede and follow the Torah reading, that reading is the main attraction of the morning. Tradition claims that revelation occurred on the Sabbath. To hear the Torah chanted aloud with its ancient cadences is to relive that revelation each week, to reenact Sinai again and again. Each week we receive the Torah anew; each week I discover a word, a phrase, a concept I had never noticed before, no matter how many times I have read this text. And as the Torah scroll is carried in procession before and after the reading, we become the Israelites in the desert, following after the ark with its two tablets of the law. The hymn that accompanies carrying the Torah out, Psalm 29, reinforces that identification. Seven times it tells of God's voice resounding through a thunderous storm, the voice that Moses interpreted to the Israelites as they stood at the foot of the mountain.

Some people lose themselves in prayer. I lose myself in the Torah reading as it circles the year.

An old belief maintains that Moses instituted the practice of chanting the Torah aloud on Saturday mornings, and the scribe Ezra began the shorter readings on Saturday afternoon. In talmudic times, the Jewish community in Babylonia read the Torah publicly over the course of a year, the five books divided into fifty-four sections. Most Orthodox and Conservative congregations continue that practice today. The community in Palestine read shorter sections each week, stretching the readings over three years. Many Reform and Reconstructionist synagogues and some Conservative ones still follow a three-year cycle, although in a different format. In either case, the weekly Torah portion is usually divided into seven sections (each known as an aliyah) during the Shabbat morning service, and people go up to the Torah to recite blessings before each (the going up is also called an aliyah). Most synagogues include special Torah readings on the Sabbath before holidays and other occasions. In Conservative and Reform synagogues, women or men may chant from the Torah or Haftarah, the prophetic portion read after the Torah. At Orthodox services only the men read or receive an aliyah, but numbers of Orthodox shuls also have separate women's prayer groups in which women lead the entire service.

In the presence of the Torah scrolls parents name their new babies, boys and girls officially come of age, brides and grooms receive honors, relatives memorialize loved ones, and congregants offer healing words for the sick. Spirituality in this religion is not simply a matter of personal aspirations or longings for union with God. One may certainly experience private spiritual moments through prayer and study—after all, we strive for such intensified moments. But the Torah reading, which invites everyone to share in prayer and study, attests to the centrality of communal time in Jewish life.

The prayer service after the Torah has been read differs from weekday services by including a final section, the *musaf* prayer. Its name, which means "additional," comes from the extra sacrifice of two lambs the priests offered in the Temple on Shabbat—another instance of Shabbat doubles. But how could the priests offer sacrifices on Shabbat? Doesn't the Bible forbid kindling a fire on this day? The rabbis, who puzzled over the same question, decided that the Sabbath laws we know did not apply to the Temple. This was God's realm, not subject to human limitations.

Reform and Reconstructionist Shabbat services usually begin later and end earlier than Conservative and Orthodox ones. In all services, some people come late, missing the early morning prayers and staying through *musaf.* Some arrive early and leave early, and the most diligent arrive early and stay throughout. (I confess to being among the late arrivers—but always in time for the Torah reading.) The midrash has some reassuring things to say about all prayers: "When the people of Israel pray . . . each congregation prays separately. . . . When they have all finished, the angel appointed over them gathers all the prayers offered in all the synagogues and weaves them into a crown that it places upon the head of the Blessed Holy One."

Another observation: "You will find that a mortal cannot absorb the conversation of two people speaking at once, but it is different with God. All pray, and God understands and receives all their prayers."

And another: "When a poor person speaks, others may pay little attention, but if a rich person speaks, others hear and listen immediately. Before God, however, men, women, slaves, poor and rich, are all equal in their prayers."

People may come early or late to Shabbat morning services, this midrash assures us, but when they pray and sing together, their words find the proper destination.

After services, congregants often gather near the sanctuary for kiddush—with wine, refreshments, and socializing—before heading home. The rites of the Shabbat afternoon meal echo the Friday evening ones. The table is set with two whole hallahs, and kiddush is recited over a cup of wine—a shortened kiddush this time. Traditional families use the afternoon to nap, stroll, visit with one another, read, or study. Emphasizing the pleasures of studying the Torah on Shabbat, the Talmud tells of Elisha ben Avuyah, a revered scholar who lost his faith and abandoned Judaism. The sages called him *Aher,* or "Other." Still, his former student Rabbi Meir—an outstanding sage in his own right—continued to study with him on Shabbat afternoon, even walking behind him while Elisha desecrated the Sabbath by riding a horse. The study was that important.

For the kabbalists, Shabbat Torah study helps transport the soul into the realm of pure spirit, offering it a glimpse of heavenly splendors. Study also expands one's Sabbath soul, which takes pleasure in every new item learned.

On a less lofty level, it is customary to study the small tractate of the Mishnah called *Pirke Avot,* "The Ethics of the Fathers," on the long Saturday afternoons in the spring and summer. The book consists of the early sages' favorite sayings and aphorisms, which their students collected over time. My father used to teach this book on Shabbat to members of his synagogue. When he became blind with age, he taught the text from memory. After he died, I found the copious teaching notes he had kept with his own interpretations of the various maxims. Sometimes on Shabbat afternoon I sit down with his notes and study a chapter or two of the ethics of those fathers and of my father.

As for napping, the disciples of the Kotzker Rebbe once asked him why he hadn't written a book with his many teachings. "Who would read such a book?" he replied, and went on to speculate. Maybe a poor Hasid who works hard all week would buy the book. But when would he have time to read it? On Friday night he would be too tired. On Saturday morning he would be in shul, praying. Perhaps he would get to it on Shabbat afternoon, after the midday meal. He might lie down on his sofa, pick up the book and open it. But, sated with Shabbat food, he would become drowsy and fall asleep. The book would slip from his hands to the floor.

The reading would end. "Now tell me," the Rebbe said, "why should I write a book?"

Then there is the mysterious dream an art dealer I know had while taking a Shabbat nap. In it he received a clear-cut message that he must help abused women. The dream changed his life. Although he has kept his business, he gives as much time and money as he can to aiding the abused and getting abusers into counseling. He has also inspired other men to take up the cause, which many had considered a "woman's issue." He can't explain the dream, but "it's significant that it came on Shabbat," he says.

Yet Shabbat afternoon is not a dream-filled idyll for everyone. A writer remembers her childhood Saturdays, when her strict Orthodox family lived in a neighborhood with few other Jewish families. "I used to open the window and lean out to listen to the radio next door," she says bitterly. "My sisters and I were so bored, we couldn't wait for the day to end."

The contemporary modern Orthodox rabbi Saul J. Berman addressed the issue of Saturday afternoon boredom, especially for young people, in a response he wrote to the question of whether it is permissible to play ball on Shabbat. It is unrealistic to suppose that drawing out meals to fill time, sleeping, praying, or studying can make Shabbat afternoon enjoyable or meaningful for children and young adults—or even many adults, he writes. It is more important to make the day a "combination of intellectual and physical activities" that convey spiritual values. After a long, scholarly search into earlier sources, he concludes that it is permitted to play ball on Shabbat. But such play can be as "vacuous" and "pointless" as sleeping all day unless parents infuse it with additional meaning. Perhaps the playing can be cooperative instead of competitive, he suggests, or through it young people can learn about the importance Judaism places on good health and well-being.

When my daughter was young, she spent every Saturday afternoon with my in-laws, who took her to free puppet shows in the nearby park or played board games with her at home. But she loved the day mostly because of the close contact she had with her grandparents, and needless to say, so did they. (She also loved the sweet gefilte fish.) Not everybody has the good fortune to live near grandparents, but Shabbat afternoon can also be family time for parents and children, a special boon for working parents. However people spend the day, it should have an atmosphere of freedom and joy, not deprivation.

In ritual practice the joy becomes more muted as the day wanes. According to tradition Moses died on the Sabbath afternoon. The Bible says "and no one knows his burial place," which the kabbalists interpreted to mean that his soul is deeply concealed within the most distant of the divine emanations, Keter. *Minhah,* the afternoon prayer service, supposedly the exact time of Moses' death, memorializes him in a hidden way. Without mentioning his name, it includes a passage that begins with the words "Your righteousness is forever," reminiscent of words used in a burial service. More secretive, the phrase "Your righteousness" appears three times, an added allusion to the deaths of Joseph and King David also believed to have been on Shabbat.

The Torah is read again at *minhah,* this time with just a

small section of the following week's portion. The week is ending, the seventh day disappearing into the dusk, but the Torah continues in its infinite cycle. The Hasidim regard the afternoon service as the most sacred part of Shabbat, when God receives the day's crown of prayers. It is the shortest service of the day, they say, because we stand in silence now, awed by God's wonder.

People who go to synagogue eat the third Sabbath meal, the *se'udah shelishit,* or in the vernacular *shaloshudas,* between the afternoon and evening services. For those at home, it usually consists of a light spread of tuna fish, egg salad, and such. If people sing, the songs are slower and more melancholy than those of the other Sabbath meals. The mood reflects the sadness at the Sabbath's imminent departure. In ceremony and prayer, thoughts turn to the coming week, but they also turn to another time, a distant time of eternal Sabbath. If the number seven stands for perfection, the number eight stands for renewal and a new beginning in that future time. Chapter 8 follows those ideas.

Eight

ETERNAL LIGHT

*And my heart's song
is an eternal Sabbath.*

KADIA MOLODOWSKY

A dam and Eve continued: In legend, the first Shabbat of
creation ended after thirty-six hours of miraculously
uninterrupted light. With the sun setting and night falling,
Adam and Eve were terrified. They could not return to Eden,
and now in the darkness Adam feared that the serpent would
attack them. God helped the first couple by pointing Adam
toward two stones, which he rubbed together. Fire burst
forth, and in gratitude Adam recited a blessing. By eating of
the tree of knowledge, Eve had opened the way for humankind to gain sexual knowledge and perpetuate itself. By
striking two stones, Adam illumined the world with fire, the
source of energy and the foundation of society.

The legend of Adam's discovery of fire contrasts with the
Greek tale of how humans acquired fire. There, Prometheus
stole the fire from the gods and gave it to humans. For this,

Zeus, the ruler of the gods, had him chained to a rock on the Caucasian Mountains, where each day an eagle tore his liver from within him and ate it. Only after many centuries did the hero Heracles rescue Prometheus from his suffering. The jealous Zeus also punished humanity by sending out a box that unleashed disease and pain in the world when Pandora unknowingly opened it.

In Jewish myth, God shared the power of fire with humans, allowing them a portion of divine creativity; in Greek myth, the gods begrudged humanity creative abilities. Though Adam created fire through his own actions, he blessed God as the ultimate source of that gift. No such blessing accrued to Zeus.

The gift of fire and productivity dominates the havdalah (separation) ceremony that marks the Sabbath's end. Along with it a softer strain of nostalgia for the Sabbath that has passed and a yearning for another that will come winds its way through the evening's proceedings, the way strands of wax wind about each other in the plaited havdalah candle.

The Sabbath ends forty-two minutes after sundown on Saturday night or when three stars appear in the sky. (One star, the rabbis said, means it is still day; two, it is twilight; three, night has arrived.) Some people extend the day by waiting an hour after sundown or longer before declaring the Sabbath over.

In many respects the havdalah ceremony, which escorts Shabbat out, parallels the Shabbat eve rituals that welcome it in. Although most people are more familiar with those welcoming ceremonies and more likely to participate in them, havdalah can be as moving and even more dramatic. Like the kiddush blessing, havdalah blessings are recited in the synagogue at the conclusion of the *ma'ariv* evening service and again at home, the more important recitation. Like the Friday evening rites, havdalah begins by lighting a candle. Many families conduct the entire ceremony by the light of that candle, which, held high, casts mysterious shadows over the proceedings. And like Shabbat eve rituals, havdalah includes wine, blessings, and songs that underline the distinction between sacred and profane time. Yet as the security of Shabbat gives way to the unknowns of the week ahead, the tensions that began accumulating in the late afternoon take hold, a throwback to the fear Eve and Adam felt when night came.

The tensions emerge in the first passage of the ceremony. "Behold, God is my deliverance; I am confident and unafraid," it proclaims, with words of reassurance, almost like whistling in the dark. As the verses continue, however, the comfort of trusting in God's providence and protection begins to outweigh anxiety about the future. Soon everybody exuberantly recites a sentence from the book of Esther that celebrates the overthrow of the wicked Haman and his plot to destroy the Jews of Persia: "For the Jews there was light, joy, gladness, and honor." Added are the words, "So may it be for us."

The tone of the evening becomes increasingly optimistic as participants move toward the heart of the ceremony—its blessings over wine, spices, and fire. Every aspect of those blessings has symbolic meaning. The first blessing, the standard benediction over wine, is recited with a brimming cup, as it was in the kiddush. Now the fullness of the cup stands for the fullness of life's blessings and the wish for a week of good fortune. (Some people substitute juice or another beverage for the wine.)

The blessing over a mixture of aromatic spices has more varied meanings. In folk belief the fires of Gehenna, shut down throughout Shabbat, begin to burn again at its conclusion. The spices conceal the stench of those fires. They also lighten the hearts of those who worry that their dear ones may now be suffering renewed punishment. Far less gruesome is the kabbalistic explanation that with the end of Shabbat, the additional soul that inhabited the body all day departs, leaving the ordinary soul "naked," as the Zohar says. Inhaling the sweet scent of the spices revives one's heart and spirits.

In this regard the Talmud records a play on the word *nefesh,* or soul. Elaborating on the Bible's use of the word *va'yinnafash* to describe God's rest and refreshment after creation, Rabbi Simeon ben Lakish said, "Once the Sabbath has ceased, *vay'nefesh,*" which means, woe (or alas) that the additional soul is lost! Passed from person to person in a special container during havdalah, the spices help to combat that woe. (Note: We are not speaking of the "high" of drugs here, only of the good feeling that breathing in the pungent spices gives. In the Middle Ages, the "spice" of choice was a myrtle branch, *hadas* in Hebrew, which is why the spice box is still called a *hadas.* The name also recalls the old man Rabbi Simeon bar Yohai met carrying two bunches of myrtle branches in honor of Shabbat. Today's spice mixture usually consists of cloves, cinnamon, and bay leaves, to which some people add dried flower petals.)

Some commentators say the havdalah spices recall the

incense used in the Temple, another reminder of the home as a replacement for the altar. In the interpretation I like best, the spices relate to the last verse in the Song of Songs, when the lovers depart from each other "on the hills of spices." The Sabbath, Israel's lover, also departs surrounded by spices. An atmosphere of sadness and loss hovers over that departure, yet the fragrance of spices floating in the air carries with it the expectation of the Sabbath's return, just as the lovers' parting in the poem anticipates their reunion at another time.

The third blessing, over the havdalah candle, symbolizes the ceremony as a whole. The sacred Shabbat has ended and lighting a fire testifies that the new week has begun. This lighting also conjures up the genesis of creation, the "Let there be light" moment when the world began. Now, with Shabbat over, we reenter that world to create once again. The colorful, braided havdalah candle with its many wicks differs in feeling from the plain white candles that welcomed Shabbat. This candle speaks to the hurly-burly nature of everyday life about to be resumed. This candle is a torch.

In a book explicating the thinking of the philosopher Emmanuel Levinas, Ira Stone analyzes a talmudic text from Levinas' point of view. The text discusses what kind of light should be used in the ceremonial search for leavened goods, *hametz*, on Passover eve. That search, which takes place after the home has been thoroughly cleaned and prepared for the holiday, symbolically pronounces it ready for Passover. In their discussion, the rabbis contrast the simple candle or lamp that should be used in the search for leaven with the torch that should be used in the havdalah ceremony. Among other things, they find that a candle can be carried into "holes and cracks" to search thoroughly for the *hametz,* whereas a torch might quickly cause a fire if placed close to a surface. At one point, the sage Rava asks, "To what may the righteous be compared in the presence of the Shekhinah?" He answers, "To a lamp in the presence of a torch." Even the most righteous persons on earth possess only a glimmer of the bountiful light of God's glory.

God is light, Stone says, taking off from this text. And the havdalah torch represents God's light, too powerful to draw close to. The light of the torch also symbolizes the extension of God's light into this world, he says, and with it the hope for redemption. He defines redemption as a reuniting with the "great light of the divine." But while we long for such reuniting, as the Sabbath ends, we find ourselves still in an unredeemed world. The best we can do is search for the spark of God within ourselves and destroy our inner *hametz,* whatever internal evil stands between us and redemption.

For Levinas, in Stone's interpretation, the torchlike havdalah candle does not simply celebrate human discovery of fire and with it our ability to transform the world. It also symbolizes our need to transform ourselves in order to redeem the world.

More prosaically, in rabbinic terms we need the bright flame of the havdalah candle and not the weaker light of an ordinary candle or lamp, because in its strength and luminosity such a flame exemplifies the clear-cut distinctions this ceremony makes between light and darkness and the sacred and ordinary. The last havdalah blessing takes up those distinctions. But first we need to look at our fingernails.

For a blessing to have meaning in Jewish tradition, it should also serve some practical purpose. Otherwise it is considered a wasted blessing. We give the blessing over the havdalah candle actual and not just symbolic purpose by using its flames to examine the nails on our fingers and the palms of our hands, or by looking at the contrast between light and shadow playing on our fingers and palms. That contrast also speaks to the separation between light and darkness fundamental to the entire ceremony.

People follow diverse customs in looking at their fingernails by the light of the havdalah candle. One custom is to raise one's hands toward the candlelight, then bend the fingers into the palm and gaze at them; another is to bend the fingers, then turn the hands over to see their backs. The Zohar gives a different explanation for the bent fingers: When Shabbat ends, the Shekhinah sends out angels to take over from her in ruling the world, although they still receive her light. The bent fingers stand for the angels and the bending demonstrates their subservience to the Shekhinah.

It's worth noting that the blessing over the havdalah candle refers to God "who creates the lights of fire." Why "creates" and not "created"? The school of Shammai actually wanted the blessing to say "created." The school of Hillel, which always won in these disputes, insisted on "creates," because creation did not end after six days, but continues as an ongoing process. And why the plural "lights"? The school of Shammai wanted the singular "light of fire." The winning school of Hillel argued that fire has many colors or lights within it. Hillel's victory became the reason the havdalah candle has at least two wicks, usually more.

The final havdalah blessing enumerates distinctions. In another parallel, both the word *kiddush* and the word *havdalah* refer to setting apart and distinguishing. Kiddush separates Shabbat from the weekdays before it and havdalah from those that follow. But havdalah goes further. It marks distinctions that form the essence of Jewish values: between holy and secular, light and darkness, Israel and other nations, the seventh day and the six days of work. Havdalah turns our attention to the biblical concept that the world began in the separation of order from chaos. As creation gets under way, God separates light from darkness, the lower waters from the upper waters, and day from night. God creates groups of animals distinct from one another, and humans distinct from the other animals.

The separations establish boundaries in the universe, and with them orderliness. The Bible echoes those separations in other areas. It forbids harnessing different species of animals together for plowing, for each species must remain distinct, its integrity intact. It also prohibits people from wearing clothing that combines wool and linen, a mixture of animal and plant products. Most far-reaching are the dietary laws, which distinguish between ritually clean and unclean animals. Long after biblical times, Jewish tradition continues to celebrate distinctions. The first in a series of blessings to be said in the morning thanks God for "giving the rooster understanding to distinguish between day and night." The rooster crows when dawn breaks, awakening humans to a new day, proof of the order and consistency in the cosmos. The blessing also hints at human understanding and human ability to distinguish between good and evil.

Ultimately, as discussed earlier, making distinctions and setting boundaries ties into the idea of reaching for holiness by imitating God, who is distinct and separate from all things in the universe. Reflecting that thought, Rabbi Judah the Prince, who lived in the second and third centuries C.E., made only one distinction in this blessing, and that was between the holy and the secular. Others later added to that category, until the sages decided that a person should recite no fewer than three distinctions and no more than seven. The four basic categories in the blessing we use today spell out the distinctions that continue to govern Jewish life. (When a festival begins on Saturday night, at the end of Shabbat, the distinction is made between "the holy and the holy." In the hierarchy of Jewish life, Shabbat's holiness outweighs that of any festival.)

At the end of the havdalah service, the reader drinks the wine in the cup, first pouring some into a saucer to be used for snuffing out the havdalah candle—an act designed to show that the candle was lit specifically for this ceremony. Some people dip a finger into the spilled wine and touch their eyes or clothes with it. This custom may have originated from a belief that the wine could heal poor eyesight. If so, nobody remembers that origin, and most interpret the gesture as a final token of love for the Shabbat commandment. A less benign old custom has women abstaining from drinking the havdalah wine, perhaps because some early mystics believed Eve had tempted Adam to eat from a grape vine, the source of wine. I've been told that this custom still persists in some places, but happily none that I know of. After havdalah, in the shtetls of eastern Europe, women would recite an additional prayer in Yiddish called *Got fun Avrom* ("God of Abraham") calling on the patriarchs to ensure a week of good health and fortune.

Havdalah closes with everybody wishing everybody else a *shavua tov*, a good week in Hebrew, or *a gute vokh* in Yiddish, and singing songs to smooth the passage into the new week. One of the most popular, "Hamavdil," praises the God of distinctions and asks to have our sins forgiven, for now that Shabbat has ended such thoughts come crowding back. The philosopher Abraham Isaac Kook writes that one must do penance at the end of Shabbat, for the day's holiness may have concealed troublesome thoughts. Freed now, such thoughts can interfere with the week's work. Be that as it may, people sing with greatest gusto the parts of the song that ask to have our children and our wealth multiply, like the sands on the beach and the stars in the sky. Nobody is embarrassed to acknowledge such down-to-earth thoughts. Although Shabbat stands apart from the six weekdays, those days have their purpose also.

Still, in their desire to extend Shabbat as long as possible, the talmudic sages instituted a fourth meal, the *melaveh malkah*, escorting the Sabbath queen out as she had been escorted in. That meal became popular among kabbalists and remains popular among Hasidim today. There is a moving story attached to it: When King David learned from God that he would die on a Saturday, he tried to hold off that decree by spending every moment of every Saturday studying Torah. He knew that the angel of death could not come close to someone engrossed in Torah study. On the designated Saturday, the angel tricked David by shaking the branches of a tree in his garden. Startled, the king went to see what was happening, and as he climbed up the stairs, one stair broke beneath him. Distracted for a moment from his Torah thoughts, he became vulnerable to the angel of death, and in that moment he died. While he was alive, David celebrated the end of each Sabbath with a feast, knowing he would live at least another week. The *melaveh malkah* commemorates the king's dinners with songs and talk that often last well into the night. In his honor it is known as *se'udat David*, David's feast.

A deeper connection to King David is the belief that from his house will come the Messiah to redeem Israel and the world. The fourth meal revolves around thoughts of the Messiah, a repast of hope and anticipation. One of the key songs Hasidim sing then and everybody sings earlier, at the end of the havdalah service, is "Eliyahu Ha'Navi," "Elijah the Prophet." Elijah has a special role in Jewish imagination as the harbinger of the Messiah. In the Bible, many miracle stories surround the life of Elijah, ending with his rising to heaven in a fiery chariot. Since then this peripatetic prophet has been symbolically present for the people of Israel at times of transition and danger. A special chair is put aside for him at every circumcision and a special cup at every Passover seder. The song in his honor after the havdalah ceremony beckons his arrival "speedily in our day" as we stand at the threshold of a new week.

Tradition suggests that Elijah will not come on a Friday, because he would not want to upset Shabbat preparations, and he cannot come on Shabbat, because even he may not travel on that sacred day. Therefore he might travel as quickly as possible on a Saturday night to announce the Messiah's arrival. His announcement will lead to redemption and an era of eternal light and peace in the world.

Less known than the fantasy of Elijah's arrival at Sabbath's end is a folk belief about the prophet Miriam that overlaps Elijah's mission. In legend, the water that sustained the Israelites in the desert during their many years of wandering came from a miraculous well created in Miriam's honor on the eve of the world's first Sabbath. Known as "Miriam's well," it irrigated the dry desert lands and supplied the people with fresh fruits and vegetables. When Miriam died her well vanished, leaving the Israelites clamoring for water. Some sources say it remains hidden in the land of Israel. Folklore holds, however, that Miriam's well becomes active again every Saturday night, after Shabbat, when it moves about from river to river and spring to spring, supplying healing waters to cure those who are ill in body or soul. In honor of Miriam and her well, people have been adding a specially designed cup filled with water to their Passover seder tables, a Miriam's cup that stands alongside the traditional wine-filled cup of Elijah.

But more than the pairing of cups connects Miriam with Elijah. The legend of Miriam's well returning after Shabbat foreshadows another legend that says that in a time to come the well with its bounty and therapeutic waters will return permanently so that nobody need ever be ill again. Moreover, in her lifetime, Miriam carried news of redemption, heralding the arrival of Israel's savior, her brother Moses. According to the midrash, she had prophesied to her parents that one day they would have a son who would redeem

Israel. In the Bible, Miriam stands at a distance to watch over her baby brother after their mother puts him in a little basket among the reeds of the Nile River. She not only protects him, she also protects her prophecy and Israel's dream of freedom from Egypt. Later, through her activities alongside her brothers Moses and Aaron, she helps redeem the Israelites, and that redemption from Egypt serves as a model in Jewish belief for the hope of a final redemption, for Israel and all humankind.

It is not too great a stretch to imagine Miriam, who heralded the birth of Israel's redeemer in Egypt, joining Elijah in heralding the ultimate redeemer some Saturday evening, as soon as Shabbat ends, when the waters of her miraculous well proffer healing to those who need it.

A Cape Cod Shabbat: My husband and I are strolling along a beach in Chatham, Massachusetts, on a Saturday afternoon. There are few people in this area, but a school of seals swims nearby, their glistening bodies flipping out of the water then disappearing beneath it, carefree, as though they owned it all. The water sparkles with light, flaunting its solar diamonds like a woman bedecked in brilliant jewelry, gaudy but gorgeous. How audacious of my early ancestors, I'm thinking, to discount gods of nature, even a god of the seas. How difficult not to worship this splendor and power, this blazing globe of gold that cannot be gazed at directly, this rippling expanse of water that has no beginning or end, this sapphire vaulting that rises far higher than the eye can see. How audacious to posit a God superior to all this, a single Being who created it all, and invisible at that.

"*Me'ein olam haba,*" my husband says, cutting into my reveries. A foretaste of the world to come. That's what it is. Too spectacular to be of this world only, the scene we're walking through is an appetizer, a whisper of a different time and place, a world the rabbis said is completely Shabbat. Perhaps this is what it will be like, that world to come. All beauty and light and the peace and serenity of Shabbat. We have been to this beach at other times, but now in the Sabbath's sanctity and tranquillity the majesty of the created world has taken on new meaning. On weekdays we witnessed the glories of nature. On Shabbat we've glimpsed beyond them.

Me'ein olam haba. Shabbat, the sages said, gives us a flavor of paradise. It carries us back to the Garden of Eden and the first Shabbat, that moment of absolute perfection after God ceased from creating and pronounced the world "very good." And it points us forward to a time to come when the world will be restored to that ideal state. "A Psalm. A Song for the Sabbath Day," the ninety-second psalm, Adam's psalm, begins. To which the Mishnah adds, "A psalm and a song for a future age, for the day that will be entirely Sabbath and rest in everlasting life." The word used here for rest is *menuhah,* the special Sabbath repose said to have been created on Shabbat itself. When the sages want to portray a future era of peace and perfection, they compare it to Shabbat, and when they want to convey the sanctity and singularity of Shabbat, they compare it to that future age. To be sure, Shabbat is only one sixtieth of the world to come, they said, along the lines of an unripened date in relation to a ripe one. Still, it anticipates the next world of perfection, and possesses a portion of its holiness.

What the tradition means to say with these comparisons is that Jews live simultaneously in two worlds, or on two levels: the real, material, here-and-now world, and an eternal world of the spirit, dreamed of and hoped for. Shabbat bridges the gulf between them, transcending the everyday to provide a taste of the ultimate.

But what really is the world to come that Shabbat foretells? The tradition is ambiguous. As often used, it refers to the world one enters after life ends—that hereafter where my hospitable great-grandmother Riva welcomes new arrivals and my parents, reunited forever now, light their Shabbat candles together. In this celestial world after death, souls rest on the wings of the Shekhinah, delighting in the sweet quietude of Eden. In regard to Shabbat, however, the world to come frequently refers to a broader vision of a national and universal period of redemption and peace heralded by Elijah (and maybe Miriam alongside him). That messianic era can be viewed almost as an eighth day of creation, a day at the end of days when the world will begin anew. Shabbat themes weave in and out of speculations about that time to come, and its theme of redemption adds yet another layer of meaning to the Shabbat celebration.

First, a small paradox: The motif of havdalah and much of Shabbat, as we've seen, is separation and the holiness that accompanies it. Yet the motif of the age to come is lack of separation, the extension of Shabbat's holiness to all eternity, with no distinctive days of the week. In fact, that vision of a continual Shabbat has a counterpart here on earth in the concept of preparing for the seventh day ahead of time and remembering it after it has ended, thus infusing holiness into the entire week. Regarding separations, the scholar Aviva Zornberg comments that the divisions occurring during creation are "achieved at some sacrifice." She cites a midrash in which the lower waters, separated on the second day from the higher waters, weep, saying, "We want to be in the presence of the King." The primal unity of the universe has been shattered, necessarily but also somewhat tragically. Applied to the ideal of an age to come, we might say that in that era a kind of unity will be restored to the world. Differences between days will dissolve and the spirit of Shabbat will pervade everything.

Speculations about the golden age ahead have never been systematized, which leads to confusion and contradictions, but also to a welcome lack of rigidity. Much depends on our own behavior. For the most part, the timing of that future world ties into Shabbat time, with elaborations on the six days of the week and the holy number seven. The most common belief, in accord with Rabbi Kattina in the Talmud, is that the world as we know it will exist for six thousand years and rest on the seven thousandth, its Sabbath. Some Jewish sources speak of the seventh millennium as the "great Sabbath," and some Christian ones as "the day of the Lord." (Based on these calculations and the Hebrew calendar, we are now in the sixth millennium, only two hundred and some years away from the "great Sabbath." This has led some commentators to label ours the "pre-Messianic era!") Many mystics, including Nahmanides, believed that the Messiah would arrive at the end of the sixth millennium, making the seventh a period of unalloyed spirituality. Others regarded the seventh as a time of desolation, with the Messiah arriving only afterward.

In almost all kabbalistic thought, the age to come will be marked by a final union between the feminine and masculine principles within God, a final restoration of the Shekhinah and Tiferet, the queen and her king only temporarily united every Shabbat. Following the teachings of Isaac Luria, the permanent coupling will be possible because the Shekhinah will have been freed from the evil forces that kept her in exile, ending Israel's exile as well. The resulting wholeness within the *sefirot* will bring lasting harmony to the cosmos.

By celebrating Shabbat every week, Jews help create that final harmony. When they light candles, study Torah, pray, rest, and eat three meals, they contribute to *tikkun,* the repair of the shattered universe and the freeing of the Shekhinah, thus hastening the messianic age. Less mystically, the talmudic rabbis regarded these acts themselves as a prelude to what future life would be like. Sometimes they compared our world to the Sabbath eve and the world to come to the Sabbath day. "A person who prepares on the eve of the Sabbath can eat on the Sabbath," they said, "but the person who has not prepared on the eve of the Sabbath, what should that person eat on the Sabbath?" How, in other words, can a person who has not made an effort to revere and enjoy Shabbat on earth be fit to enjoy eternal Shabbat in another era and place? Sometimes they emphasized the scrupulous observance of Shabbat as a clear path to redemption, and they used the next world to illustrate that idea. In this world, Rabbi Simon said, if a person gathers figs on the Sabbath, the fig tree says nothing. In the time to come, however, the tree will call out "Stop. It is the Sabbath!"

Carrying through on that thought, Rabbi Johanan said, "If Israel were to keep just two Sabbaths properly, the Messiah would come immediately." The implication is that by observing two Sabbaths, with all their sanctity and serenity, the Jewish people can create a messianic age during their own lifetimes here on earth. Rabbi Levi had a more liberal outlook. He was willing to accept one well-observed Shabbat as a harbinger of paradise.

Occasionally the rabbis felt despairing. A midrash tells that on every Shabbat, Israel's early leaders—Moses and Aaron, David and Solomon, and all the prophets—sit and wail with the Messiah. Then they comfort him and wish him well, saying, "Have patience, your time is near."

More than anything else, Shabbat hymns and prayers mirror Jewish longing for the Messiah and for the age of peace and accord that will follow. The words and tunes of some of these prayers have become so familiar over time that many people (I among them) recite them routinely, without noticing their far-reaching meanings. But those meanings are there if one looks, adding depth to the prayers. Here are some samplings:

On the Sabbath, the *birkat hamazon,* the grace after meals, has an additional section not included in the weekday version: "May the All-merciful God cause us to inherit the day that will be entirely Sabbath and rest in everlasting life." The request is for an inheritance not of material possessions but of Israel's most spiritual possession, Shabbat everlasting.

The mystical Lekha Dodi poem, so adoring of the Sabbath queen, actually devotes six of its nine verses to visions of the people of Israel returning from exile to Jerusalem. This Jerusalem is a city of dreams, restored to the glory it boasted in the days of King David. This Jerusalem is "a royal sanctuary, seat of God's kingdom." Why such emphasis on a restored Jerusalem of the future, and with it the Temple, in a poem about greeting the Sabbath here and now? Because Shabbat and Temple are always interlocked, both symbols of God's creation and love. Shabbat symbolizes the creation of the natural world, the Temple the re-creation of the world, the home where God's Presence once dwelled on earth. Going out to welcome Shabbat in the present, the poet catches sight also of the future age that Shabbat promises, when the Temple will again crown Jerusalem, David's majestic city. At that time God will rejoice over Zion and Jerusalem as God rejoices over the Sabbath, as "a bridegroom rejoices over a bride."

In the psalms recited on Shabbat we witness an era to come when God's sovereignty will extend to all of humanity, not only the people of Israel. "The Eternal is a great God, the great ruler beyond all that is worshiped," says one psalm. "Declare among the nations, 'the Eternal reigns!' . . . God judges the peoples with equity," states another. Some Bible critics view such passages as parallels to hymns of other early peoples that portray their gods' triumph over the forces of nature. But tradition regards these psalms as jubilant predictions of another age, when, in keeping with the words of Isaiah, ". . . Sabbath after Sabbath, all flesh shall come to worship before Me, says the Eternal."

The Sabbath hymn, Psalm 92, raises the universal problem of evil that goes unpunished and righteousness too often repaid with suffering. In lyrical Hebrew it promises that a time will arrive when "The righteous shall flourish like the palm tree / they shall thrive like a cedar of Lebanon.... They shall bear fruit even in old age." The psalmist wants to assure us that although we may not see the results in the course of our lives, in the end wickedness will be punished and goodness rewarded.

Finally, a blessing for a "sukkah of peace" ends the Friday evening prayer, *hashkiveinu.* The kabbalists equated the image of a canopy of peace with both Shabbat and the Shekhinah and the peace that alights on Sabbath homes. This blessing thanks God, who "spreads a sukkah of peace over us, over all the people Israel, and over Jerusalem." Again, these words carry us to a future age when the Shekhinah will shelter a redeemed Israel and with it a redeemed world in her sukkah of peace. A fragile structure that housed the Israelites in the desert under God's protective care, the sukkah serves as a symbol of peace for an era of pure spirit devoid of strife.

Me'ein olam haba. Shabbat is a semblance of that age of the spirit. But Shabbat is even greater than that age, the Hasidic Medzibozer Rebbe said, because the future world takes its source from the Sabbath and is therefore just an offshoot of it. Over millennia, Jews who lived in poverty and under the constant specter of prejudice and persecution could take comfort in finding within their one unique day of rest intimations of a better life in a messianic period to come. Those intimations still apply to us today, as aspirations, goals yet to be achieved of a world freed from evil and drudgery, where respect and cooperation replace bitterness and hatred among Jews themselves and among all people.

* * *

Light revisited, one more time: Of all the symbols of the new age to come, light most captures the ideal. As discussed before, in the biblical story of creation, the seventh day is the only one that does not end with the formula "and there was evening and there was morning." That open-endedness stirred some commentators to read into the biblical description an allusion to a time and place where darkness never falls and light shines eternally, a luminous world beyond this one. In that world, Isaiah proclaims, "No longer shall you need the sun for light during the day, / Nor the shining of the moon for radiance; / For the Eternal shall be your light everlasting. . . ." God's infinite radiance will brighten the skies in that future time, eliminating the need for any other light.

Even so, legend says, the sun and moon will shine during that perpetual Sabbath as never before, restored to their original state when first created as "two great lights" of equal size. God lessened the moon, one midrash explains, because it complained about having to share the heavens with the sun. Another ascribes its punishment to its callous laughter when Eve and Adam wept after they had sinned. But all that will be forgotten in the new age, when, in Isaiah's words again, "The light of the moon shall become like the light of the sun, and the light of the sun shall become sevenfold, like the light of the seven days. . . ."

In rabbinic thought the "light of the seven days" alludes to yet another source of illumination in the future era. That is the primordial light that came into being with God's first words, "Let there be light." After allowing the light to shine for Adam and Eve throughout the first Sabbath, God concealed it so that the wicked would never gain control of it. That light will reveal itself in the next world, in a new Eden, where the righteous will bask in its warm glow, fulfilling the words of the psalmist that "Light is sown for the righteous, and joy for the upright of heart."

Me'ein olam haba. The world to come is Shabbat writ large. The joy and holiness, the freedom from toil, the sense of equality, the lack of strife, the oneness of God, and mostly the light that is so much part of the Shabbat spirit—all will come into being eternally, the tradition teaches, when the world is redeemed, beginning perhaps one Saturday night after the havdalah service.

Yet here is something the Zohar says about this world, the real world in which we live, and the primal light God hid after creation: "Had the light been totally concealed the world could not have existed for even a single moment. Yet it was concealed and sown like a seed that produces offspring, other seeds and fruit, and because of it the world is sustained. Every day some part of that concealed light emerges into the world, preserving everything in it; and with that light, God nourishes the world. . . . Since the first day the light has never been completely revealed, but it has been essential to the world, each day renewing the work of creation."

As hidden away as it may be for the righteous in paradise, this passage asserts, the concealed light still affects our world. It sustains and inspires us, as partners with God, constantly to renew creation, and through our own acts of righteousness to return the world to the perfection with which it began. How do we know that concealed primal light beams here on earth? It partially reveals itself on Shabbat, the rabbis

say, in the study of Torah, in the prayers recited, and especially in the candles we kindle to illumine the day.

I watch my grandchildren's eyes as they stare in awe and
wonder at the Shabbat candles. I hope someday to tell them
about the secret light hiding within the flames. I hope to tell
them about my mother's candlesticks and my own and why
the Sabbath lights are part of a larger whole that every day
enriches my life. But meanwhile, the reflection of those Shabbat flames dancing in their eyes is eternity enough for me.

Appendix

The Ten Commandments

I the Eternal am your god who brought you out of the land of Egypt, the house of bondage:

You shall have no other gods beside Me. You shall not make for yourself a sculptured image, or any likeness of what is in the heavens above, or on the earth below, or in the waters under the earth . . .

You shall not swear falsely by the name of the Eternal your God . . .

Remember the Sabbath day and keep it holy. Six days you shall labor and do all your work, but the seventh day is a Sabbath of the Eternal your God . . .

Honor your father and your mother . . .

You shall not murder.

You shall not commit adultery.

You shall not steal.

You shall not bear false witness against your neighbor.

You shall not covet your neighbor's house; you shall not covet your neighbor's wife, or his male or female slave, or his ox or his ass, or anything that is your neighbor's.

EXODUS 20: 2–14

Shabbat Blessings

CANDLELIGHTING

בָּרוּךְ אַתָּה יהוה אֱלֹהֵינוּ מֶלֶךְ הָעוֹלָם,
אֲשֶׁר קִדְּשָׁנוּ בְּמִצְוֹתָיו, וְצִוָּנוּ לְהַדְלִיק נֵר שֶׁל שַׁבָּת.

*Barukh atah Adonai, Eloheinu melekh ha'olam, asher
kid'shanu b'mitzvotav v'tzivanu l'hadlik neir shel Shabbat.*

Blessed are You, Eternal our God, Ruler of the universe, who
sanctifies us with the commandments, and commands us to
kindle the Shabbat lights.

BLESSING THE CHILDREN

Traditionally parents place their hands on a child's head
while reciting the blessing.

For daughters

יְשִׂימֵךְ אֱלֹהִים כְּשָׂרָה רִבְקָה רָחֵל וְלֵאָה.

Y'simeikh Elohim k'Sarah, Rivkah, Rahel v'Leah.

May God grant you the blessings of Sarah, Rebecca, Rachel,
and Leah.

For sons

יְשִׂימְךָ אֱלֹהִים כְּאֶפְרַיִם וְכִמְנַשֶּׁה.

Y'simkha Elohim k'Efrayim v'khiMenashe.

May God grant you the blessings of Ephraim and Manasseh.

For all children

יְבָרֶכְךָ יהוה וְיִשְׁמְרֶךָ.
יָאֵר יהוה פָּנָיו אֵלֶיךָ וִיחֻנֶּךָּ.
יִשָּׂא יהוה פָּנָיו אֵלֶיךָ וְיָשֵׂם לְךָ שָׁלוֹם.

Y'varekh'kha Adonai, v'yishm'rekha.
Ya'eir Adonai panav eilekha vihunekha.
Yisa Adonai panav eilekha v'yaseim l'kha shalom.

May God bless you and guard you.
May God show you favor and be gracious to you.
May God show you kindness and grant you peace.

KIDDUSH

וַיְהִי עֶרֶב וַיְהִי בְקֶר
יוֹם הַשִּׁשִּׁי.
וַיְכֻלּוּ הַשָּׁמַיִם וְהָאָרֶץ וְכָל־צְבָאָם.
וַיְכַל אֱלֹהִים בַּיּוֹם הַשְּׁבִיעִי מְלַאכְתּוֹ אֲשֶׁר עָשָׂה,
וַיִּשְׁבֹּת בַּיּוֹם הַשְּׁבִיעִי מִכָּל מְלַאכְתּוֹ אֲשֶׁר עָשָׂה.
וַיְבָרֶךְ אֱלֹהִים אֶת־יוֹם הַשְּׁבִיעִי וַיְקַדֵּשׁ אֹתוֹ,
כִּי בוֹ שָׁבַת מִכָּל־מְלַאכְתּוֹ, אֲשֶׁר בָּרָא אֱלֹהִים לַעֲשׂוֹת.

Vay'hi erev vay'hi voker yom ha'shisi. Va'khulu ha'shamayim
v'ha'aretz v'khol tz'va'am. Vay'khal Elohim ba'yom ha'sh'vii
melakhto asher asah, vayishbot ba'yom ha'sh'vii mi'kol m'lakhto
asher asah. Vay'varekh Elohim et yom ha'sh'vii vay'kadeish
oto, ki vo shavat mi'kol m'lakhto, asher bara Elohim la'asot.

And there was evening and there was morning, the sixth day. The heaven and earth were finished, and all their array. On the seventh day God finished the work of creation, and ceased on the seventh day from all the work that had been done. And God blessed the seventh day and declared it holy, for on it God ceased from all the work of creation that God had done.

בָּרוּךְ אַתָּה יהוה אֱלֹהֵינוּ מֶלֶךְ הָעוֹלָם, בּוֹרֵא פְּרִי הַגָּפֶן.

Barukh atah Adonai, Eloheinu melekh ha'olam, borei p'ri ha'gafen.

Blessed are You, Eternal our God, Ruler of the universe, who creates the fruit of the vine.

בָּרוּךְ אַתָּה יהוה אֱלֹהֵינוּ מֶלֶךְ הָעוֹלָם,
אֲשֶׁר קִדְּשָׁנוּ בְּמִצְוֹתָיו וְרָצָה בָנוּ,
וְשַׁבַּת קָדְשׁוֹ בְּאַהֲבָה וּבְרָצוֹן הִנְחִילָנוּ
זִכָּרוֹן לְמַעֲשֵׂה בְרֵאשִׁית.
כִּי הוּא יוֹם תְּחִלָּה לְמִקְרָאֵי קֹדֶשׁ,
זֵכֶר לִיצִיאַת מִצְרָיִם.
כִּי בָנוּ בָחַרְתָּ וְאוֹתָנוּ קִדַּשְׁתָּ מִכָּל הָעַמִּים,
וְשַׁבַּת קָדְשְׁךָ בְּאַהֲבָה וּבְרָצוֹן הִנְחַלְתָּנוּ.
בָּרוּךְ אַתָּה יהוה מְקַדֵּשׁ הַשַּׁבָּת.

Barukh atah Adonai, Eloheinu Melekh ha'olam, asher kid'shanu b'mitzvotav v'ratzah vanu, v'Shabbat kodsho b'ahavah u'v'ratzon hinhilanu, zikaron l'ma'aseh v'reshit. Ki hu yom t'hilah l'mikra'ei kodesh, zekher litzi'at mitzrayim. Ki vanu vaharta v'otanu kidashta mikol ha'amim, v'Shabbat

*kodsh'kha b'ahavah u'v'ratzon hin'hal'tanu. Barukh atah
Adonai, m'kadesh ha'Shabbat.*

Blessed are You, Eternal our God, Ruler of the universe, who
sanctifies us with the commandments and cherishes us. Lovingly and willingly You have given us the holy Shabbat as
our inheritance, a reminder of the work of creation. It is first
among our sacred days of assembly, recalling the going forth
from Egypt. For you chose us and sanctified us from among
all peoples, granting us your holy Shabbat lovingly and gladly.
Blessed are You, God, who makes Shabbat holy.

WASHING HANDS

Participants pour water over each hand, beginning with the
right hand, alternating hands two or three times. The blessing is recited silently.

בָּרוּךְ אַתָּה יהוה אֱלֹהֵינוּ מֶלֶךְ הָעוֹלָם,
אֲשֶׁר קִדְּשָׁנוּ בְּמִצְוֹתָיו וְצִוָּנוּ עַל נְטִילַת יָדָיִם.

*Barukh atah Adonai, Eloheinu Melekh ha'olam, asher
kid'shanu b'mitzvotav v'tzivanu al n'tilat yadayim.*

Blessed are You, Eternal our God, Ruler of the universe, who
sanctifies us with the commandments and commands us to
rinse our hands.

HA'MOTZI — BLESSING OVER BREAD

בָּרוּךְ אַתָּה יהוה אֱלֹהֵינוּ מֶלֶךְ הָעוֹלָם,
הַמּוֹצִיא לֶחֶם מִן הָאָרֶץ.

*Barukh atah Adonai Eloheinu Melekh ha'olam, ha'motzi lehem
min ha'aretz.*

Blessed are You, Eternal our God, Ruler of the universe, who brings forth bread from the earth.

KIDDUSH FOR SHABBAT DAY

וְשָׁמְרוּ בְנֵי יִשְׂרָאֵל אֶת-הַשַּׁבָּת, לַעֲשׂוֹת אֶת-הַשַּׁבָּת
לְדוֹרוֹתָם בְּרִית עוֹלָם. בֵּינִי וּבֵן בְּנֵי יִשְׂרָאֵל אוֹת
הִיא לְעֹלָם, כִּי שֵׁשֶׁת יָמִים עָשָׂה יהוה אֶת-הַשָּׁמַיִם
וְאֶת-הָאָרֶץ, וּבַיּוֹם הַשְּׁבִיעִי שָׁבַת וַיִּנָּפַשׁ.

עַל כֵּן בֵּרַךְ יהוה אֶת-יוֹם הַשַּׁבָּת וַיְקַדְּשֵׁהוּ.

בָּרוּךְ אַתָּה יהוה אֱלֹהֵינוּ מֶלֶךְ הָעוֹלָם, בּוֹרֵא פְּרִי הַגָּפֶן.

*V'shamru v'nei Yisrael et ha'Shabbat, la'asot et ha'Shabbat
l'dorotam brit olam. Beini u'vein b'nai Yisrael ot hi l'olam,
ki sheshet yamim asah Adonai et ha'shamayim v'et ha'aretz,
u'v'yom ha'sh'vi'i shavat va'yinafash.*
    Al ken berakh Adonai et yom ha'Shabbat va'y'kadshehu.
    *Barukh atah Adonai, Eloheinu Melekh ha'olam borei
p'ri ha'gafen.*

The people of Israel shall keep the Sabbath, observing the Sabbath through all generations, an everlasting covenant. It is a sign for all time between Me and the people of Israel. For in six days God made the heaven and the earth, and on the seventh day ceased from work and was refreshed.
    Therefore God blessed Shabbat and made it holy.
    Blessed are You, Eternal our God, Ruler of the universe, who creates the fruit of the vine.

HAVDALAH SERVICE

הִנֵּה אֵל יְשׁוּעָתִי, אֶבְטַח וְלֹא אֶפְחָד. כִּי עָזִּי וְזִמְרָת יָהּ יהוה,
וַיְהִי לִי לִישׁוּעָה. וּשְׁאַבְתֶּם מַיִם בְּשָׂשׂוֹן מִמַּעַיְנֵי הַיְשׁוּעָה.
לַיהוה הַיְשׁוּעָה עַל עַמְּךָ בִרְכָתֶךָ סֶּלָה. יהוה צְבָאוֹת עִמָּנוּ,
מִשְׂגָּב לָנוּ אֱלֹהֵי יַעֲקֹב, סֶלָה. יהוה צְבָאוֹת, אַשְׁרֵי אָדָם
בֹּטֵחַ בָּךְ. יהוה הוֹשִׁיעָה, הַמֶּלֶךְ יַעֲנֵנוּ בְיוֹם קָרְאֵנוּ.

*Hinei eil yeshuati evtakh velo efkhad. Ki azi v'zimrat Ya
Adonai, va'y'hi li li'shuah. Ushavtem mayim b'sason mi'ma'nei
ha'y'shuah. La'adonai has'y'shuah al amkha birkhatekha selah.
Adonai tz'va'ot imanu, misgav lanu elohei ya'akov selah.
Adonai tz'va'ot ashrei adam botei'akh bakh. Adonai hoshiah
hamelekh ya'aneinu v'yom kareinu.*

Behold, God is my deliverance; I am confident and unafraid.
God is my strength and my might, and will be my deliverance. With joy shall you draw water from the wells of your
deliverance. Deliverance is God's; may You bless your people.
God is with us; the God of Jacob is our fortress. God, blessed
is the person who trusts in you. Help us, God; answer us,
O Ruler, when we call.

לַיְּהוּדִים הָיְתָה אוֹרָה וְשִׂמְחָה וְשָׂשׂוֹן וִיקָר.
כֵּן תִּהְיֶה לָנוּ.
כּוֹס יְשׁוּעוֹת אֶשָּׂא וּבְשֵׁם יהוה אֶקְרָא.

*La'yehudim ha'y'tah ora v'simkhah v'sason vee'y'kar; kein ti'yeh
lanu. Kos yeshu'ot esa, uv'sheim Adonai ekra.*

For the Jews there was light, joy, gladness, and honor. So may
it be for us. I lift the cup of deliverance and call upon God.

בָּרוּךְ אַתָּה יהוה אֱלֹהֵינוּ מֶלֶךְ הָעוֹלָם, בּוֹרֵא פְּרִי הַגָּפֶן.

*Barukh atah Adonai, Eloheinu Melekh ha'olam borei p'ri
ha'gafen.*

Blessed are You, Eternal our God, Ruler of the universe, who
creates the fruit of the vine.

בָּרוּךְ אַתָּה יהוה אֱלֹהֵינוּ מֶלֶךְ הָעוֹלָם, בּוֹרֵא מִינֵי בְשָׂמִים.

*Barukh atah Adonai, Eloheinu Melekh ha'olam borei minei
v'samim.*

Blessed are You, Eternal our God, Ruler of the universe, who
creates fragrant spices.

בָּרוּךְ אַתָּה יהוה אֱלֹהֵינוּ מֶלֶךְ הָעוֹלָם, בּוֹרֵא מְאוֹרֵי הָאֵשׁ.

*Barukh atah Adonai, Eloheinu Melekh ha'olam borei m'orei
ha'eish.*

Blessed are You, Eternal our God, Ruler of the universe, who
creates the lights of fire.

בָּרוּךְ אַתָּה יהוה אֱלֹהֵינוּ מֶלֶךְ הָעוֹלָם, הַמַּבְדִּיל בֵּין קֹדֶשׁ
לְחוֹל, בֵּין אוֹר לְחֹשֶׁךְ, בֵּין יִשְׂרָאֵל לָעַמִּים, בֵּן יוֹם
הַשְּׁבִיעִי לְשֵׁשֶׁת יְמֵי הַמַּעֲשֶׂה. בָּרוּךְ אַתָּה יהוה הַמַּבְדִּיל
בֵּין קֹדֶשׁ לְחוֹל.

*Barukh atah Adonai, Eloheinu Melekh ha'olam, hamavdil bein
kodesh l'hol, bein or l'hoshekh, bein Yisrael l'amim, bein yom
ha'sh'vi'i l'sheishet y'mei ha'ma'aseh. Barukh atah Adonai,
hamavdil bein kodesh l'hol.*

Blessed are You, Eternal our God, Ruler of the universe, who distinguishes between the holy and the mundane, between light and darkness, between the people of Israel and other peoples, between the seventh day and the six days of the week. Blessed are You, Eternal our God, who distinguishes between the holy and the mundane.

Notes

꒒

Grateful acknowledgment is made for permission to reprint biblical passages from the *Tanakh: A New Translation of the Holy Scriptures According to the Traditional Hebrew Text*. Copyright © 1985 by The Jewish Publication Society. Most biblical passages in the book are based on this translation, but I have translated some passages myself according to my understanding of a text, to use gender-neutral language where appropriate, or to fit with a rabbinic interpretation.

Prologue: SABBATH LIGHTS

1 Franz Rosenzweig: "The Secret of the Sabbath," in *Sefer Ha'Shabbat,* ed. H. N. Bialik (Tel Aviv: Dvir, 1938), 539 [Hebrew].

2 Josephus: Cited in Abraham E. Millgram, *Sabbath: Day of Delight* (Philadelphia: Jewish Publication Society, 1952), 218.

3 To thirteen-year-old Ozzie: Philip Roth, "The Conversion of the Jews," in *Goodbye Columbus and Five Short Stories* (New York: Meridian Fiction, 1960), 143.

3 "the mystery of the fire . . .": Zelda, in *Kol Haneshamah: Shabbat Eve* (The Reconstructionist Press: Wynocote, PA, 1989), 4.

3 "As long as Sarah was alive . . .": Rashi on Gen. 24:67.

4 The command to Aaron: Num. 8:2 and Nahmanides' commentary on it.

5 Karaite betrothal contract: "Karaite Deed of Betrothal," Fustat, ca. 1030, in *Scripture and Schism* (New York: Library of the Jewish Theological Seminary, 2000), 79.

5 "Lighting the Sabbath lights . . .": Maimonides, *Mishneh Torah,* Laws of the Sabbath 5:1.

6 Hebrew letters for light: Gershom Scholem, "The meaning of the Torah in Jewish Mysticism," in Scholem, *On the Kabbalah and Its Symbolism* (New York: Schocken Books, 1996), 63.

7 "What is twilight . . .": *Shabbat* 34a–34b.

7 "Let there be light": Gen. 1:3.

7 light illumined the universe: *Leviticus Rabbah* 11:7.

9 "I form light . . .": Isa. 45:7.

9 God blessed the day with light: *Genesis Rabbah* 11:2. This is also the source of Rabbis Levi and Liezer's statements and the legend about Adam.

10 "Light is sown . . .": Ps. 97:11.

11 "The lamp of my holy day . . .": *Selected Poems of Jehudah Halevi,* ed. Heinrich Brody (Philadelphia: Jewish Publication Society, 1974), 141.

11 "wrapped in a robe of light": Ps. 104:2.

12 Shekhinah's rule: Isaiah Tishby, *The Wisdom of the Zohar: An Anthology of Texts,* trans. David Goldstein (London: Littman Library of Jewish Civilization, 1994), 3:1296.

12 "You are the light of the world . . .": *Numbers Rabbah* 15: 5.

13 "I told you to kindle . . .": Ibid., 15:7.

13 "The lifebreath . . .": Prov. 20:27.

13 "commandment is a lamp . . .": Ibid., 6:23.

13 "If My light will be in your hand . . .": *Exodus Rabbah* 36:3.

13 Extra souls: The various images of the extra souls are discussed fully in Elliot K. Ginsburg, *The Sabbath in the Classical Kabbalah* (Albany: SUNY Press, 1989), 127–131. This is a superb, scholarly source for understanding the kabbalistic Sabbath.

14 Adam's face beamed: *Genesis Rabbah* 12:6.

14 light of a person's face: Ibid, 11:2.

17 Why do I: I thank Anne Roiphe for raising the question of whys.

One: SPANNING HEAVEN AND EARTH

---

18 Legend of the cow: *Pesikta Rabbati,* piska 14:2.

21 "No, the thing . . .": Deut. 30:14.

22 "If in the Ten Commandments . . .": Bialik in *Sefer Ha'Shabbat,* 519.

22 Shabbat commandments: Ex. 20:8–11; Deut. 5:12–15.

24 Early Islamic texts: *Encyclopedia of Islam, CD-ROM Edition,* vol. 10, s.v. Sabt.

24 Moshe Weinfeld suggests: Cited in Jon D. Levenson, *Creation and the Persistence of Evil* (Princeton, NJ: Princeton University Press, 1988), 124–25.

24 "The Lord is God from of old . . .": Isa. 40:28.

25 how much more do humans . . . : *Mekhilta,* Bahodesh 7.

25 "saw the thunder . . .": Ex. 20:15 and Rashi on this verse.

26 "It is clear to me . . .": Moses Maimonides, *The Guide for the Perplexed,* trans. M. Friedlander (London: Pardes Publishing House, 1904), bk. 2, ch. 33. My thanks to Rabbi Harlan Wechsler for this insight.

27 "enough": Hagigah 12a.

28 "holy Sabbath": Ex. 16:23.

28 "God blessed it with manna . . .": Rashi on Gen. 2:3.

30 "great sea monsters . . .": Gen. 1:21.

30 a place . . . to hide in: Kotzker Rebbe in Martin Buber, *Tales of the Hasidim: The Later Masters* (New York: Schocken Books, 1948), 288.

31 Jon Levenson has shown . . . : Levenson, *Creation and Persistence of Evil,* 100–107.

31 insight and creativity: Rashi on Gen. 1:26.

32 Saadiah suggested: Robert Gordis, *A Faith for Moderns* (New York: Bloch Publishing House, 1960), 192.

32 "fill the earth and master it": Gen. 1: 27.

32 "What are humans . . .": Ps.8:5–6.

33 one-seventh of their lives: Judah Halevi, "Kuzari," ed. Isaak Heinemann, in *Three Jewish Philosophers* (Cleveland and New York: World Publishing Company, 1961), 91.

33 "I the Eternal am your God": Deut. 5:6.

34 Moses and the angels: *Shabbat* 88b–89a.

36 "They are My servants": Lev. 25:42.

37 Ezekiel condemns: Ezek. 22:7–8.

37 "what is right . . .": Isa.56:1–2.

39 *va'yinnafash*: Ex. 31:17.

39 God gave the world its soul: Rabbi Solomon ben Abraham Adret, cited in Abraham Joshua Heschel, *The Sabbath: Its Meaning for Modern Man* (New York: Farrar, Straus and Giroux, 1951), 83.

40 "A *kugel* fit for a king": Josef Erlich, *Sabbath* (Syracuse, New York: Syracuse University Press, 1999), 146.

40 "two wrinkles": Ibid., 178.

40 "more than Israel has kept the Sabbath . . . :" Ahad Ha'Am, cited in Millgram, *Sabbath,* 253, among many other sources.

41 Remember and Observe as one: *Shevuot* 20b.

41 As two sets of tablets: *Pesikta Rabbati,* piska 23:2.

42 Legend of Rabbi Simeon bar Yohai: *Shabbat* 33b.

43 "If ever a doubt arises . . .": Nahmanides on Deut. 5:15.

44 Being who continues to act: Joseph Albo, *Book of Principles,* trans. Isaac Husik (Philadelphia: Jewish Publication Society, 1930), 3: 246–48.

45 Sabbath equal to all the laws: *Exodus Rabbah* 25: 12.

Two: SACRED SEVENS/SACRED SIGN

46 "All sevens are beloved": *Pesikta de Rav Kahana,* piska 23:10.

47 Cure for tertian fever: *Shabbat* 67a.

47 sevens in creation narrative: See Umberto Cassuto, *A Commentary on the Book of Genesis,* trans. Israel Abrahams (Jerusalem: Magnes Press, 1961), 1:7–13.

48 "I am the seventh": Buber, *Tales of the Hasidim, Later Masters,* 273.

48 Sumerians, Babylonians, and others: For a discussion of the number seven

in other cultures, see Nahum Sarna, *Exploring Exodus* (New York: Schocken Books), 147.

49   the seven planets: Eleanor Munro, *On Glory Roads: A Pilgrim's Book About Pilgrimage* (New York: Thames and Hudson, 1987), 40.

49   music of the spheres: *Dictionary of Scientific Biography,* s.v. Pythagorus.

49   "eyes of the Eternal . . .": Zech. 4:10.

49   "seven planets in the firmament": *Zohar* I, 188b.

49   seven maidens: Tishby, *Wisdom of the Zohar,* II, 665.

51   the "decade": In Raphael Patai, *The Hebrew Goddess* (New York: Ktav Publishing House, 1967), 248.

52   Moses invented Shabbat: *Exodus Rabbah* 1:28.

53   *sabbatosis:* Peter Schäfer, *Judeophobia: Attitudes Toward the Jews in the Ancient World* (Cambridge: Harvard University Press, 1997), 29.

53   days of "ill omen": For theories about origin of the Sabbath, see Mayer Gruber, "The Source of the Biblical Sabbath," *Journal of the Ane Society* 1, no. 2 (Spring 1969): 14–20.

53   feminist theorists: Elyse Goldstein, *ReVisions: Seeing Torah Through a Feminist Lens* (Woodstock, VT: Jewish Lights, 1998), 161–62.

54   God spoke Egyptian: *Tanhuma,* Jethro.

54   common source: Jacob Milgrom, *Leviticus 23-27: The Anchor Bible* (New York: Doubleday, 2000), 1960.

55   Sabbath has no mate: *Genesis Rabbah* 11:7.

55   birthday of the world: In *Sefer Ha'Shabbat,* 14.

56   Lord's Day: Daniel Harrington, "Sabbath Tensions," in *The Sabbath in Jewish and Christian Tradition,* eds. Tamara Eskenazi, Daniel Harrington, and William Shea (New York: Crossroad Publishing, 1991).

56   moral and ceremonial: Samuele Bacchiocchi, "Remembering the Sabbath," in Ibid., 86.

57   Sabbath as punishment: *Encyclopedia of Islam,* 10.

58   Sambatyon legend: Louis Ginzberg, *The Legends of the Jews* (Philadelphia: Jewish Publication Society, 1968) 4:316–17.

59   "Proclaim Liberty . . .": Lev. 25:10.

59   Six years . . . Six days: Ex. 23:10–12.

59   Sabbath of the Lord . . . : Lev. 25: 2, 4.

60   Rabbi Kattina: *Sanhedrin* 97a.

60   cosmic cycles: Scholem, "Meaning of the Torah," 77–81.

61   replenished the soil: Baruch A. Levine, *Leviticus: The JPS Torah Commentary* (Philadelphia: Jewish Publication Society, 1989), 170.

61   "the land is Mine . . .": Lev. 25:23.

61   man from Laodicea: *Pesikta Rabbati,* piska 23:7.

62   "Be fertile . . .": Gen. 1:28.

62 "See My works...": *Ecclesiastes Rabbah* 7:13.

63 "till it...": Gen. 2:15.

64 return to God: Moshe Weinfeld, *Deuteronomy 1–11: The Anchor Bible* (New York: Doubleday, 1991), 306.

64 laws modified: A good summary of the history of the sabbatical and jubilee is Jeffrey H. Tigay, *Deuteronomy: The JPS Torah Commentary*, Excursus 16.

65 "charms of indolence...": In Schäfer, *Judeophobia*, 87.

68 "a sign": Ex. 31:17.

68 "community of Israel": *Genesis Rabbah* 11:8.

69 circumcision as a sign: George Foot Moore, *Judaism* (Cambridge: Harvard University Press, 1946), 2:24.

69 the covenant: Sarna, *Understanding Exodus.*

70 parallel tablets: *Mekhilta*, Bahodesh 8.

70 belief in creation: Don Isaac Abrabanel, *Mifalot Elohim* 1:20. With thanks to Maud Kozodoy.

71 "all the days of the world": Nahmanides on Gen. 2:3.

71 "order of creation": *Shabbat* 53b.

72 basic numbers and laws: Martin Rees, *Just Six Numbers* (New York: Basic Books, 1999).

73 creating and destroying worlds: *Genesis Rabbah* 3:7.

74 Elijah and rain: *Pesikta de Rab Kahana* 28:4.

74 "no seven... days...": *Leviticus Rabbah* 27:10.

Three: HOLINESS IN SPACE AND TIME

76 "The meaning of the Sabbath...": Heschel, *The Sabbath*, 10.

76 "holiness in time...": Ibid., 8.

76 "our great cathedrals...": Ibid.

77 "Thing is a category...": Ibid., 5.

77 "We are all infatuated...": Ibid.

77 "the coronation of a day...": Ibid., 18.

77 "Time and space interrelated": Ibid., 6.

78 "enslavement to things": Ibid.

78 "make Me a sanctuary...": Ex. 25: 8–9.

79 God's Shekhinah moved: *Genesis Rabbah* 19:7.

81 out of order: Rashi on Ex. 31:18.

81 "the glory of God abode...": Nahmanides on Ex. 25:1.

82 timing of events: Nahmanides on Lev. 8:2.

82 "Nevertheless...": Ex. 31:13 and Rashi on that passage.

83 gods, creation, and shrine: Stephen A. Geller, *Sacred Enigmas* (London: Routledge, 1996), 66–68.

NOTES to pages 83–100

83 link between Tabernacle and creation: critical thought summarized in Nehama Leibowitz, *Studies in Shemot* (Jerusalem: World Zionist Organization, 1981), 471–86. The verses cited are, respectively, Ex. 24:16; Ex. 31:17; Gen. 2:1–2; Ex. 39: 32; and Ex. 40:33.

84 sages noted comparisons: *Numbers Rabbah* 12:13.

85 *ohel: Sefer Ha'Shabbat,* 179.

85 "keep My Sabbaths...": Lev. 19:30.

85 *la'asot:* In Leibowitz, *Shemot,* 475, 538–39.

88 "I am Holy": Lev. 19:2.

88 "As God is gracious...": *Shabbat* 133b.

88 "as I am separated...": In Milgrom, *Leviticus* 17–22, 1603.

88 Cassius Dio: In Schäfer, *Judeophobia,* 45.

89 "Choose...": Kadya Molodowsky, "God of Mercy," in *Modern Poems on the Bible: An Anthology,* ed. David Curzon (Philadelphia: Jewish Publication Society, 1994), 167.

89 "kingdom of priests...": Ex. 19: 6.

90 God's treasure house: *Betzah* 16a.

90 "Why is Sabbath different...": *Sanhedrin* 65b.

91 "table makes atonement": *Berakhot* 55a.

93 *shamir: Sotah* 48b.

93 "Sabbath clothes": *Shabbat* 113a.

93 "Sabbath 'delight'...": Isaiah 58:13.

94 "my honorers": *Shabbat* 113a.

95 walking on Shabbat: Ibid.

95 Shabbat speech: Ibid., 13b.

95 three meals: Ibid., 117b.

95 "dish of beets...": Ibid., 118b.

95 garlic: J *Megillah* 75:1.

96 Sabbath spice: *Shabbat* 119b.

97 Baal Shem's dream: Based on story in Louis I. Newman, *Hasidic Anthology* (New York: Schocken Books, 1963), 411–12.

99 The Tall Rabbi: In Freema Gottlieb, *The Lamp of God* (Northvale, NJ: Jason Aronson, 1989).

99 *va'y'kholu: Shabbat* 119b.

100 whose deeds are finer: *Tanhuma,* Tazria 5 and *Pesikta Rabbati* 23:4.

Four: WOMEN AT THE CENTER

I'm indebted to three main sources for much of the background information in this chapter: Gershom Scholem, "Tradition and New Creation in the Ritual of the

Kabbalists," in *On the Kabbalah and Its Symbolism*; Elliot Ginsburg, *The Sabbath in the Classical Kabbalah*; and Ginsburg's companion book, *Sod Ha-Shabbat: The Mystery of the Sabbath* (Albany: SUNY Press, 1989).

106 *"the day ..."*: Scholem, "Tradition and New Creation," in *Kabbalah and Its Symbolism*, 139.

108 "the Shekhinah went with them": *Megillah* 29a.

109 A rainbow: Tishby, *Wisdom of the Zohar* 2:667.

110 what is it lacking: *Genesis Rabbah* 10:9.

110 "Come O bride ...": *Shabbat* 119a.

111 "Arise, shine ...": Isaiah 60:1

111 Deborah: Judges 5:12.

112 "Why does it say ...": In Ginsburg, *Sod Ha-Shabbat*, 86.

113 "Angels of peace": *Shabbat* 119b.

113 "Woman of Valor": Prov. 31: 10–31.

114 "holy souls": *Zohar* I, 89b.

114 "marital duty": Mishnah, *Ketubbot* 5:6.

114 "prepare themselves for intercourse ...": *Zohar:* I, 89a.

115 souls soar: Ibid., 136a.

117 "I will espouse you ...": Hosea 2:21.

118 "when male and when female ...": Zohar I, 232b.

118 "then her face is dark": In Scholem, "Kabbalah and Myth," in *Kabbalah and Its Symbolism*,107.

119 Wolfson stresses masculinity: Elliot R. Wolfson, *Circle in the Square* (Albany: SUNY Press, 1995).

120 "Women die in childbirth ...": Mishnah, *Shabbat* 2:6.

120 women must observe laws: *Genesis Rabbah* 17:8.

121 "rise up . . .": Esther Ettinger, "The Sadness Cage," in *The Defiant Muse: Hebrew Feminist Poems*, eds. Shirley Kaufman, Galit Hasan-Rokem, and Tamar S. Hess (New York: Feminist Press, 1999), 161.

121 American poet: Merle Feld, "The First Time We Made Shabbos Together," in *A Spiritual Life* (Albany: SUNY Press, 1999), 88.

122 "The lifebreath ...": Prov. 20:27.

122 "The soul ...": *Shabbat* 32a.

122 groundbreaking book: Chava Weissler, *Voices of the Matriarchs* (Boston: Beacon Press, 1998).

123 "Send an angel ...": Weissler, *Voices*, 33.

123 "And when the woman kindles ...": Ibid., 97.

124 "humble dish": *Shabbat* 118b.

125 woman and Rabbi Meir: J *Sotah* 1:4, 16d.

128 "Many daughters ...": Prov. 31: 29.

129 Canopy of peace image: *Zohar* I, 48a–b.

Five: OF LABOR AND LAWS

132 his own sin: Num. 27:3.

132 man gathering wood: Ibid., 32–36.

132 "the wood gatherer was . . .": *Shabbat* 96b.

132 "you will have to account . . .": Ibid.

133 tale of pious man: Ibid., 150b.

133 Zelophehad's soul: Nogah Hareuveni, *Tree and Shrub in Our Biblical Heritage*, trans. Helen Frenkley (Kiryat Ono, Israel: Neot Kedumim, 1984), 42–53. All the elements of the wood gatherer's story are pulled together here. My thanks to Dr. Terry Krulwich.

134 specific Sabbath rules: Aside from the Fourth Commandment, Sabbath laws or admonitions appear in these biblical sources: Ex. 16:23–30, 23:12, 31:13–17, 34:21, and 35:2–3, Lev. 19:30 and 23:3, Num.15: 32–36; Isa. 58:13; Jer. 17:21–24; Amos 8:5; Neh. 10:32 and 13:15–22.

134 the wood gatherer's sin: *Shabbat* 96b.

135 mountains by a hair: Mishnah *Hagigah* 1:8.

135 "On the seventh day . . .": Gen. 2:2.

136 demons: *Genesis Rabbah* 7:5.

136 *menuhah:* Ibid., 10: 9.

137 hair's breadth: Ibid.

137 part of scheme of creation: See Yosef Yitzhak Lifshitz, "Secret of the Sabbath," *Azure*, 10 (Winter 5761/2001), 85–117.

137 "just as the Torah . . .": *Fathers According to Rabbi Nathan*, ch. 11.

137 "Even Adam . . .": Ibid. Biblical verses cited from Gen. 2:15–16.

138 Rabbi Dostai: *Fathers According to Rabbi Nathan*, ch. 11.

138 "All study of Torah . . .": *Ethics of the Fathers* 2:2.

138 "to study Torah and not work . . .": Maimonides, *Mishneh Torah*, Laws of Torah Study 3:10.

138 Simeon bar Yohai: *Shabbat* 33b.

140 days of the week: Nahmanides on Exodus 20: 8.

141 "Whoever has to 'Observe' . . .": *Berakhot* 20b.

142 thirty-nine categories: Mishnah *Shabbat* 7:2.

143 "They sowed . . .": *Shabbat* 49b.

143 allusion to prohibited labors: *Shabbat* 97b.

143 "these are the things . . .": Ex. 35:1.

143 thirty-nine lashes: Tishby, *Wisdom of Zohar*, 3:1228–29.

144 purposeful work: The best discussion of this concept is Isidor Grunfeld, *The Sabbath* (New York: Feldheim, 1954).

145 creative craft: Ex. 31: 3.
147 intentionally cooked food: Shabbat 38a.
148 French *cassoulet*: Claudia Roden, *The Book of Jewish Food* (New York: Knopf, 1997), 146.
150 "guard yourselves...": Jer. 17:21–22.
151 "the whole world belongs...": *Pesikta Rabbati*, piska 23:8.
151 two women: J *Eruvin* 3:2.
152 "magic schlepping circle": Calvin Trillin, "Drawing the Line," *The New Yorker* (Dec. 12, 1994), 50–62.
153 Conservative controversy: See Neil Gillman, Conservative Judaism (New York: Behrman House, 1993), 95–96.
155 Yalta: *Hullin* 109b.
155 "betrothal of a young girl...": Maimonides, *Mishneh Torah*, Laws of the Sabbath, 24:5.
155 carry arms: Mishnah *Shabbat* 6:4.
156 "will not lift up sword...": Isaiah 2:4.
156 "all Israel...": Mishnah *Shabbat* 14: 4.
156 "live by them...": *Sanhedrin* 74a.
157 "wipe us off face of earth...": I Macc. 2:41.
157 "instead of protecting...": Agatharchides in Schäfer, *Judeophobia*, 83.
157 "Sabbath made for man..." Mark 2:27.
157 "Sabbath given to you...": *Mekhilta*, Shabbata 1.
158 "allowed to do good...": Matthew 12:12.
158 "Son of Man...": Ibid., 12:8.
158 blind woman: *Shabbat* 128b.
159 contrasting rules with legends: H. N. Bialik, "Halakhah and Aggadah," in *Modern Jewish Thought*, ed. Nahum N. Glatzer (New York: Schocken Books, 1977), 55–64.

Six: THE SABBATH JEW AND THE SABBATH GENTILE

161 "call Sabbath delight": Isa.58:13
161 "despised My holy things...": Ezek. 22:8.
162 prophets put greater emphasis: Discussed fully in Moshe Greenberg, "The Sabbath in Jeremiah," in *Studies in Jeremiah* [Hebrew], ed. B. Z. Luria (Israel: Society for Biblical Research, 1971), 2:38–52.
162 "hallow the Sabbath...": Jer. 17: 24–25.
163 "men in Judah...": Neh. 13:15–22.
163 "ranged round the greasy...": In Schäfer, *Judeophobia*, 90.
164 "Sabbath adds holiness...": *Mekhilta*, Shabbata 1.
164 Joseph Who Honors...: *Shabbat* 119a.

165 "I sinned . . .": Trial of Juana Martínez in Renée Levine Melammed, *Heretics or Daughters of Israel?* (New York: Oxford University Press, 1999), 196–97.

168 "*goy shel Shabbat*": Melammed, *Heretics,* 24.

169 "If a gentile lights a lamp . . .": Mishnah *Shabbat* 16:8.

170 "Every Friday I lock it . . .": In Jacob Katz, *The "Shabbes Goy"* (New York: Jewish Publication Society, 1989), 56.

170 "profaning the Sabbath . . .": Hirschel Levin sermon, c. 1757, in Marc Saperstein, *Jewish Preaching* 1200–1800 (New Haven, CT: Yale University Press, 1989), 356.

170 On a different tack: I. L. Peretz, "The "Shabbes Goy," in *The I. L. Peretz Reader,* ed. Ruth R. Wisse (New York: Schocken Books, 1990), 131–138.

172 response to Hatzolah members: *Responsa of Rav Moshe Feinstein,* vol. 1, trans. Moshe Dovid Tendler (Hoboken, NJ: Ktav Publishing House, 1996), 111–17. With thanks to Dr. Neil Schluger.

173 Reb Ya'akov: Rabbi Oshry's response in Irving J. Rosenbaum, *The Holocaust and Halakhah* (Hoboken, NJ: Ktav Publishing House, 1976), 92–95.

175 man with a pipe: Based on anecdote in Elie Wiesel, *Souls on Fire,* (New York: Touchstone, 1972), 89.

176 first Sabbath transgression: Sholom Aleichem, *From the Fair,* trans. Curt Leviant (New York: Viking Penguin, 1985).

179 "Does she look back . . .": Tillie Olsen, *Tell Me a Riddle* (New York: Delta, 1984), 81.

179 Rachel Lazarus: In *The Jew in the American World: A Source Book* (Detroit: Wayne State University Press, 1996), 142.

179 Jewish peddler: Ibid., 342.

181 dialogue group: The Jewish Women's Dialogue meets under the auspices of the New York Chapter of the American Jewish Committee.

181 "discover within ourselves . . .": Mordecai M. Kaplan, *The Meaning of God in Modern Jewish Religion* (Detroit: Wayne State University Press, 1994), 62.

181 "only when unseen": *The Journals of Mordecai M. Kaplan,* vol.1, ed. Mel Scult (Detroit: Wayne State University Press, 2001), 452.

182 Franz Rosenzweig: In Nahum N. Glatzer, *Franz Rosenzweig, His Life and Thought* (Philadelphia: Jewish Publication Society, 1953).

183 "Is it possible . . .": *Mekhilta,* Bahodesh 7.

184 "Remove . . .": Ex. 3:5.

186 ruler in his palace . . . : Maimonides, *Guide,* bk.3, ch. 51.

Seven: THE LOVELIEST OF DAYS

187 "With what . . .": Mishnah *Shabbat* 2:1.

188 Gemara defines: discussion, from *Shabbat* 20b-26b.

189 "only with olive oil": Mishnah *Shabbat* 2:2 and Gemara discussion.

190 teaching from memory: David Weiss Halivni, *The Book and the Sword* (New York: Farrar, Straus and Giroux, 1996), ch. 3.

190 "all your children...": Isa. 54:13.

190 your builders: *Berakhot* 64a.

191 Hillel and Shammai: *Betzah* 16a.

191 Rabbi Hanina's wife: *Ta'anit* 24b–25a.

192 God would repay: *Betzah* 15b.

192 "treat Sabbath like a weekday...": *Pesahim* 112a.

194 sages' preparation: *Shabbat* 119a.

195 home is bridal chamber: Scholem, "Tradition and New Creation," in *Kabbalah and Its Symbolism.*

195 "to set a banquet": Maimonides, *Mishneh Torah,* Laws of the Sabbath 30:4.

195 "welcome in Tiberius": *Shabbat* 118b.

196 Count off six days: Ibid., 39b.

196 six blasts: Ibid., 35b.

197 "My old grandmother...": Isaac Babel, "Gedali."

198 Sabbath angel upon a throne: Ginzberg, *Legends,* 1:84–86.

200 "Songs of the Sabbath Sacrifice": *The Dead Sea Scrolls,* trans. Michael Wise, Martin Abegg, Jr., and Edward Cook (New York: HarperCollins, 1999), 365–69.

201 may not weep: Norman Lamm, *The Religious Thought of Hasidism* (New York: Yeshiva University Press, 1999), 389.

202 "By you shall Israel...": Gen. 48:20.

203 "May God bless...": Num. 6:24–26.

204 "Remember it over wine": *Pesahim* 106a.

205 "Not even a Jew...": Gaius Suetonius Tranquillus, *The Twelve Caesars,* trans. Robert Graves (Middlesex, England: Penguin Books, 1973), 93.

205 groups of ascetics: See David Kraemer, "The Spirit of the Rabbinic Sabbath," *Conservative Judaism* 49, no. 4 (Summer 1997): 46–47.

207 "God forgets...": In *Open Closed Open,* trans. Chana Bloch and Chana Kronfeld (New York: Harcourt Brace, 2000), 42.

207 revelation on Sabbath: *Shabbat* 86b.

210 the midrash on prayers: *Exodus Rabbah* 21:4.

210 *Aher: Hagigah* 15a.

211 "Who would read...": Based on story in Buber, *Tales* 2: 288.

212 play ball: Rabbi Saul J. Berman, "Playing Ball on Shabbat and Yom Tov," *Edah Journal* 1, no.1 (2000): 1–13.

213 no one knows: Deut. 34:6.

Eight: ETERNAL LIGHT

215 Adam and Eve terrified: *Genesis Rabbah* 11:2.

216 One star, two...: *Shabbat* 35b.
218 *vay'nefesh:* Betzah 16a.
219 "hills of spices": Songs 8:14.
219 from Levinas' point of view: Ira F. Stone, *Reading Levinas/Reading Talmud* (Philadelphia: Jewish Publication Society, 1998), 72–79.
219 search for leavened goods: *Pesahim* 7b–8a.
221 bent fingers: Tishby, *Wisdom of Zohar* 3:1296.
221 "creates the lights": Mishnah *Berakhot* 8:5.
223 only one distinction: *Pesahim:* 103b.
223 no fewer than three: Ibid.
223 wine heal eyesight: Joshua Trachtenberg, *Jewish Magic and Superstition* (Cleveland, OH: Meridian Publishing Co., 1961), 195.
223 women abstaining: Ginsburg, *Sod Ha-Shabbat,* 235.
224 do penance: Abraham Isaac Kook, *The Lights of Penitence,* trans. Ben Zion Bokser (New York: Paulist Press, 1978), 108.
224 King David's story: *Shabbat* 30a–b.
226 Miriam announces redeemer: Adin Steinsaltz, *Biblical Images* (Northvale, NJ: Jason Aronson, 1984), 95–97.
228 "song for future age...": Mishnah *Tamid* 7:4.
228 one sixtieth: *Berakhot* 57b.
230 lower waters weep: Avivah Zornberg, *Genesis* (Philadelphia: Jewish Publication Society, 1995), 5.
230 for six thousand years: *Sanhedrin* 97a.
230 "great Sabbath": Ginzberg, *Legends* 5: 128, n. 140.
231 desolation: Ginsburg, *Sod,* 53–5.
231 *tikkun:* Scholem, "Kabbalah and Myth," in *Kabbalah and Its Symbolism,* 117.
231 "person who prepares": *Avodah Zarah* 3a.
232 "Stop": In H. N. Bialik and Yehoshua Ravnitzky, *The Book of Legends* (New York: Schocken Books, 1992), 493.
232 two Sabbaths: *Shabbat* 118b.
232 comfort the Messiah: *Sefer Ha'Shabbat,* 173.
233 "a great God": Ps. 95:3.
233 "with equity": Ps. 96:10.
233 "Sabbath after Sabbath...": Isa. 66:23.
234 "The righteous...": Ps. 92: 13, 15.
234 Shabbat is greater: *Hasidic Anthology,* 408.
235 "No longer...": Isa. 60:19.
235 "light of the moon...": Ibid. 30:26.
236 "Light is sown...": Ps. 97: 11.
236 "world could not have existed...": *Zohar* II, 148b–149a.

Suggested Readings

꙳

Abrahams, Israel. *Jewish Life in the Middle Ages.* New York: Atheneum, 1973.

Artz, Max. *Joy and Remembrance: Commentary on the Sabbath Eve Liturgy.* Hartford, CT: Hartmore House, 1979.

Biale, Rachel. *Women and Jewish Law.* New York: Schocken Books, 1984.

Cox, Harvey. *Common Prayers: Faith, Family, and a Christian's Journey Through the Jewish Year.* Boston: Houghton Mifflin, 2001.

Donin, Hayim Halevy. *To Pray as a Jew: A Guide to the Prayer Book and the Synagogue Service.* New York: Basic Books, 1980.

Dresner, Samuel H. *The Sabbath.* New York: Burning Bush Press, 1987.

Elbogen, Ismar. *Jewish Liturgy: A Comprehensive History.* Translated by Raymond P. Scheindlin. Philadelphia: Jewish Publication Society, 1993.

Elkins, Dov Peretz. *A Shabbat Reader: Universe of Cosmic Joy.* New York: UAHC Press, 1998.

Erlich, Josef. *Sabbath.* Edited and with an introduction by Hana Wirth-Nesher. Syracuse, NY: Syracuse University Press, 1999.

Eskenazi, Tamara, et al., eds. *The Sabbath in Jewish and Christian Traditions.* New York: Crossroad, 1991.

Finkelman, Shimon. *Shabbos: The Sabbath—Its Essence and Significance.* New York: Artscroll Mesorah Series, 1991.

Ginsburg, Elliot K. *The Sabbath in the Classical Kabbalah.* Albany, NY: SUNY Press, 1989.

———. *Sod Ha-Shabbat: The Mystery of the Sabbath.* Albany, NY: SUNY Press, 1989.

Glatzer, Nahum. *Franz Rosenzweig: His Life and Thought.* Philadelphia: Jewish Publication Society, 1953.

Gottlieb, Freema. *The Lamp of God: A Jewish Book of Light.* Northvale, NJ: Jason Aronson, 1996.

Greenberg, Irving. *The Jewish Way: Living the Holidays.* New York: Simon & Schuster, 1988.

Greenberg, Moshe. *Studies in the Bible and Jewish Thought.* Philadelphia: Jewish Publication Society, 1995.

Grunfeld, Isidor. *The Sabbath.* New York: Feldheim, 1988.

Hammer, Reuven. *Entering Jewish Prayer.* New York: Schocken Books, 1994.

Heschel, Abraham Joshua. *The Sabbath: Its Meaning for Modern Man* (1951). New York: Farrar Straus Giroux, 1993.

Ilan, Tal. *Jewish Women in Greco-Roman Palestine.* Peabody, MA: Hendrickson Publishers, Inc., 1996.

Jacobson, B. S. *The Sabbath Service.* Tel Aviv: Sinai Publishers, 1981.

Jewish Publication Society. *Torah Commentary.* 5 vols. Nahum M. Sarna, general editor. Philadelphia: Jewish Publication Society, 1989–1996.

Kaplan, Mordecai M. *The Meaning of God in Modern Jewish Religion.* Detroit: Wayne State University Press, 1994.

Katz, Jacob. *The "Shabbes Goy:" A Study in Halakhic Flexibility.* Philadelphia: Jewish Publication Society, 1989.

Klagsbrun, Francine. *Jewish Days: A Book of Jewish Life and Culture Around the Year.* New York: Farrar, Straus and Giroux, 1996.

Levenson, Jon D. *Creation and the Persistence of Evil.* Princeton, NJ: Princeton University Press, 1988.

———. *Sinai and Zion: An Entry into the Jewish Bible.* San Francisco: Harper-Collins, 1985.

Melammed, Renée Levine. *Heretics or Daughters of Israel? The Crypto-Jewish Women of Castile.* New York: Oxford University Press, 1999.

Millgram, Abraham E. *Sabbath: The Day of Delight.* Philadelphia: Jewish Publication Society, 1952.

Peli, Pinchas H. *Shabbat Shalom: A Renewed Encounter with the Sabbath.* Washington, DC: B'nai B'rith Books, 1988.

Sarna, Nahum. *Studies in Biblical Interpretation.* Philadelphia: Jewish Publication Society, 2000.

Schäfer, Peter. *Judeophobia: Attitudes Toward the Jews in the Ancient World.* Cambridge, MA: Harvard University Press, 1997.

Scholem, Gershom. *On the Kabbalah and Its Symbolism.* Translated by Ralph Manheim. New York: Schocken Books, 1965.

Steinsaltz, Adin. *A Guide to Jewish Prayer.* New York: Schocken Books, 2000.

———. *The Candle of God: Discourses on Chasidic Thought.* Northvale, NJ: Jason Aronson, 1998.

Tishby, Isaiah. *The Wisdom of the Zohar: An Anthology of Texts.* 3 vols. Translated by David Goldstein. London: Littman Library of Jewish Civilization, 1994.

Waskow, Arthur, ed. *Torah of the Earth: Exploring 4,000 Years of Ecology in Jewish Thought.* Woodstock, VT: Jewish Lights, 2000.

Weissler, Chava. *Voices of the Matriarchs: Listening to the Prayers of Early Modern Jewish Women.* Boston: Beacon Press, 1998.

Wolfson, Ron. *The Shabbat Seder.* Woodstock, VT: Jewish Lights, 1996.

Zerubavel, Eviatar. *The Seven Day Circle: The History and Meaning of the Week.* Chicago: University of Chicago Press, 1989.

Acknowledgments

I'm grateful to the many friends and scholars who generously offered suggestions and advice about what they would like to see included in a book on Shabbat. I cannot thank them all in print, but I do want to thank several people who led me to source materials and pathways I might have missed.

Chancellor Ismar Schorsch of the Jewish Theological Seminary supported the concept of this book from the time it was germinating in my mind, and later met with me to discuss it at length. Professor Raymond Scheindlin of the Seminary steered me to the mystics, whose theories and thoughts are essential to understanding the Shabbat, and he shared his knowledge on Muslim attitudes toward the Sabbath with me. Rabbi Harlan Wechsler has been a continual source of learning and inspiration for me.

Eleanor Munro's enthusiasm for the Jewish Sabbath and particularly for the Sabbath lights and her generosity in making her files on light available to me meant a great deal to my work on this book. Gloria Goldreich constantly kept an eye out for writings and literary materials that would be useful to me, and Rudi Wolff volunteered aid and advice when I most needed them.

I thank Linda Loewenthal, executive editorial director of Harmony Books and my esteemed editor, for her mixture of encouragement, prodding, and superb judgment. She is a joy to work with. Cara Brozenich has been an intelligent, calm, and efficient presence throughout this project, and I thank her. Charlotte Sheedy helped turn my thoughts about Shabbat into an idea for a book, and has, as always, been my friend as well as my agent. And my husband, Samuel Klagsbrun, once again sustained me with his love and care through a challenging writing project.

Index

INDEX

About the Author

FRANCINE KLAGSBRUN is the author of more than a dozen books on social and religious issues, including *Jewish Days* and *Voices of Wisdom,* and was the editor of the bestselling *Free to Be . . . You and Me.* She is a columnist for *The Jewish Week* and for *Moment* magazine, and has contributed numerous articles to national publications. Among many awards, she holds an honorary doctorate degree from the Jewish Theological Seminary. She and her family live in New York City.